Captured
in
Liberation

ANDREW BAJDA

PAGE PUBLISHING, INC.
New York, NY

First originally published by Page Publishing, Inc. 2016

ISBN 978-1-68409-042-6 (Paperback)
ISBN 978-1-68409-043-3 (Digital)

Book cover designed by Reg Springer.

Printed in the United States of America

Contents

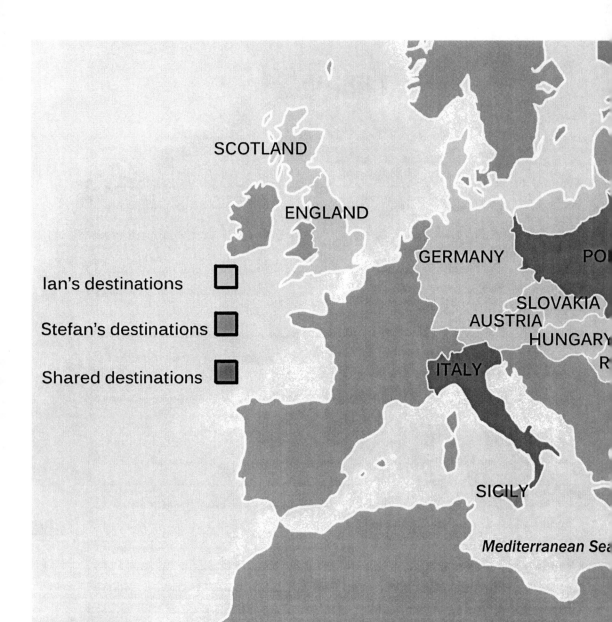

SCOTLAND

ENGLAND

GERMANY   PO

SLOVAKIA

AUSTRIA

HUNGARY

ITALY   R

SICILY

Mediterranean Sea

Ian's destinations ☐

Stefan's destinations ☐

Shared destinations ☐

Pre - World War II Map of Europe
and Surrounding Areas

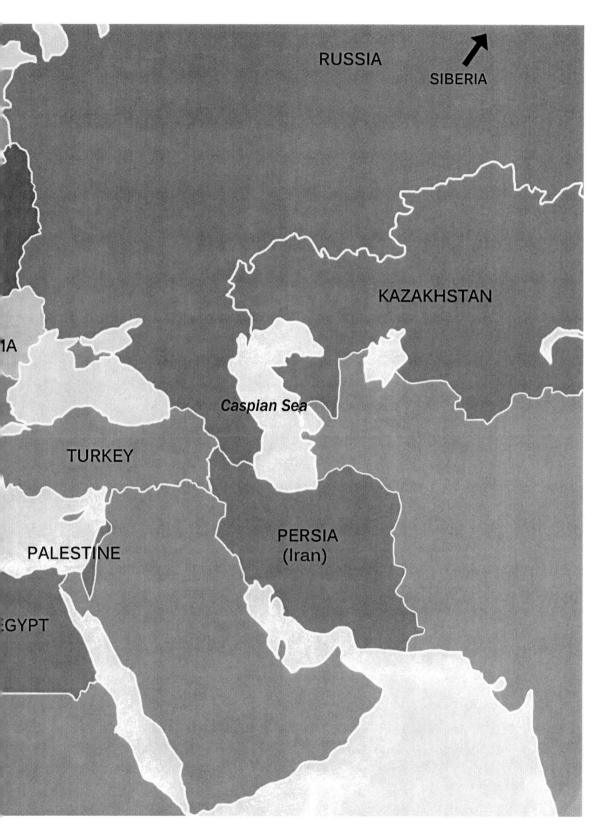

RUSSIA

SIBERIA

KAZAKHSTAN

Caspian Sea

1A

TURKEY

PALESTINE

PERSIA
(Iran)

EGYPT

Preface

Elyria, Ohio USA

"Grandma, have you ever been accused of being a spy?"

Little could I have imagined when my daughter Lauren lightheartedly asked that question that an unexpected response would open up the floodgates. That it would generate a wake-up call to begin a project that I had been thinking about for years. A project that I had pretty much resigned myself to the fact that I had waited too long to begin and would never complete. And little could I imagine how that project would change my life, but then came the response to that question.

Before that response, I always knew my parents had a story. I suspected theirs was a colorful one filled with adventure, intrigue, searching, and discovery. As the years unfolded and life happened, elements of their story came to life, but I never fully understood their story until it was almost lost forever.

Their story first came to me during my childhood. Growing up the middle child in the warmth of a happy home in Elyria, Ohio was a true blessing. Before turning six years old and entering school, I enjoyed listening to my mother's songs and stories of family "back home." The characters became fixated in my mind; Auntie Pauline and Auntie Ethel were household names. A salt sea breeze over the seaside town of Millom could almost be felt, and the rolling hills of England's Lake District seemed just beyond the horizon.

My father's story was more of a mystery. He would come home from work, typically in a pleasant mood but often looking tired with sleeves rolled up on his faded blue work shirt. He'd clean up for a well-rounded dinner that my mother always had prepared, and alertly listen to the day's events over the dinner table from his son and two daughters. Little was shared of his day, and he spent many evenings reading, studying, or writing letters to family members back home in Poland.

As the years crept by, more was revealed. Every Christmas Eve was spent with a family that moved into our fresh new subdivision; they also immigrated to the States. Their son Gary became my close friend and, like me, arrived by ship as a toddler from England. Gary's mom was from Ireland's Achill Island, and his father from Nottingham England. His parents also met following the war. We would all sit around the cozy addition in the basement built by my father, the gas fireplace lit, the adults reminiscing about wartime England. When the eccentric Amy and Al stop over, things would really perk up. Amy with her Lancashire accent kept everyone laughing. Al would break into wartime songs that they all merrily joined in. Before the song's ending, Al often found himself in tears, and the adults appeared lost in their collective thoughts and memories of England during the war.

All, that is, with the exception of my father. He appeared content listening to the others, dutifully mixing drinks to make sure that everyone was comfortable. Before the night was over, they'd ask him to sing a song or two in his native tongue. He'd initially scoff at the idea, before singing a song that always had me mesmerized with its mysterious language and melodic tone. After receiving polite applause and answering a few questions, he'd drift back into the background as the mood lightened once again amidst hearty laughter that combined four distinct British accents with a lilting Irish accent.

The next we would hear from my father was an urgent need to get ready for Midnight Mass. The memory remains etched in my mind.

Two families squeeze into one car, singing carols on the drive across town to Holy Cross, a Catholic Polish church and school surrounded by a corner store and tired wood frame homes in the old neighborhood. The church is decorated with an endless array of bright red poinsettias filling up the altar area. Familiar Polish tunes sung in melodic measured tones drift from the hidden upstairs choir and envelops the quickly overflowing church. A priest ceremoniously enters, surrounded by altar boys, one in front carrying a large cross and the others handling rich bronzed lanterns swinging on decorative chains. They lead a procession around the aisles; smoke wafts through the pews as the hypnotizing scent of incense fills the church.

The mass commences in Latin, more Polish songs, followed by a Polish sermon repeated in English. Much of my time spent viewing an oversized painting on a rounded concave wall high above the altar. Also visible were life-sized statues of saints, a realistic-looking manger scene, and colorful stained glass windows. Thoughts of waking up in the morning to the feel of an overstuffed stocking at the foot of my bed, wondering what gifts might be awaiting me. I glance over at my parents. My mother returns the look with a warm smile and a nod. My father peers straight ahead, listening intently and appearing deep in thought. What could he be thinking?

My father's story remained a mystery throughout my youth. Hints of a prison escape and nostalgic reminders of camaraderie slipped out as we enjoyed watching together the many TV shows and war movies popular at that time: *Combat, Stalag 17, The Great Escape, The Bridge Over the River Kwai,* to name a few. Even *Hogan's Heroes* became a favorite; my father would fondly recall a good-natured guard and rough-hewn barracks looking "just like that," while enjoying Hogan's obvious ploys to trick the unsuspecting Sergeant Schultz and Colonel Klink.

However, much more frequent was a serious tone, a silence, perhaps even a hidden wound. While cousin Janek sent photos and news from England as my pen pal, I knew very little of my family in Poland. I recall the evening my father received an urgent message from Western Union. He sat in silence reading an official-looking document that stated his mother Jozefa had passed away. I'm not even sure that I initially made the connection she was my grandmother. We didn't see much of my father that evening, but I'm pretty certain that I caught a glimpse of him through the partially opened door to my parent's bedroom, knelt down in prayer at the foot of the bed.

About the only other childhood memory I recall related to my Polish family was reluctantly selecting some of my favorite items to send away each year around Christmas. My father would expertly pack our clothes and small gifts into a tightly bound and secure package, an exotic collection of letters and numbers painstakingly printed in bold block letters. Some years later, we learned that the more expensive items and tucked-away bills were never found in the poorly wrapped packages eventually received by family members.

As an adult, I had the good fortune of visiting England on two occasions, as well as Poland once on a trip with my father. Having actually experienced the salt sea breeze and meeting the aunts, uncles, and cousins in England cemented the familiarity that I already held. And having stepped on Polish soil and sensing a natural belonging, I felt that the family was always part of my life. Over the years, my parents occasionally received family members who crossed the Atlantic on holiday, so subtle elements of their story crept to fruition.

But it was only in recent years that the depth of my father's story began to emerge. A walk together on a September afternoon along Sandy Ridge rekindles memories of the sunny days when his family hastily traveled east by horse carriage to avoid the Nazi invasion. A full Christmas tree in my house reminds him of the tree he risked arrest to cut down for the family's first Christmas under German occupation. A menagerie of events that occurred during the war began to surface, but little if anything connected the pieces of the puzzle.

One day my daughter Lauren and I stopped over for a visit. Lauren had just come home from a year of voluntary service in Alaska (late August 2013) and was eager to see her grandparents. I also knew that my father was excited to see Lauren. Resembling his sister Krystyna in both appearance and personality, it was easy to sense a special bond between the two.

Over the years, my four daughters came to know their grandparents' home as a special haven in their lives. My father built the house after retiring from years as a laborer, in which he held jobs ranging from a welder in the Lorain shipyards to a millwright at local factories. It would be quite misleading to view my father as your typical blue-collar worker. Even as a college professor, I've never met a person with more knowledge in such a wide range of topics, or who is more attuned to the social, economic, and political impact of both past and current world affairs. Neither liberal nor conservative, his views are guided by values based on a strong work ethic and individual freedoms, and balanced with simple common sense. But I suppose that not having a formal college degree limited his options in finding work as an immigrant.

I should also clarify just what I mean by "built the house." Now when some people say they build a home, they in reality oversaw construction or coordinated the effort with a group of fellow tradesmen. But after having the basement dug and concrete poured, my father and I placed the steel beams, after which he literally carried every board and pounded every nail. Drawing blueprints, framing, drywall, carpentry, plumbing, electrical work, landscaping. Not one detail ignored, every minute task completed. I would often stop on Saturdays to help out but at times felt more a hindrance than help. He had everything orchestrated to do it just the right way with engineering feats that would have appeared magic had I not seen how he pulled it off.

He completed the entire project in one year, visibly aging in the process. Stress and long hours from the need to meet delivery dates and coding inspections. But from the completed task emerged a fountain of youth and renewed vigor, continual tinkering and projects that unfold to this day. When not at the college gym down the street, he's adding an office behind the garage, laying new tile in the foyer, constructing an oak cabinet to fit an empty corner. Where did all this knowledge and energy come from?

So on this day we comfortably settled in the family room enjoying a cup of tea. My mother as typical made us laugh with whimsical comments, prompting Lauren to jokingly ask, "Grandma, have you ever been accused of being a spy?"

Grandpa sat stoically on his chair holding a cup of tea and calmly answered, "Well, I have." From there he mesmerized us with a matter-of-fact description of how he and a friend named Artur were accused of being spies after capture along the Romanian countryside near the Hungarian border.

I finally got off my seat and scrambled to find a notepad and pen, beginning the first of many memorable visits to learn the story of my parents and family. A story that would lead to discovery not only of my relationship with them but also personal discovery and lasting relationship with faraway family. A personal quest that will lead me across Europe to see first-hand the places and even one person still alive who was part of their story. Learning about life and myself from family members, both the living and the dead, who remained overseas in the faraway places of my ancestry.

As soon as I returned home that evening, I began typing my handwritten notes, and unknowingly embarked on a journey to capture the story of my family, a story that has forever changed my life.

Part 1

Iris and Jean Graham. Iris is upset because Jean still has her apple while Iris has already eaten hers.

Mary (Minnie) Graham, with daughters Iris and Jean in Burgh by Sands, England

CHAPTER 1

Orphaned

Burgh by Sands and Millom, England
Summer Holiday – September 1938

Silence fell prey to the measured beat of a ticking clock. The dark-haired figure might have been convinced that time had already drifted away if not for the clock's pretentious warning, or was it the beating of a heart that stirred her senses? Mary Graham fought to prop up on her bed in the simple but reposeful cottage, keenly aware that time was indeed alive, and offering what she feared might be the most difficult moment in her life. Her senses were further heightened by the kiss of a breeze that danced around a flower vase sitting under an open window. Its drying bouquet of English bluebells and white orchids drooped as if genuflecting to cottages along the rolling countryside symbolic of a Lake District postcard.

Mary, more affectionately known as Minnie, had long succumbed to her cancer, but fought to generate a spark of energy, a battle to appear strong for her youngest child. Just turned thirteen years old, Iris sat close by her side, staring at a sheet of paper with an ink blot pen in hand. She barely moved. Her concentration dulled from conflicting thoughts, torn between staying with Mum and moving in with family members in Millom. The bus was scheduled to arrive sooner than they wished, so Iris focused on the right words to ease their pain, a poem she desperately wished would both please and comfort her mother. Completing the final line, she handed over the sheet of paper, intently studying dark tired eyes breathe in every word:

> *I will write to you a lot*
> *And will not make any blots*
> *But will tell you all the news*

And you'll be waiting in the queues
And when I've wrote to you just once
You'll be writing in response
To your happy daughter fair
Who is waiting in despair.

Minnie thoughtfully folded the paper to view her daughter, who looked to be more an innocent child than a rebellious teen. Iris remained still. She was wearing her favorite dress. The pretty face emerging from a shadow behind darkening wavy hair could not hide concern, such a contrast from her trademark joyful appearance. To see Iris so lost and confused sliced through her heart. Minnie was overcome with an urge to wrap her daughter tightly in her arms, but that would have to wait.

"Why did you write 'in despair'? You'll be with Pauline and Ethel, and Grandma will be with you."

"Why of course I'll be in despair. I'll be thinking about you every day."

Silence returned. Only when the clock's familiar chimes broke their shared anfractuous trance did the two look up to take note of the time. The bus was scheduled to arrive, and the moment for mother and daughter to bid their farewells was upon them. Iris hugged her mother tightly, desperately wanting to make everything all right and have their family back together the way it used to be. Minnie leaned back from the embrace. A genuine smile radiated life and warmth to her drawn face. "Tata Pet. Always know that I love you and hold you more precious than anything in the entire world. Now off with you, and please be a dear for your poor Uncle Will."

Reluctantly, the troubled daughter arose to leave the room, a whirlwind of thoughts running through her head. She had no way of knowing that the precious time just spent together would be their last.

Iris Graham (right) with cousin Pauline shortly after arriving
in Millom, England. When this photo was taken, Iris had
no idea that she would never see her mother again.

A week later in Millom, Iris was alerted to a rude knock at the front door. She rushed to answer before her uncle abruptly stopped her. "Don't answer, it's probably Salvation Army wanting money."

Iris considered ignoring the order, hoping it might be the postman with a letter from Mum, but chose against crossing Uncle Will and retreated upstairs. Since losing his wife to complications with appendicitis, her uncle was even more ornery than normal, and his mood was not much improved after the spirited Iris joined a household already populated with mostly females.

Despite concern for her mother and the bitterness that her uncle exuded, Iris was happy and settling seamlessly into the familiar home on One Oxford Street, just a few blocks from the seaside town square. Her outgoing and attractive cousins Ethel and Pauline were like sisters to her, the three inseparable. Mary was the oldest of the cousins and more reserved, spending most of her time tidying up and staying in the house. It seemed that Mary was always berating her brother Frank for one thing or another, but he was always pleasant around Iris. She found her cousin Frank to be like a brother, although nobody could be quite like her brother Wilf (Wilfred).

Just last night Iris had the most fun since her arrival in Millom. Frank's antics had her, Pauline, and Ethel laughing so hard that her stomach ached as joyful tears blurred her vision. He was impersonating different people from the neighborhood,

some of them with made-up songs that he sung off-key with exaggerated manner-
isms. Uncle Will was not amused. He yelled downstairs for everyone to go to bed and
get to sleep. Iris bit into her fists to muffle laughter as Frank pantomimed his father's
anger and yelling. The four stayed up well past midnight immersed in laughter and
cheer, but what Iris remembered most was the one serious message that Frank relayed
to her. Just before retiring to her room, he spoke in a soft voice for only Iris to hear,
"One day, Pet, I'm going to get married, and we'll adopt you." Iris was touched by
his words, warmed by the acceptance in her new home, and reminded of the loss she
felt in not having her own brother around.

Thoughts of him generated both tears and smiles. When Wilf was selected
as a schoolboy for the renowned boys' choir at the prestigious Carlisle Cathedral,
shock waves reverberated among the locals. During his concerts, the family gathered
around the radio, listening to the choir with glowing pride. Wilf would come home
later looking like a proper choirboy in his pressed shirt and navy blazer sporting the
cathedral emblem, but then he'd laugh while showing Iris the chocolate drops hidden
in his cap and thrown at the other boys while not being watched. He did have a mar-
velous voice. Guests visiting the house always requested that he sing a song for them.
Wilf reluctantly agreed to the requests, but typically only after money was offered for
his efforts. As he reached puberty, a penchant for cigarettes coupled with a change in
tenor ended his time with the school and the choir.

An innocent-looking Wilf Graham, well before his troublemaking adolescent years

18

Iris was forever coming up with excuses to be around her older brother. They often played a game where she sat on his lap, trying to snatch the gum out of his mouth as he'd chew and tantalizingly stick it out. While their sister Jean sat quietly nearby reading a book, Iris enjoyed the roughhousing and teasing. "Ewe, I can smell you've been smoking, I'm going to tell Mum."

"You'll do nothing of the sort." She would jump off screaming as Wilf chased her around the house.

She recalled the day the police came to the house, giving Wilf a good talking to for some mischief he'd been accused of. It seemed that Wilf was always taking the blame for any trouble that occurred in the village. Maybe the police felt they were doing Minnie a favor, with knowledge that she was a widow having to raise her troublemaking son and two daughters all by herself. After the police left, Mum really let Wilf have it, striking him as he walked away fending the blows. However, within minutes the four were amused at the sight of Mum struggling to reach up and discipline a son who had grown into a young man. It was as if the realization hit her for the first time that Wilf was no longer the schoolboy with the alto voice. The image of them all united in laughter was a reminder that Iris clutched on to. She yearned to remember a time and place when her family was happy and together.

But now, Wilf and her sister Jean were seldom seen around the house in Millom. With growing rumors of the possibility for war with Nazi Germany, he was contemplating joining the Royal Navy and Jean the WAAFs (Women's Auxiliary Air Force).

Despite all the changes, there was a rock in her life, a foundation that assured Iris things were going to turn out all right. For what truly made her stay in Millom special was sharing a room with Grandma. Iris always felt a close bond with her Grandma, and now the two became even closer as they openly talked about anything that Iris wished to discuss long into the night.

Sensing an eerie silence in the normally boisterous household, Iris cautiously walked down the stairwell to view a most sobering sight. Everyone was seated in the living area, vacant stares, speaking in hushed tones. Uncle Will spotted Iris and directed her to Grandma, who enveloped her granddaughter in a tight embrace with tear-filled eyes. "Your mum has gone to heaven."

It took a moment for the words to sink in. Iris felt in a daze. Her mind went blank as the room spun around her. Sharp white specks of light filled her head. Breaking from Grandma in search of her mother's arms, faces spun around her as tears further blurred her vision. "No! Mum's not gone. She can't be gone!"

While the room stood still, only Pauline reacted. She approached her cousin with a sympathetic tone. "Well, you know, Pet, I also don't have my mum anymore."

Uncle Will stopped Pauline, suggesting that she not say anything and just leave Iris be. Iris had just sent her mother a card and was waiting for a reply, but there would be no return letter, and there was indeed despair.

* * *

Despair and darkness prevailed in the household, and continued until the occurrence of a most unexpected parley. Uncle Will's mood only worsened as he spiraled into a similar pattern of dealing with his sister-in law's death that he did with the loss of his wife. Iris wasn't certain if he was overwhelmed with loss or the realization that he was now responsible for her care. He spent his days sitting alone at the dining room table, a bottle of whiskey his sole companion before his drunken head found the table. Nobody dared to speak or approach him. In the evenings, he'd go out to drink in the pubs. One evening, he left and didn't come back for days. When he finally returned, he said nothing, simply retreated to his room. Iris clutched to Grandma for support and comfort to cope with the changes around her, and as typical, Grandma convinced her that everything was going to be all right.

The morning after his return, she dressed for school while quietly talking with Grandma, not wanting to stir or awaken her Uncle. Their conversation was interrupted by rustling and a voice from his room that caused her to freeze. "Iris, come in here. There's something I need to tell you!"

With a fearful expression, Iris peered toward his room. "Grandma, it's Uncle. What do I do?"

In a forceful measured whisper, Grandma's smile invited an element of ease. "Go! It's all right, Pet, there's nothing to worry about. Go to your uncle, maybe he's going to give you some money, or maybe he just has something to tell you." With a raised voice and motion of her hands she whisked away her wide-eyed granddaughter. "Go! Just GO!"

Heavy steps led her toward Uncle's room. The hallway never seemed so long, his doorway appearing closer yet distant at the same time. Iris felt the coldness of the door handle before slowly opening to enter a room cast in darkness. A dim light filtered through closed shades before her eyes adjusted to view Uncle looking up from his bed. He appeared normal, somehow looking more alive than at any time she'd seen him since the loss of Mum. "Come closer, Iris, there's something I need to tell you."

What could it be? What could be wrong? Iris felt the beating of her heart, fearing yet more bad news. The floor creaked from several cautious steps before she came to a stop at the foot of his bed.

"Pet, I want you to know that everything's going to be all right from now on."

That was it? *Everything is going to be okay?* Iris felt a surge of relief, a giant weight released from her body. Not knowing what to do or say, she thanked her uncle and left in a rush to share the encounter with Grandma. From that day on, Iris never saw her uncle so much as touch a bottle of liquor while in the household.

Iris walked to school that day as if on air, for the first time realizing that she actually enjoyed her new school. It was fun to study fresh new faces, and she had almost immediately established a friendship with a girl named Ida. Following the first day of school, she approached the bespectacled girl, short like herself and with a quiet but friendly demeanor, and asked if she'd like to walk together. Ida replied that she couldn't because of piano lessons, prompting Iris to feel like the new girl who everyone avoided. But Ida approached her after school the following day and asked if she could join her on the walk home. The two became instant friends.

Iris picked up her step; because of the unexpected meeting with Uncle Will, she was running late. The school bell was about to ring when she hastily entered the classroom, the other students mingling and settling in their seats. Standing toward the back of the room was Ida and another girl, looking so prim and proper in their smart uniforms. Buoyed by her exhilaration and seizing an opportunity to have some fun, Iris rushed up to push Ida just as she was about to sit down. Caught by surprise, Ida tumbled forward in an awkward manner that seemed to send her spiraling throughout the classroom, capturing the attention of the entire class. The room grew stone silent. Dreadful reality crept in that Iris was suddenly the object of everyone's attention. Soon enough, harsh words hit her like a shock of ice water running through her veins.

"Be seated, class. Oh, not you, Iris Graham. Remain standing right where you are. Iris Graham! I was led to believe that you had come from a good family, that you were a nice girl. Well then, what would your mother be thinking right now if she were here and could see you pushing down other students in the classroom?"

The words bounced off her like white noise, drowned out by the hum that pounded in her head. Iris simply looked down, well aware the entire class was staring; she could feel her face burn in humiliation. She wanted to cry but fought the urge for tears to flow. Emotional wounds reopened with a vivid image of her mother and insult added with the suggestion of her mother's disapproval. The stinging words directed toward her continued. "This is not the proper way for a young lady to act. We do not accept such behavior here."

Remaining standing, thoughts drifted far from the classroom. She hated this school. Why did Mum have to die and leave her in this dreadful place? Why did this teacher have to be so mean? She wished she were home, far away from the school and this cruel teacher. She wanted to be with Grandma. Surely, she would not divulge why she got into trouble, but at least she'd be someplace where she felt loved. The teacher's parting shots slowly crystalized back into her consciousness. "You may be seated, Ms. Graham. You've done enough to disrupt the classroom for one day. Now open your textbooks class to chapter 2. We shall resume Scripture lessons."

Millom, England
Summer Holiday 1939

Posing before the full-length mirror in their shared room, Iris tipped her hat forward in a most fanciful manner. "What do you think, Grandma, should I wear it like this?"

Grandma tried to appear upset but was unable to conceal a smile, enjoying her granddaughter's light-heartedness and sense of fashion. "Oh, don't make such a scene. Just wear the outfit and make your Auntie Gertrude happy."

Iris had just received the outfit in a package sent by post from her Auntie Gertrude, who was on her way to visit from near Burgh by Sands. The entire household speculated that her aunt would request that Iris move in with her to help relieve Uncle Will of the crowded household. But Iris was feeling a sense of confidence spurred by strong vocal support from within the household. The normally mild-mannered Pauline had suddenly turned adamant and quite serious about not allowing Iris to leave, and she even overheard Uncle Will convincingly state in a private conversation one evening, "She's just fine to stay here." Iris confided with Grandma that there was no way she could leave their current arrangement. The two had discussed the matter at great length, and Grandma suggested that if Iris proudly wore the outfit upon her aunt's visit, it might soften the blow of her desire to stay in Millom.

Leaning forward from her chair, Grandma took on a serious tone and shared that she's been doing some thinking. "What would you think about us getting a nice place of our own? We've been sharing this room for almost a year, and having our own place to live might be quite nice. You could even have your own room, and that would allow your uncle some freedom and get back to his normal pace."

"Oh no, Grandma! We can't do that. I can't leave Pauline and Ethel. I like it here just fine." Grandma sat back and smiled. "It's quite all right, Pet. We can stay here." Iris glanced back at the mirror, placing the hat at an even more severe angle. "What do you think of this look, Grandma?"

Several weeks later, exactly one year to the day after her mother's death, Grandma joined Minnie in heaven. Throughout her life, two events would go on to pose a profound impact on Iris's worldview. One was leaving her family behind when she crossed the Atlantic for America, and the other was losing Grandma so close to the loss of her mother, on the one year anniversary of her mother's death.

Grandma

CHAPTER 2

Escape from the Blitzkrieg

Bochnia, Poland, and Eastern Poland (Ukraine)
3 September – 15 September 1939

While England and the rest of the world braced for the outbreak of war, Poland had no such luxury. The war found Poland. In the year 1939, the town of Bochnia, Poland, lay directly between Germany and the Russian front, off a roadway just east of Poland's cultural capital and second largest city, Cracow. A roadway eyed as crucially important to German chancellor Adolf Hitler for plans that would soon be revealed. On a Sunday afternoon in early September 1939, elements of the Fuhrer's unpredictable strategy were finally exposed. Where it would lead was still unknown to a world on edge, though the danger signs were crystal clear. The town of Bochnia knew the momentary calm was preceding a mountainous storm.

Two middle-aged women conversed in the garden of a yellow stucco home, facing a street uncharacteristically void of life. The normally bright yellow color of the house appeared washed out, matching a mood that strained the flow of conversation between two close friends.

"Please consider taking Victor with you, Jozefa. I assure you he'll be no trouble. He's seventeen now, you know, and I fear could be in great danger if left behind. He won't cause problems. In fact, he'll provide added protection and help out in any way you need him to."

Jozefa Bajda knew she could not refuse the impassioned plea from her neighbor and close friend Pani Dobranovsky. Although conveying outward appreciation for the promise of protection and help, she was not overly concerned about those needs. Her own sons were quite capable. Henryk was now twenty-three and had always been a responsible son. Standing tall in stature, his gruff appearance belied a gentle and caring nature. Stefan was the same age as Victor but seemed much older. He possessed an outgoing personality and fluid athleticism that made him popular and a natural leader among his peers and even adults in the community. Everything seemed to come so easy for him. Jozefa always felt comforted when she thought of fifteen year-old Marian (Ian), who was more than capable of helping out. An avid reader of books and historical novels, his clear blue eyes reflected an inquisitive mind and adventurous spirit, reminding Jozefa so much of herself with his resourceful ways, unassuming personality, and quiet strength.

Her concern was not for needing help, but in adding yet another passenger to a carriage growing more and more crowded. She had already agreed to bring along her two young nieces Alexandra and Zofia. While twelve year-old Krystyna took this news with delight that she was no longer the only girl, Jozefa pondered in her mind just how they would make this work. Her youngest sons at least would not take up much space. Eleven-year-old Jerzy would be no trouble; he'd be content as long as he had a book to read. However, her two youngest sons, Zdislaw and Stanislaw were more rambunctious and required extra attention. Perhaps Victor could help to keep an eye on her two youngest sons.

Jozefa took quick inventory: her six sons, one daughter, and two nieces made for nine travelers. Adding herself and the driver made for eleven. She glanced over at the open-bed wagon hitched behind two stout workhorses. There appeared to be ample space for all of them. Why not an even dozen? Twelve seemed a good omen.

"Of course we will be happy to have Victor join us. He will indeed be a big help to us."

"Oh thank you, dear Jozefa! You will not be disappointed. May the Lord stay with you!

Jozefa watched her friend run toward the house down the street to fetch her son and share the good news, and for the first time allowed the reality of the moment to sink in. Hitler's feared blitzkrieg had begun. The German Army was expected to storm in any day to capture the town of Bochnia, unless the undermanned Polish Army received much needed support from their allies or could somehow manage to hold the Germans off.

Ian was pleased when his mother came inside the house to inform them all that Victor would be joining them. Victor's mother was also Ian's godmother, so he felt a natural kinship with his neighbor from down the road. Having Victor join them removed at least a sliver of the tension that was steadily building all around them.

A family photo, taken several years before the German invasion. Back row (left to right) Stefan, Jozefa, and Henryk. Middle row (left to right) Jerzy, Krystyna, and Ian. Front row, Zdislaw and Stanislaw.

Just two days earlier, German planes finally broke the dreaded anticipation of war when they bombed an apartment building in town. The bombed building resembled an army barracks with several long structures sitting side by side, and Ian was certain that the Germans believed they had destroyed a military building. Fortunately, there were no civilian or other fatalities, but the building sustained severe structural damage. Then the following day, planes were again heard, and this time the train station was targeted. After the planes departed, Ian and others from the neighborhood raced for the plume of smoke to assess the source of raging fire and resulting damage. Surprisingly, the station survived with minimal damage and no fatalities. Bochnia remained intact, but the reality of war coupled with fear of the unknown gripped the community.

Even in their home, the threat of war had been mounting. During the past week, he'd only seen his father Stefan Senior two or three times. Father would stop at the house only to clean up and gather a change of clothes before heading back to his office where he'd spend the night. His father was the head of the county law department but now Ian learned also acting as military head for the entire district. As such, he was responsible for logistical arrangements involving military personnel, the county's government officials, and their families.

Stefan Senior shown working at his law office in Bochnia

Another recent change in the household was the presence of Ian's grandfather and cousins Zofia and Alexandra. His aunt, Jozefa's sister, had recently passed away, and his uncle was an officer in the army, so the three moved in several days earlier. The cousins were now preparing to join the family on their upcoming journey.

A local farmer commissioned by the army had abruptly appeared in the horse-drawn carriage earlier that Sunday afternoon with orders to collect the family and escort them out of Bochnia. "I don't know how long we'll be gone or where we'll end up, so bring your necessities, but please do it fast, and make sure there's enough room for everyone."

Jozefa directed everyone to lay out just enough clothes to cover all possible weather conditions, from rain to snow, heat to cold. Ian sorted out a heavy pair of trousers, extra shirts, his jacket, and a thick vest. He wasn't sure at the time why his mother insisted that he include his long heavy coat with the high school insignia but would come to learn that coats will prove to be lifesavers.

With clothes for all the travelers sorted out by family member in neat stacks, Jozefa began the process of wrapping each stack in a separate blanket, held in place with string expertly knotted in the four corners. The area began to resemble a collection of oversized gifts decorating the room on Christmas Day. Before finalizing his personal stash, Ian searched out several items of necessity. Included among them were the family's five revolvers, one of which he tucked securely inside his pants pocket.

Ian's father was once again with them and provided a calming presence as they all finalized their preparation. He assured his son that that they would be safe and travelling with fellow families of government officials. However, Ian was surprised when his father informed them that he would not accompany them. "As soon as I complete some business in town, I'll catch up and join you. And once Bochnia is safe and secure, we'll all be able to return home. In the meantime, your grandfather will be staying here to take care of the house. Now let's finish packing so that you can meet up with the rest of the convoy."

A convoy? Travelling across the country on an open wagon as part of a convoy actually sounded intriguing. With handsome boyish features and a taste for adventure, wavy-brown-haired and blue-eyed Ian was actually feeling a sense of anticipation and nervous energy, as if embarking on a new adventure, but there also remained some apprehension. Up to that point, his entire life had been spent in Bochnia, surrounded by the warmth of family and friends, and where he had access to everything that an adventurous teenage boy could possibly ask for.

Their house on Fifty-Eight Brzeznicka Street was indeed a handsome home. The cheerful one-story yellow stucco structure lay just inside the city limits. Their neighborhood was close enough to the active city center but also distant enough to have its own unique neighborhood feel and charm. Built on a sloping lot fifty meters wide by three hundred meters deep, the house was accented by a lavish flower garden decorating the front lawn. A well-maintained vegetable garden and hen house took up a section of the back yard, with over fifty fruit trees populating the property. Across the street stood a well-maintained red brick factory with neat homes for the workers tucked tidily along a wooded hillside. The factory contained a brickyard and a flourmill, the cylindrical smoke stack towering as a neighborhood landmark. Living in one of the factory homes was Ian's close friend Samuel (Mulek) Dienstag. Mulek's father was the superintendent of the factory, and they were just one of many Jewish families who made up the neighborhood.

Throughout the year, Ian and Mulek tirelessly explored the numerous areas of interest. A gradual hillside emerging behind the factory provided entrance into a forest densely populated with birch and pine trees. By cutting through the factory and climbing several flights of stairs, they simplified an entrance to a shaded path that led to a rustic chapel. Farther down from the chapel, the wooded path opened up to offer a view of two inviting ponds at the bottom of a valley. Water was pumped up for use by the factory, but the ponds also provided the boys a year-round haven for fishing, swimming, and ice-skating.

Even with no shortage of outdoor activities, the youth in the community still managed to create a variety of fun and competitive events. Henryk organized a neighborhood Olympics every summer. He'd mark off distances in the nearby Raba River for swimming, one-hundred-meter sprints on an open field, even set up a high-jump pit and makeshift stations for other field events. Boys and girls throughout the neighborhood would compete, and Ian quickly gained a reputation as among the swiftest of swimmers and runners regardless of age. Farther down the road was an open field where his brother Stefan often led a group of older teens and young men in rough-and-tumble soccer matches. Stefan enjoyed quite a reputation as the town's soccer star with lightning speed, crafty skills, and aggressive play.

During the winter, children of all families spent entire days together sledding down hills forming a range of shapes and sizes. Some days they would sled or don snow skies and glide down the narrow winding road that pointed them to the city of Bochnia, a bustling town known for a famous salt mine and with its own charm and personality.

The skiers had to maneuver a sharp left turn before freely gliding to their destination. Slowing to a crawl at the bottom of the hill, a town square teeming with villagers of all ages came alive to greet them. Beyond the square lay narrow streets filled with small shops and cafes, the upstairs apartments decorated with cheerful flower boxes outside their windows. Streets beyond the city center hugged the Carpathian Mountain foothills, resulting in a maze of winding elevated roads. This topography, combined with the elegant architecture of government buildings and centuries-old churches, made for a charming city with both history and personality.

As Ian finished packing his personal belongings, he wondered what was to become of Bochnia. Was there a chance the city would be destroyed and disintegrated into rubble? Would Bochnia remain intact but taken over by German residents? Would they even be allowed back if the German Army were victorious? Lost in the uncertainty of what might happen, his mother Jozefa sensed his concern and brought him back to the task at hand. "Everything is going to be just fine, son. I need you to be strong. Now see if you can find a favorite toy for Stanislaw while I wrap your clothes. We need to finish up here and get going."

Jozefa Bajda posing in ~~the family living room prior to~~ the Nazi invasion of Bochnia
a studio after

Taking one final inspection while searching out the figurine of two small wooden soldiers, Ian claimed the toys along with his wrapped luggage and walked outside to a carriage now fully loaded with neat stacks of clothing. The carriage actually appeared cozy, their luggage set up as makeshift furniture that could be repositioned for bedding. Everyone stood in silence, gazing at the fully packed carriage as if not sure what to do. Handing over the toy soldiers to Stanislaw and Zdislaw, he lifted them onto the wagon before climbing aboard, and listened to his father pass out some final instructions. "You are in good hands. The driver will take you into town where you'll be united with other families. There you will receive further instructions and supplies. Please pay close attention but know that the convoy will travel east to avoid any possible danger. I'll come and join you as soon as I complete my work here. May God be with you."

The driver cracked his whip as the loaded carriage creaked its way along the road and down the winding descent that took them into Bochnia. However, upon reaching the meeting hall in town, they were greeted to the first of what would be many surprises. The family did not pack fast enough. As scheduled, they arrived at dusk, but the designated meeting place was empty. The other families, in their alacrity, had already departed. Without benefit of extra supplies, information, or security in travelling with the larger group, the carriage hastily headed east in hope of separating from the approaching German invaders and catching up with the convoy.

Ian never slept that first night. A balmy evening, bright stars dotted the ink-black sky as the carriage moved steadily along the wide-open country road. In the middle of the night, their driver stopped to take a break. He filled a bucket with water from a larger container stored behind his seat and grabbed the lantern to step down and provide water for the horses. Stefan took the reins as soon as he climbed back aboard, allowing the fatigued driver much-needed rest. The clip-clop of horse hooves blended with an orchestra of insects, providing a rhythmic backdrop as they continued their journey uninterrupted. Observing everyone else deep in slumber and seeming quite comfortable in their makeshift beds, Ian finally lay down to attempt sleep. Finding difficulty in keeping his eyes closed, he was rewarded with a magnificent display. Shooting stars. The entire sky lit up with a spectacular show of shooting stars dancing to the music from below.

The wagon continued moving through the starlit night and kept going right on through the next day, stopping only occasionally so they could stretch and feed the hungry horses. As the eastern sky faded into darkness following their first full day of travel, they reached a monastery. Jozefa knew the abbot, so they were invited to stay overnight, able to enjoy a warm meal and sleep on shared cots. They awoke early to a simple breakfast, which the nuns prepared in virtual silence. Jozefa conversed quietly with the mother superior as the appreciative family finished up their breakfast. Ian actually found himself eager to get back on the trail.

Once on the road, it wasn't long before evidence of the German invasion and its accompanying dangers reached them. Echoes from shelling disturbed the road's serenity while plumes of smoke provided clear indication and location of the nearby towns that surrounded them. These indicators proved invaluable in steering clear of vulnerable targets, but even the lonely road proved to be no safe haven. Stefan was the first to spot the danger. He urgently brought to everyone's attention, two German fighter planes approaching from the western skies. They had earlier observed such smaller planes accompanying the larger bombers, but now these two rogue planes approached like fluttering bees moving in their direction, dipping in altitude as if guided directly toward their path.

The planes continued their descent with a buzzing sound that grew in intensity, and it soon became apparent that the road travelers were the objects of the gunners aim. "Run for cover!" Everyone scrambled off the wagon, running for cover under nearby trees as the sound and sparks of gunfire splattered all around them. The planes circled somewhere overhead as Ian checked to make sure that everyone was okay. Henryk hovered near Krystyna and his cousins, while Jozefa stayed near her youngest sons. Stefan stepped out toward the road before proclaiming, "Everyone, stay down, they're coming back" Again, a low buzz grew in intensity, preceded by random gunfire that splattered along the road and all around them. Stefan stepped out once again following a period of silence and announced this time that the coast was clear.

One by one family members walked out toward the roadway, visibly shaken by the unforeseen attack. Jozefa was the last to join them and brought everyone together in the middle of the dusty road. She appeared calm as she brushed herself off, looking around as if they were embarking on a family holiday. "Everyone is okay and everything is just fine. Now let's get back on the carriage and continue our journey."

For several days, they travelled nonstop day and night. Days were warmed with brilliant September sunshine and evenings decorated with an endless display of shooting stars. One afternoon, Ian and Victor sat at the end of the wagon keeping watch, their legs lazily dangling below them. Stefan was again at the reins as Henryk and the driver stood toward the front of the wagon engaged in conversation. The driver pointed to a landmark in the distance, perhaps indicating their intended destination. Krystyna and her cousins sat huddled together in animated conversation, intermittent giggles mixed in with occasional laughter. Jerzy sat next to Jozefa reading a book while Zdislaw and Stanislaw were close by her side contentedly playing with their wooden soldiers. Had they not been on the run from an invading army, the setting could have been described as idyllic.

Ian and Victor were on the alert for nearby shelling or the buzz of invading airplanes. Since the air attack after leaving the convent, German pilots continued to slow down their travel every day by shooting wildly at anything in sight. Initially they would hear a distant hum, quickly followed by the scattered formation of rogue fighter planes that appeared with an angry buzz. They were now joined by fellow travelers who dotted the roadside, all prepared to scramble in the event of planes approaching with random gunfire. The pilots, it was later learned, were German teens not trained to be disciplined fighter pilots. However, they earned a reputation as reckless young fighter pilots who seemed to derive joy in wreaking havoc on the road-weary travelers.

Although Ian was well attuned to the dangers, he was also invigorated by the journey. There was a sense of exhilaration in travelling out in the open air, unaware of what lay ahead. He gained a sense of responsibility and pride as he felt the revolver tucked safely away and close at hand, knowing that he was helping to protect the family.

Keeping their eyes and ears open for any sign of danger, the teens took note of the increased activity around them. More and more wagons and travelers, lugging whatever they could carry, appeared on the roadway, all headed east to avoid the approaching German Army. Little if any traffic headed west. Occasionally, an over-crowded bus would pass them, open windows exposing anxious passengers stuffed inside. Hearing the moan of an approaching bus, Ian observed a farmer along the roadside. He looked to be supervising several workers along a wooden fence, and his appearance was strikingly familiar. Studying the face and movement of the farmer, Ian's view was instantly blocked by the bus, which passed them at a snail's pace as the driver grinded gears to make it up a gradual incline. Just as the bus painstakingly passed, Ian managed to catch one last glimpse of the farmer and was convinced that he recognized the face.

"Stefan, stop! I believe we know that man."

Stefan brought the wagon to a halt, and the farmer looked up with a surprised expression. "Pani Bajda!"

Upon being recognized, Jozefa stood and smiled. The farmer enthusiastically guided Stefan to steer the wagon toward the barn and instructed his workers to collect water and feed for the horses. "Come, come! You are my guests for the evening."

Later that evening, Ian realized just how much he enjoyed the simple meal that was prepared for them after days of limited rations on the road. They learned over dinner that their former neighbor took an offer from the Polish Government several years earlier. The young farmer was able to purchase land with assistance from Ian's father Stefan and was now operating a sugar beet farm in eastern Poland. Once again, the dozen travelers were provided a place to sleep and offered a tasty breakfast containing sliced ham, fresh beets and tomatoes, pickled cucumbers, and bread with butter and strawberry jam, before continuing on their journey.

Back on the road, the volume of families and travelers populating the roadside continued to increase with each passing day. They had now been on their journey for over a week, and even their own travel party had increased. During a stop while passing through a small village, Stefan struck a conversation with an anxious university student who expressed concern over the impending Nazi invasion. After learning of his concern and having no place to go, Jozefa extended an invite for the young man to join them. The travel party had now grown to thirteen.

Gradually, the echoes from shelling became more distant while the threat from fighter planes mysteriously stopped. Ian watched stunned as planes that once attacked them now circled back, as if bounced off an invisible wall before reaching them. Replacing the fear of German invasion arose a new fear, an element of uncertainty now posing as danger. In stark contrast to the darkening mood that covertly strangled the surrounding countryside, the weather remained absolutely perfect. Blue skies and brilliant sunshine warmed the crisp September air while shooting stars continued to decorate balmy evening skies.

Once again, Ian and Victor sat at the end of the carriage keeping watch. Their driver rigidly peered straight ahead, tightly holding the reins. Stefan and Henryk stared intently beyond the distant horizon, their thoughts hidden in silence. Krystyna and her cousins sat huddled in idle conversation void of giggles or laughter. Jerzy sat next to Juzefa reading a book. Zdislaw and Stanislaw were stretched out, fast asleep with the wooden soldiers visible by their side. The university student was also sleeping, his folded jacket serving as a makeshift pillow. They were now a travel party of thirteen. Nothing was shared in spoken words, but everyone wondered in nervous silence what fate lay around the corner.

Historical Perspective

World War II commenced with the German Army invasion of Poland on 1 September 1939. Hitler's blitzkrieg into Poland would not come without significant cost to the Third Reich. Over 16,000 German soldiers would be killed, hundreds of aircraft lost, and heavy damage inflicted upon their armored vehicles. The German Army was forced to use double the ammunition that would be required to take France one year later. But the vastly undermanned and underequipped Polish Army was no match for the powerful war machine constructed by Hitler over years of meticulous planning and preparation. Defending their country alone, the Polish Army suffered over 60,000 casualties and more than 400,000 soldiers were captured.

All across Poland, civilians fled major cities under attack, aided by the shelter of forests and fellow Poles. Many more stayed behind to defend their homeland. In Warsaw alone, over 40,000 civilians were killed in a desperate attempt to defend their city from German tanks.

The family expected to find refuge by travelling east to avoid the invasion, but there was good reason for their growing apprehension as they separated from the German Army. Unknown to the scores of families escaping invasion from the west, Germany and the Soviet Union (under Josef Stalin) had been engaged in a secret and devious plot. Under Hitler's grand plan, Poland would cease to exist after the blitzkrieg. As agreed upon by the unlikely collaborators, German troops invading Poland would halt their blitzkrieg at a zone considered to be of interest to the Russians.

With an undermanned Polish Army defending from the west, Red Army troops surprisingly waged their own attack against softened targets from the east. These unexpected attacks brought about by the improbable alliance surprised and further weakened the Polish Government and their military, playing tactically into Hitler's plot to have Poland wiped right off the map. An already spread-thin Polish Army was now required to reallocate much-needed resources to the east.

Defending on the eastern front, once again all alone, up to 7,000 additional soldiers lost their lives in battle, and over 240,000 captured. Virtually every Polish officer captured was murdered by the Russians in and around the Katyn Forest in Russia. The bloody massacre in Katyn took place on 5 March 1940, resulting in the loss of an estimated 8,000 Polish officers. In addition, 6,000 policemen and thousands of Polish intelligentsia representing landowners, accused saboteurs, factory owners, lawyers, officials, and priests were executed.

Not every Polish soldier was killed or captured. An estimated 100,000 Polish soldiers escaped to neighboring countries, where they regrouped to join the fight against Germany. The largest number of Polish soldiers risked great danger to enter France, where the German Army amassed in force following their defeat of Poland.

By 6 October 1939, Germany and the Soviet Union occupied the entirety of Poland.

CHAPTER 3

Russian Occupation

Eastern Poland (Ukraine)
15 September 1939 – Early December 1939

The hidden presence of an enemy was lurking in their midst and would soon reveal itself to Ian in a most chilling manner. For now the family was ready to take a break. They anticipated travelling into Romania when they initially set out, but getting split up from their fellow travelers before even leaving Bochnia changed everything. Unable to learn of shared plans or arrangements, they headed east in hope of catching up to the convoy. The travel party stayed on course, continuing east to separate from the invaders after it became apparent they were unlikely to meet up with the convoy. All the while, they sought out information to determine their own optimal plan.

After twelve days on the run and under constant exposure to the open air, the road-weary family decided to seek refuge in the quiet village of Podwoloczysko, mere kilometers from the Russian border. Gone were the sounds of shelling and threats from fighter planes. Still feeling some apprehension, they at least felt safe from the German invaders. The village they arrived at was a border town in an area that before World War I was part of the Ukraine, populated roughly half by Polish residents and half by residents of Ukrainian descent.

Their driver dropped them off at the village police station where they collected their belongings and went their separate ways. Ian couldn't help but feel a sense of loss as the horse-drawn carriage disappeared from view and the university student sought out his own lodging. However, Jozefa wasted no time in planning their next step.

After conferring with the head of police, Jozefa and Henryk gathered them all to share the arrangements. They were being provided an opportunity to stay in three different homes hosted by local families.

Home 1 – Jozefa, Krystyna, Jerzy, Dzislaw, Stanislaw, Alexandra, and Zofia
Home 2 – Henryk and Stefan
Home 3 – Ian and Victor

Ian and Victor were to stay in a farmhouse owned by a Ukrainian farmer, as were Henryk and Stefan. The rest of the family would be staying in the home of a Polish schoolteacher just outside of the village. The loss of the horse-drawn carriage was instantly forgotten. Ian had already formulated dozens of questions for his unsuspecting host, based upon initial observations of the border town.

* * *

The broad-faced farmer's open smile transformed to guarded concern as he read the sheet of paper Ian handed to him. Early that morning, he was surprised to awake and see his young guest seated at the old wooden table in the small kitchen, full of questions about the farm and surrounding area. They spoke in Polish, but the teen was more than eager to learn new Ukrainian words for much of their conversation. If only he had an apprentice who was as curious and attentive.

He rather enjoyed how the Polish teen showed a keen interest in not only the operations of the tobacco preparation process but also even in the financial aspects of the business. The farmer happily gave Ian a tour, proudly displaying long narrow leaves hanging in the open shed. He explained how once dried sufficiently, each leaf is placed flat on a table to be cured, sprinkled with sugar before another leaf is placed on top; stacked like a deck of cards. When the curing process is complete, government officials will visit the tobacco plantations, identifiable by a black sign posted in front of the house. If the tobacco leaves pass inspection, the plantation owners were sure to receive good prices for their operations. Tobacco and alcohol production were among the few industries that the Polish government held as a monopoly, and small businesses contributing to those industries were paid handsomely. The region around Podwoloczysko was populated with a large number of small tobacco plantations, but the future of those operations now seemed very much in jeopardy.

"Tell me again, where did these leaflets come from?"

Ian explained how after leaving the farm earlier in the afternoon with Victor, they met up with his older brothers to explore the area. Stefan had apparently also toured a tobacco plantation, as evidenced by a freshly rolled cigarette he was smoking. When Ian asked how he managed to obtain the dark-looking tobacco, Stefan simply winked and smiled.

Ian was not surprised by Stefan's ability to obtain the tobacco. He recalled a time where he, Stefan, and Mulek all set out to build kayaks. Stefan bargained for a low price at a local lumberyard but was rebuffed. Undeterred, he shopped with another merchant and soon had both vendors dropping their prices to compete for his business. Mulek, who was Jewish and well versed in the art of negotiation, appeared to be in awe of Stefan's skills. Upon their purchase of the lumber at a bargain price, Mulek smiled in admiration and shared with Ian, "Do you know, I believe that your brother could buy and sell a Jew."

Leaving out the fact that his brother managed to obtain enough tobacco to roll an entire pack of cigarettes, Ian went on to inform the farmer what they saw in the village. Shortly after their arrival, a low-flying airplane dropped leaflets, one of which he now shared with the farmer. Later in the day, small gangs of young men showed up and appeared to be looking for trouble. The local police remained out of sight as a sense of lawlessness seeped into the village.

Recognizing the Russian word for "LIBERATION" smattered in bold letters across the leaflet, Ian asked the farmer, "Just who is being liberated?"

The farmer's face contorted into a curious smile. The lines on his weathered face took on even deeper wrinkles, but the sudden coldness of his eyes struck like blue ice sharply visible in their narrowing crease.

"Ah, that is the question. Outside of jailed Communist troublemakers, just who is being liberated?

"These young men that you saw in the village today are radical Nationalists. They are fools to believe they will be liberated, or that the Soviets will allow an independent Ukraine state. Our life here is good. I work hard to earn an honest living for my family. My children go to school where they learn to read and write both Polish and Ukrainian. These leaflets that were dropped, there is nothing good that can come from this."

The farmer brushed back thick strands of sweaty black hair with both hands, his calloused fingers resembling stubby sausages. After a pause, he dropped his hands on the table. A craggy smile reappeared. Beefy forearms moved apart as if sweeping away all potential troubles. "Enough of such talk. Go fetch your friend. I'll have my wife prepare something for us to eat."

The following morning, 17 September 1939, introduced a frightening image that would remain forever etched in Ian's mind. He ventured out in the early morning, a Sunday, to explore the surrounding countryside. While the village slept, he walked toward a field by the main road where he viewed a solitary soldier surveying the area on horseback. The soldier spotted Ian, and eventually approached as close to fifteen meters, observing from the saddle of his sturdy Russian Don horse. Ian froze as the two made eye contact, but the Russian soldier made no menacing gesture. He was not concerned with a teenage boy wandering alone in the countryside. The purpose of his mission would soon be revealed. Spotting nobody else in the vicinity he kicked his horse and, with a harsh command, sped past Ian in a westerly direction. The encounter cast a disturbing feeling, but what followed was even more troubling. A tremor, it sent shivers through Ian's entire being. The ground began to shake as a distant rumbling mysteriously blended into the landscape. It started as a low rumble barely discernible but grew in intensity as the mounted soldier disappeared beyond the western horizon. Ian could feel the ground shake below him. The vibration increased as the object of the rumbling slowly emerged into view. His heart raced as a column of tanks surfaced, rising above the fog slowly clearing along the eastern horizon. The line of tanks appeared endless, rolling in single file over the open fields and knocking down fences, trees, anything in sight, right alongside the same roadway they travelled only days earlier to reach this destination. Ian felt as if he'd been kicked in the gut, a sense of betrayal. He was well aware of the Russian intentions. Poland was once again under attack, and now surrounded by enemies from both east and west.

There is, of course, no way to verify the fact, but Ian may have indeed been the first independent source to spot Russian tanks entering Poland. Though impossible to share this revelation with anyone outside Podwoloczysko, he needed to immediately inform his family. Meeting up at the main house and conferring with their mother, the family took note of the unsettling occurrences. The homeowner was also openly concerned upon hearing Ian's account, especially following the prior day's events. Fully aware that Ian, Victor, Stefan, and Henryk were all staying in farmhouses owned by Ukrainian families, he insisted that they all move in with him, believing there was added safety in numbers. The homeowner was a Polish schoolteacher who lived just outside the village with his wife and two daughters. He ignored the threats around them and was more than willing to provide refuge for the large travel party. By that evening, the entire family was once again united and under one roof.

Following weeks of brilliant sunshine, the rains finally arrived. Amid darkening clouds, Stefan and Alexandria left early in the morning on bicycles to visit a nearby town, the bikes made available by their host. A cold front blew in a thunderstorm that lasted the entire day, heavy raindrops diminishing visibility to a stone's throw. When a drenched Stefan and Alexandria finally arrived back to the house in the twilight hour, the road was so muddy they were unable to ride the bikes, having to walk them back to the house. That image was how Ian recalled autumn's arrival in the year 1939.

Emblematic with darkening weather was increased levels of lawlessness in the village. Under a veil of raised threats, the family rarely ventured far from the home, spending most of their days huddled around the radio in the cramped living quarters. Radio Warsaw continued to provide news around the clock, and they were all thrilled after learning of reports that both England and France had declared war against Germany. There was renewed hope and a belief that Allied forces would soon aid the undermanned Polish troops, thereby enabling the family's safe passage back home to Bochnia. But all enthusiasm and reason for optimism soon faded with the reality of two stark occurrences. First, Radio Warsaw was abruptly taken down, meaning their only news came from intermittent reports out of London. While the ability to receive news was much welcomed, reports that were communicated from Polish correspondents were not very promising. Poland stood alone in defense of a country now under attack by two enemies. Second, lawlessness in the community appeared to be growing at a disturbing pace. Young men, who Ian identified as the radical Ukrainian Nationalists, were spotted in the neighborhood. And it looked as if they were up to no good.

Tension filled the household. The young radicals grew more aggressive as rumors spread of Russian authorities intimidating Polish officials and select landowners. Their gracious host was visibly concerned. One evening, as he stepped outside to use the outhouse, he was attacked. A local gang had been hiding in the yard, and they proceeded to pummel him with rocks. Running back into the house, he displayed a heavy jagged rock that was aimed at his head but fortunately just missed hitting him. They all scrambled to hang heavy blankets over the windows. The owner sat by the front door with his rifle, Ian loaded and clutched his revolver, and everyone was on high alert. Nobody slept as they heard continuous rustling and noises, but they survived the night without further incident.

The household remained on alert. Strangers remained visible during the day and were obviously observing all movement in and around the house. The family kept a round-the-clock vigil to guard the house, keeping eyes and ears open for any sign of trouble. The owner believed that as a Polish educator, he was the object of the radical Nationalists' attention. Two days later, they awoke to learn that their host was gone. Sensing imminent danger for his family with his presence, he fled during the night to avoid impending attack or arrest. Following his departure, the radicals were seldom seen around the neighborhood.

Jozefa had enough. She defiantly walked into the village and demanded assistance from someone who could help them. The nervous mayor shared her concern over the attack. Having managed to retain his position for the time being, he promised to assist her. Several days later, he arranged for a local farmer to transport the family to the larger town of Tarnopol. The travel party once again prepared for journey on a horse-drawn carriage, this time heading west.

Stefan had also had enough. He was seventeen and nearly of age to join the army. Believing the family would find safety in Tarnopol, he decided to return to Bochnia, determined to find a way to join the Polish Army or underground movement. Once again, Ian was not surprised by Stefan's actions. He was well aware of Stefan's passion and drive, always wanting to make things happen and never accepting no for an answer.

Before departing, Ian was concerned that the family revolvers would be confiscated, possibly causing complications or arrest. He sought out a farmer, a trusted friend of their host family who often stopped to visit, joining them as they listened to the radio reports. The farmer lived just outside the village not too far from where they stayed. Ian stopped to visit the day before they departed, asking him to hold on to the weapons. The farmer agreed to do so, hiding them in the attic of his thatched roof. Ian informed the friend that he'd be back as soon as possible to pick them up, but that was the last he saw of the trusted family weapons. Many years later, Ian often pondered over what happened to the five revolvers; were they found by an unsuspecting party or simply lost in the history of the thatch roof house?

Brisk autumn winds locked in cooler air and extended darkness. The family had now been away from home for well over a month when they left the village of Podwoloczysko. In contrast to the carriage ride from Bochnia, their journey to Tarnopol was marred by steady rain mixed with chilling drizzle. Whenever travel was slowed, Ian took the opportunity to jump off the carriage, observing wagon wheels half stuck in mud. Yet the horses continued their determined pursuit, and the family moved slowly but steadily in the direction of their destination.

As the beleaguered family finally approached Tarnopol under the cloak of a threatening sky, they congregated along the driver's seat to view a somber sight. The city was bereft of life. Few townspeople were visible, and the town's church steeples stood scarred with bullet holes. City officials offered some assistance, directing them to the local high school where they were provided shelter and a place to sleep. Fellow refugees spread out across the entire gymnasium floor as the family searched for an opening to claim as their own. Stumbling over the entire area, they negotiated enough movement to secure a tight space, where Ian felt fortunate for their blankets to shield them from the cold, hard floor. Although not the best of conditions, the family at least took solace and felt some measure of safety in sharing space with the large number of fellow Polish refugees.

Ian ventured out with Henryk and Victor the following morning to learn what they could about life in Tarnopol. Scores of Russian soldiers were visible throughout the city, identifiable from their khaki green uniforms with a red band or a red star on the cap. Although the soldiers had a gruff and unkempt appearance, they did not appear to be the object of fear within the community. The Secret Police held that distinction. Ian observed many soldiers wandering around the city in a somewhat curious manner, eager to visit shops and observe the surroundings of a foreign city.

All across the city were signs to register with the Russian authorities, a process to receive a passport-like document that seemed to be a step toward eventual Soviet citizenship. The young men entered a building where they had their photos taken and filled out an application form. They were told to come back in several days to pick up their paperwork and complete the process. Departing the building with some apprehension, they decided to take their chances and not return. Given the uncertainty and rumors of arrest that were spreading throughout the city, it seemed in their best interest to remain incognito from the Russian authorities.

For their meals, the family welcomed the support of a local charity. They were provided a small allowance, which enabled them to fill up a jug of coffee and purchase slices of bread at a nearby church every morning. In the afternoon, they were offered helpings from a pot of soup, which they brought back to the high school to share among themselves. Fortunately, no papers were required to receive the servings. The small amount of money provided by the charity was all that was needed.

Within days of their arrival in Tarnopol, Jozefa ventured out to meet some of the local townspeople, and one of the ladies she befriended was a Jewish woman. The woman shared that her fifteen-year-old son was in need of friends. Aware of her son's appetite for adventure and thinking this would give Ian something to do, they arranged for the boys to meet up. Unfortunately for Ian, the young lad was quite different from himself or his Jewish friend Mulek. Expecting to see and learn of places to explore in Tarnopol, the boy was instead immersed in talk of science projects and dreams of becoming a scientist. Ian suspected that he now understood why the boy had so few friends.

Ian soon observed another difference between Jewish families in Tarnopol and those back home in Bochnia. Some of the young Jewish men were provided an opportunity from the Russian authorities who now occupied the town. These young men were provided arms and given authority to serve as a militia, replacing the Polish police officers that had been arrested following Russian occupation. Perhaps some took on this assignment with excessive vigor due to the limited prospects available to them or the threat of what awaited them if German troops eventually occupied Tarnopol. But the militia established a tarnished reputation with the locals. A few of the men developed a swagger, exhibiting an aggressive attitude toward residents in the town. Ian was well aware that the militia was made up of a small number of Jewish residents and did not represent the actions of the larger Jewish community. His own experience with Jewish families was borne of friendship and community. However, in Tarnopol, the actions of this small group did not endear the Jewish community to the troubled Polish and Ukrainian citizens.

The family stayed in Tarnopol for several weeks before making a decision to travel back to Bochnia. There they hoped to reunite with their father, whom they suspected had at least made an attempt to return in wait for them. Further, there was a desire to sleep on real beds in their own home in lieu of living as refugees. Although a seeming difficult decision based upon the unknown of what awaited them, they also sensed imminent danger in Tarnopol and considered being home under German occupation to be the lesser of two evils. This sentiment was shared by many, as sounded in a common refrain heard among fellow refugees: "Better to die with your head on a stone under German occupation than with your head on a loaf of bread under Russian occupation."

Clearly, there was concern that living in Tarnopol under Russian occupation would result in extreme hardship and little hope, if not fatal consequences. The family had only a small amount of money left but found the means to purchase train tickets for their return home to Bochnia.

Historical Perspective

Although not fully aware at the time, the family's decision to leave Tarnopol would prove to be both timely and fortuitous. The entire Tarnopol region was a diverse ethnic mix that included Poles, Jews, and Ukrainian nationalists. Following World War I, the region changed hands several times during the course of the Polish/Soviet War. When Polish field marshal Josef Pilsudski took control of Tarnopol in 1919, he offered assurance to the Ukrainian nationalists that there would be no peace with the Russians without creating an independent Ukrainian state. However, that promise was never realized, and for twenty years, Tarnopol remained under Polish control while the Ukraine was effectively partitioned between Poland and Russia.

With Russia now occupying Tarnopol, their aggression, as around Podwoloczysko, proved to be swift and heavy-handed. They would go on to arrest and execute Ukrainian

Nationalist leaders before implementing a program of mass arrests, torture, and deportation of Poles, Ukrainians, and "enemies of the working class." As for the militias and Jewish population, their reprieve would also prove to be short-lived. Ignoring his earlier agreement with Stalin, Hitler would ultimately invade from the west. By the time Germany occupied Tarnopol in 1942, they continued the practice of exterminating the population. German forces proceeded to murder thousands of Jewish citizens in Tarnopol, and send Poles, Jews, and Ukrainians to forced labor camps across Germany and their occupied territories.

Though unaware of the full extent of atrocities that were about to occur, the family sensed a need to leave Tarnopol. There was lingering doubt and the unknown of what awaited them back home, but they were ready and willing to take the risk.

Przemysl, Poland
Early December 1939 – April 1940

In the early morning hours, Jozefa led their party of ten to a dark, desolate train station populated with a handful of nervous travelers, Russian soldiers visible everywhere around the city. Their scheduled morning departure was delayed, and it was not until late evening that they were able to board a late-arriving train. It was only when the train steamed west in the direction of Bochnia that they felt some sense of relief. However, after several hours of travel, the family was denied their intended destination. The train made a sudden stop during the middle of the night in Przemysl. Ian and his family arrived at the precarious border that separated Russian and German occupation, and the train would travel no farther.

Detraining on the Russian side of the border, they searched and found shelter in a monastery situated just around the corner from the train station. Next to a smart-looking church tucked inside a street corner stood a white L-shaped three-story monastery, where up to a thousand refugees had already arrived. Conditions in the Przemysl monastery were even more overcrowded than what they experienced in Tarnopol. People and families spread out on the floors, hallways, stairs, wherever they could find an open space, leaving only a narrow opening along the walls so others could maneuver along the corridors. The family negotiated as best they could before they secured a spot on the second floor, steps away from the lone bathroom. Again, they felt fortunate to have extra clothing and blankets, providing some semblance of comfort on the hard, cold floors.

Przemysl was geogrphically a city divided. The San River, which cuts right through the city, separated German and Russian occupation. Ian observed their side of the river full of chaos and disorder, while the view across the river appeared much more neat and orderly. The only way to reach the German side was by crossing a narrow railroad bridge. The main bridge had been destroyed during the Polish Army's defense of the city. Fully aware that they had no other choice, the family settled as best they could, bracing for the coming winter and seeking information that would enable them to cross the border in hopes of returning home.

The European winter of 1940 proved to be extremely harsh, the coldest that Ian had ever experienced in his fifteen years. Some days approached 30 degrees below 0 F. Fortunately, the family had packed winter clothing, and Ian was relieved to have his long winter coat, which he layered over a heavy shirt, vest, and jacket. Despite the conditions imposed upon the family, Jozefa once again proved to be a beacon of strength, always lifting everyone's spirits. Meanwhile, she encouraged Ian to apply his resourcefulness and come up with his own enterprising ways to help support the family.

Shortly after arriving in Przemysl, Jozefa befriended the owner of a hotel that sat close to the city center. The owner was a generous man, and he proudly treated the entire family to dine at a nearby restaurant. Paying close attention to the conversation over dinner, Ian learned of the hotel's difficulty in distributing adequate water supplies for the guests. So he and Victor devised a plan to help out. Using spare parts that they managed to scrounge, they constructed a sled capable of holding two large containers. Pushing the sled, they would glide the containers to the village pump, where local residents queued up to fill their water jars. Along with the water containers, the two also managed to pick up and load firewood on the sled. With a bundle of firewood and two large containers filled and brought back to the hotel for use by his guests, the gracious owner happily provided meals for the teens to share with the family.

Unfortunately, their partnership with the hotel owner was short-lived. Russian officials had no tolerance for private enterprise, and they were in need of a building to house their operations. The authorities abruptly took over the hotel and forced the owner, his wife, and two children out of their private lodging. The proud and generous hotel owner and his family were now relegated to a single hotel room and required to labor for the Russian authorities.

Ian and Victor soon came up with another enterprising way to earn money and help feed the family. Braving the cold, they would leave the monastery in the middle of the night while everyone was asleep. The only sign of life in the frigid mornings were drivers transporting goods on their horse-drawn carriages. Every morning, Ian and Victor managed to hitch a ride with a driver who was transporting loaves of bread, offering their assistance. The driver made frequent stops in town, where the two filled large baskets with loaves of bread to be taken to a local store. Because Ian and Victor assisted the driver, they were allowed inside the store, unloading the baskets and helping fill the shelves. Once stocked, the stores opened around 7:30 am, allowing the queues of people outside to enter. Ian and Victor were each provided with a loaf of bread for their assistance. Venturing out onto the streets, they searched out buyers willing to pay good prices for their bread on the black market. With money in their pockets, the two repeated the process, again locating a driver to help fill baskets for delivery to a local store. Their second loaves of bread earned that day were taken back to share with the hungry and appreciative family.

In addition to providing a means to earn bread and money, the brutal winter also enabled another opportunity. By mid-January the San River was frozen solid. Vicor met a local resident who assured them that for a small fee he'd lead them across the border and safely into German occupation. The teens conferred with Jozefa, and all agreed for Ian and Victor to make the trip so that they could arrange for the entire family's safe return to Bochnia. The border crossing did not come without some apprehension. Ian observed that almost overnight, heavy Russian artillery had been installed and manned along the hilly banks on the Russian side. The guns pointed directly at the tidy and orderly-looking side of town across the river. Ian suspected that the Germans and Russians might not be on such good terms with one another after all.

Daylight was losing grip under a mass of gathering clouds as the suddenly nervous local led Ian and Victor downstream from the city center and past the train station. They came to a stop along the river's edge, separated from the German border by only a wide blanket of windswept ice, gusts of snow swirling around them. Expecting to cross with further help and direction, their guide simply pointed to a barely visible guardhouse across the river, stating "There it is" before doing an abrupt about-face and running back toward the direction from which they came. They didn't even have time to ask a question. Suddenly unsure, the two looked at one another before moving with caution to cross the frozen gateway.

They barely moved two steps before they heard a commotion. Shouts and threats coming from a distance but directed toward them and getting closer. The two looked up to see a group of young men sprinting away from a patrol of Russian soldiers, the chase approaching rapidly. Stepping away from the river, crisp gunfire echoed above them as the two joined the fleeing men before breaking off and turning down a side street. With the narrow street made up of storefronts and residences, they banged on the entrance of the first doorway, pleading with the startled owner to allow them inside. A balding man showed fear. He barely opened the door, refusing entrance, but they managed to hold him in conversation, calming down as much as possible to reassure him of their friendly intentions. Spotting several heavy-breathing Russian soldiers screech to a halt at their street corner, they continued engaging their host in jovial conversation. The soldiers regained their bearings to view the surroundings, and paused for what seemed an eternity. Ian could feel their gaze, but the two continued light-hearted conversation complete with backslaps and laughter. Finally, appearing satisfied, the soldiers rushed off to inspect the next street. Ian and Victor cheerily wished the perplexed homeowner a pleasant evening, tipping their caps as they hurriedly left to depart a nervous street slipping into darkness. Their return to Bochnia would have to wait.

Welcome signs of spring introduced hints of warmth and extended daylight, their cold, gray world animated with the brush of a slow, methodical thaw. Ian and Victor were now able to venture and explore more of Przemsyl, where threatening changes cast images both loud and subtle over the scenic city.

They walked along narrow streets from the city center to a clock tower perched atop a hill, and climbed to the top of the tower, where spectacular panoramic views of the city and surrounding area greeted them. Farther up the hill stood a well-maintained medieval castle that offered equally breathtaking views, offering yet further evidence of what lay both below and beyond the San River. Not everything they viewed was welcoming. Visible along the city square were oversized loudspeakers spewing Russian propaganda. Patriotic songs mixed with fiery speeches eschewing the greatness of Russia suffocated the area. A distressed pull drew them away from the hill and toward the train station, where they observed a most disturbing scene. Dozens of Russian soldiers guarded a cattle car train that extended far around the bend; they could not see the end of the line. The boxcars contained no windows, only a narrow opening toward the top of each car, so they were unable to see inside. But the sounds emanating from inside were unmistakable. A continuous drone of muffled conversation breathed fear and desperation. Ian learned from onlookers that entire families filled the boxcars. Families of Polish officials, select landowners, shop owners, even anyone deemed a threat to Russian authorities. The authorities were known to pay informers to identify any person considered a threat to Communist ideologies. No trial was conducted; people were arrested on mere suspicion. Ian felt quite certain that the hotel owner and his family were suffocating in fear somewhere inside the train.

The haunting sounds continued nonstop day and night, the hum a tortuous reminder of capitulation and uncertainty that befell the community. It echoed all around them for several days before the ghostly train mercifully pulled out of the station, the haunting drone replaced with an eerie silence.

In contrast to the forced removal of families, an increased presence of Russians now populated the cityscape, and the inclusion of Russian women wove into the city's fabric. Many of the officers and authorities now had their families living with them, their wives and girlfriends easily identified. Few townspeople had the means or opportunity to purchase goods, but Russian women freely shopped and gobbled up items from the small storefronts that remained open. Ian observed that the transition for many of these women and their families might not be so simple, perhaps some living in a city for the first time. Popular among the items that Russian ladies frequently purchased were lacy gowns proudly worn while shopping or dining. Ian and Victor enjoyed the sightings but mused it would be best to not inform the officers that their wives were actually wearing nightgowns in public, not evening dresses. A number of the soldiers and new arrivals also appeared quite awkward when viewed through grainy windows dining out for their meals, as displayed by table manners void of proper etiquette.

Occasionally, the two managed to engage some of the Russian soldiers in conversation. Ian made a point of reading the propaganda newspapers on a daily basis in an attempt to learn Russian, and there were many common phrases between the two Slavic languages. The Russian soldiers exhibited bravado, a fierce pride that everything was a little bigger and better in their native Russian homeland. One day, Ian and Victor purchased some fruit at the market, the pickings not the best. Standing close to them was a young soldier outwardly complaining to anyone within earshot, lamenting on the slim pickings of ripe fruit. Victor asked the soldier, "Do you have oranges in Russia?" The abrasive soldier proudly stuck out his chest, broke into a clamor describing the most delicious-tasting oranges that you can ever imagine. With everyone forced to listen in silence, he closed his oratory with "Our orange factories produce the largest and finest-tasting oranges in the world."

Ian was unable to contain himself, the comic visual of an orange factory filled his brain. He bent over and broke into uncontrolled laughter that had the entire crowd, including the Russian soldier, staring at him. Feeling the soldier's glare, he attempted to stifle laughter but only managed a stoic smile that continued blurting out uneven chuckles.

Doubt and unease crept into the face of the proud soldier, so Ian thought it best to discontinue the exchange and move on. He did his best to straighten up, motioned for Victor to join him, and spoke in almost perfect Russian, "Enjoy your day, sir, hopefully we will have the good fortune of tasting your delicious factory-made oranges one day."

By April, seven months after leaving their home to escape German invasion, the border to German-occupied Poland finally opened. The Russians and Germans coordinated a reentry that would allow Polish refugees back across the border, relieving the Russian side of the overcrowded conditions.

German SS officers were brought over to the Russian side where they set up an office and questioned Polish citizens wishing to cross the border and return home. The smart-looking officers conducted interviews, checking for documents to ensure proof of nationality and residence. Ian was surprised to observe that the officers were actually polite and professional, much different from the Russian soldiers they had encountered over the past few months. Unfortunately for Victor, he did not possess the required documents to allow entry. He was forced to remain back in the monastery on the Russian side while the rest of the family collected their few belongings, this time in hopes of finally returning home. Before leaving, Ian promised his friend that he would stop at his house first thing to secure and send him the required documents.

Ian's document issued by the SS, allowing entry into German occupation. Included were instructions for him to immediately report for work duty.

Against the backdrop of a pale yellow sky in the early evening hour, the entire family walked along the narrow railroad bridge to reach the German side of Przemysl. They carried their clothing, again tied in blankets, but lighter than the load brought over on the carriage. Worn and tattered clothing had to be discarded without replacement due to a lack of funds. With his free arm, Henryk carried their youngest brother Stanislaw, who had taken ill during the winter and was too weak to walk. Reaching the German side of the San River, everything appeared more orderly as they boarded the westbound train to Bochnia. Following seven months of living as refugees, they were finally returning home.

Arriving in the early morning hours, Ian breathed a sigh of relief when his father rushed to greet them as they entered the house. However, that relief was tempered by foreboding news. Young Stanislaw was fighting for his life. He became ill during the winter, a seven-year-old forced to sleep every night on a hard, cold floor and with substandard rations. A doctor in Przemysl diagnosed that he had come down with tuberculosis but was only able to provide basic medicines. After the family arrived back in Bochnia, they immediately brought in their family doctor in a desperate attempt to save him. They were too late. Their doctor walked out of the room with his head down and quietly delivered the prognosis. "There is nothing more that can be done. The best thing that you can do now for Stanislaw is simply make sure he's comfortable. May God be with you."

Refusing to allow anyone to sulk, Jozefa wasted no time in arranging a schedule to ensure that someone was always with Stanislaw throughout the day. Ian agreed to serve the evening shift before blowing out the lights and retiring to bed.

On a damp April evening, Ian entered the room to spend time with his young brother. Seated alongside one bed was Henryk, leaning over and speaking to Stanislaw in a gentle tone. Zdislaw rested comfortably near Henryk, his eyes barely open in an attempt to fight sleep. Ian carried the wooden soldier with him and placed it on the bed right next to Stanislaw. His little brother showed a peaceful expression.

"I see that he looks quite peaceful. You've been here a long time, Henryk, I'll watch him now."

"It's okay, Ian, I want to stay with him tonight. I think he needs company through the night, and I'm quite comfortable here. Why don't you take Zdislaw to his bed and get an early night yourself. I'll be just fine."

Ian walked over to the side of Stanislaw's bed and placed a hand on his brother.

"Sleep tight, little Stanislaw. Your soldier will keep watch over you."

Lifting Zdislaw and laying him in the bed next to Stanislaw, Ian left the room, wishing his brothers a good night.

Ian awoke well before dawn to the sound of sobs. Rushing from his cot to reach Stanislaw's, he came to a stop at the doorway entrance. There he viewed the candle-lit shadow of his mother kneeling alongside the bed, clutching her youngest son, loving words spoken through tears. Henryk and his father stood above them. It wasn't clear if Stefan's hand on Henryk's shoulder was intended to comfort his son or to remain upright. Henryk's words were spoken with calm and clarity. "He went in peace. I leaned over, and he simply looked at me with a smile as if to say 'Goodbye.'"

The family arranged a proper funeral for their little soldier. Stanislaw's body was laid out for three days in the house, where friends and family grieved his loss under the close watch of German soldiers. A splendid horse-drawn glass carriage carried the casket, leading a procession to the cemetery where Stanislaw was laid to rest. It was an ominous sign upon their return to Bochnia.

CHAPTER 4

Captured by the Red Army

Bochnia, Romania, Kiev, and Moscow
Autumn 1939 – Early Spring 1940

Separated from his family, Stefan could never have imagined that his quest to join the fight for Polish freedom would ultimately lead him across three separate continents. After the late-night attack on the family in Podwoloczysko, he grew restless, tired of feeling helpless while Russian soldiers and authorities took over Eastern Poland. He met up with another young Pole who shared his frustration. They made a decision to retreat back to Stefan's home in Bochnia. Once there, they would remain in hiding to elude the German occupiers and join the underground, or perhaps find a way to join the Polish Army. Heading back west without constraints of a large travel party, they easily slipped back into Bochnia where Stefan was reunited with his father, who had also safely returned and was back in their house. Also at the house was his grandfather, who remained in Bochnia throughout their departure.

Stafan Sr. felt blessed to be joined in his home at a dining table populated with three generations of male lineage. He thirsted to learn everything of his family's plight after they left Bochnia and needed to lay plans for their safe return. Since returning to Bochnia, Stefan Sr. took careful measures to avoid unnecessary contact with the German authorities. He avoided going back to his office and blended in as best he could while German officers and officials took over the community. His son's arrival back at the house however was more precarious. If Stefan Jr. was seen, he'd immediately be taken away for work assignment, or more likely arrested for suspected activities against the Third Reich.

Despite concern for his family and a strict rationing of food in the community, Stefan Sr. was anxiously awaiting another delicious meal. He watched his son deftly mix eggs from their hen house with measured dabs of flour and water, and expertly flatten the mixing into fine dough. From there, he sliced extra thin strips with a sharp knife, each strip perfectly matched. The strips would eventually be cooked and sprinkled with small amounts of available cheese and salt to create a delicious spaghetti meal just as tasty as any ever served in the finest local restaurants. Of course, there were no restaurants available to dine in, so Stefan's anticipation was even higher than normal. Coupled with every meal was conversation and information sharing that was vital to them all.

"My understanding is that a large number of Polish troops have made their way to France in support of the French defense against the German Army. But there's virtually no way you can successfully get there by travelling west. You'd be traversing directly into enemy territory. You'll need an alternate route."

"What if I can make it to the Mediterranean? I can find passage on a ship and enter France from the south."

"That's quite lengthy, but it is a possibility. The best route is to go through Romania. Their government is neutral, and it was discussed that our government officials not already in France initially seek refuge there if Poland falls to the Germans. Romania is also the location that your convoy was headed to, as we had officials there in place to assist families on their arrival. I can provide you with some contacts, but you'll have to memorize them."

"I can do that with no problem. You know we were prepared and planning to go to Romania. We just decided to take a break in Podwoloczysko. Father, we didn't realize we were so close to the Russian border. But as I've told you, there is nothing to worry about. They were on their way back west, and I'm sure will make it safely."

Despite the risk and danger awaiting his son, Stefan Sr. had no qualms over his son's decision to seek out and join the Polish Army in France. He knew his son well enough to understand his courage and conviction, and besides it seemed that anything Stefan did or touched always worked out. Perhaps more important, Stefan Sr. knew that it was the right and honorable thing to do. Poland was at war, their way of life now compromised, and his son was determined to do whatever was required to liberate Poland and restore their freedom.

Rich aromas filled the room. One thing they would surely miss was Stefan's creative cooking. Grandfather finally spoke, "Stefan, if you don't get that spaghetti cooked and served soon, the war will be over and you'll be going nowhere."

Stefan turned to his grandfather with a hearty laugh followed by a genuine smile that warmed the room. "Now you just relax, General, dinner will be served in due time."

It was early December 1939 when Stefan began his quest. He and the friend who joined him back to Bochnia finalized plans to join the Polish Army following his father's suggested route. They would travel through Slovakia, Hungary, Romania, and Yugoslavia, skirt Italy by boarding a ship on the Mediterranean, and enter France from the south. Although this added a significant amount of time and travel to reach their destination, they would at least avoid unfriendly and more dangerous territory.

Travelling on foot in freezing temperatures, they made it through the mountains of Poland and Slovakia, through Hungary, and into Romania. But there they stumbled upon an unexpected event. Even though believed to be far from the Russian border, Russian soldiers or border guards spotted them, yelling and firing shots in their direction. Sprinting for cover, Stefan quickly separated and thought he'd eluded them, until he heard threatening growls and soon reconciled that the guard dogs would deprive him of his quest to join the Polish Army.

Historical Perspective

For a Pole to be captured by Russian soldiers was near tantamount to a death sentence. Beginning with the Soviet occupation of Polish territory, approximately 1.7 million Poles were arrested and sent to labor camps across desolate locations in Siberia. This total number included not only soldiers, or in the case of Stefan, political prisoners, but also civilians (including children). Hundreds of thousands of Poles perished from the oppressive conditions imposed upon them. While soldiers and political prisoners were arrested for being enemies of the Red Army, citizens were arrested for simply enjoying basic freedoms that were seen as an affront to Soviet Communism.

Following his capture, Stefan was sent to Kiev, where he was housed in a castle-like dungeon with other suspected enemies of the Red Army. Prisoners were housed inside stark barren rooms that connected to a long hallway. The echo of pain and suffering mixed with an eerie silence. There was nothing to do but sit and wait for their turn to be called in for questioning. Every prisoner was gripped with fear and wonder in the unknown of what awaited him. Outside of being served with several meager rations, Stefan was left alone pretty much during the day, but nighttime took on a much different and more sinister twist.

Jangling of keys interrupted a dream-filled sleep. Stefan looked up to see several armed guards roughly grab and march him to the commander's office. Stepping inside cold walls, he was blinded by a bright light coming from behind a heavy wooden desk, the interrogator's face obscured from the light. The only thing Stefan could make out from the desk was a revolver and a stack of official-looking documents. The questions and accusations began, and were repeated over and over. "You are a spy against Russia. Make your life easier and sign your confession here."

Stefan refused to sign, explaining that he was no spy but simply traveling across Europe to avoid the Nazi occupation. Harsh words came back accusing him of a litany of offenses, but after about thirty minutes they were at a standstill. The interrogator called for the guards to take their prisoner back to his cell.

Stefan lay on the cold concrete floor, but sleep was no ally. Pained screams and yells crept into his cell from every direction, other prisoners going through their own interrogations. There was no time to register his thoughts, for he soon heard heavy boots marching toward his cell, clanging of keys opening the cell door. Stefan was once again grabbed and taken to the commander's office for more questioning. The same format repeated, accusations and denials. Over and over the process was repeated into the night. Five times, maybe six, he lost count. Stefan could barely speak or keep his eyes open. The interrogator repeated over and over that there is no hope. "Make your life easy and sign the papers, you have a way out." But again, Stefan refused to sign. The guards dragged him back to his cell, Stefan barely able to stand or walk. He lost all track of time and found himself dizzy and confused by the sequence of events. Losing sense of surroundings, he fought to focus on his predicament, where he was, how he got here, how he can survive. Expecting the guards to enter and take him for questioning with the echo of every sound in the cavernous dungeon, he was instead left to his own devices. As the hollow sound of silence tantalizingly breathed hope into his cell, Stefan believed he had survived the night. However, sleep never came. The chilling threat of heavy boots and clanging keys haunted his every thought.

For six nights Stefan was subjected to the same cruel questioning. Even though losing strength and hope, he refused to agree to the offenses. The interrogations took on different tactics. Harsh intimidating threats coupled with severe blows all over his body intended to break him, followed by an interrogator with calming words to put an end to his hell. Every time, Stefan refused to sign. It was not until the seventh day of questioning that they finally broke him. Unable to sleep or think clearly, and in a desperate attempt to maintain his sanity, Stefan confessed to all accusations and signed the documents.

For his offenses, he was sentenced to five years' hard labor to be served in a Siberian labor camp. From Kiev, Stefan was forced to march over 850 kilometers to Moscow in the middle of winter. The journey lasted well over a month, and many prisoners did not survive the grueling march. Every day on the march, exhausted prisoners fell to the ground, unable or unwilling to continue. An impatient guard would immediately order them to get up with angry threats and jabs from the butt of his rifle. Sometimes the prisoner managed to get back on his feet to continue the march. If unable to do so, they were shot dead and left behind on the roadside. One day a prisoner spotted a small cart along the edge of a hill. In a desperate attempt to flee he raced for the cart in hopes of escape by rolling down the hill. Just before reaching the cart, he was struck down by multiple bullets and left to die.

Once in Moscow, conditions only deteriorated. Stefan was held in the notorious Lubyanka prison where cells were packed so tight that it was virtually impossible to even lie down. Prisoners were forced to stand or crouch in tight areas in the most unsanitary conditions, and given only one hour each day to stretch and move freely in an outdoor yard. After one month in Lubyanka, Stefan and his fellow prisoners were transported by rail, filed onto cattle cars, from which they were shipped to the hinterlands of Siberia.

CHAPTER 5

German Occupation

Bochnia, Poland
April 1940 – December 1942

Bold red flags hung like threatening daggers outside of government buildings that now housed German military personnel. The flags displayed a thick black swastika over a white circular background hung taut in a vertical manner, a constant reminder of forced occupation and strict authority. So different from the Polish flags they replaced, with its white eagle appearing a symbol of freedom flapping in the wind. Outside of the derided flags, the city of Bochnia under German occupation appeared much the same visually. But in ways that a city breathes life and bares its soul, it may as well have been a different place altogether. Bochnia was void of life, its beating pulse ripped from the city's core. The few residents who could be seen moved quickly with heads down, so as not to make eye contact with German soldiers or officials who now owned the city. Shops stood largely vacant, if they were open at all. Strict food rationing forced residents to purchase only the most basic food supplies one day of the week, and required long waits in queue for a chance to select from the meager rations left over from their German occupiers. A strict curfew was now imposed, and anybody seen outside their home after curfew was immediately arrested and sent to jail. Citizens were not allowed to meet up or congregate. Any citizens seen talking in groups were arrested for conspiring against their German occupiers.

The locals were also required to move and make way for any German soldier or official walking down the street. Failure to do so could result in arrest. Ian quickly learned that the German officers were lax to this law and tended to be more tolerant of the citizens. However, the SS officers, gestapo, and youngest soldiers, many of whom were trained as Hitler Youth, were extremely arrogant, looking for any excuse to arrest or intimidate the local citizens. Ian learned this in his attempt to gain a small measure of self-respect. He would often test the patience of oncoming soldiers by looking down as if not noticing who was approaching, thereby avoiding a show of respect or fear in having to move out of their way. It was a dangerous game, and he quickly learned just how far he could go with each of the rank and file.

Another disturbing change were policies that led to growing division among residents in the community. Some of the changes were covert and subtle, but others clearly intended to create isolation and direct fear into a segment of the community.

German authorities introduced a practice of recognizing and favoring German nationals, or Volksdeutsche. Many families in the community were known to be of German lineage. Their ancestors immigrated to Poland to escape religious persecution that took place in Germany during the seventeenth century. There was even a small German community of thirty to forty families in the city who freely practiced their faith and clung to their way of life. Ian learned of this community just prior to the war. He volunteered at his high school to communicate warnings of a possible German attack. Officials expressed concern that the Germans may use gas in their attacks, so Ian memorized the safeguards and tips for homeowners to keep their homes safe and secure. The neighborhood he was assigned was this German community. While most were quite appreciative, he did recall that some families were not so keen or friendly in receiving the information.

Among the privileges that Volksdeutsche families received were improved food rations and access to available jobs under the authority of German occupiers. Volksdeutsche residents took over the many positions that were originally held by Polish residents who lost their jobs, including the position once held by Ian's father in the law department. A number of Volksdeutsche men also took over jobs as police under the direction of German authorities. The German gestapo established their own office in town to conduct surveillance and prosecute citizens for suspected crimes against the German Army. But some Polish men of German ancestry, who now felt allegiance to their German occupiers, replaced the disfavored officers of the local police department.

Most of the families who registered as Volksdeutsche came as no surprise to the local residents, but there were some surprises. The Novakowski family who lived down the street from Ian's family never gave any indication of their German ancestry, but seemingly out of nowhere they were afforded special privileges. The youngest son was often seen walking down the street, proudly speaking aloud in an obvious display to learn his newfound German language. However, much more common in the community were the German families who refused to sign up as Volksdeutsche.

They viewed themselves as Poles whose families lived free in their adopted country for generations, and they joined other residents in their distrust and contempt of local citizens who now received special privileges from the foreign occupiers.

Life in Bochnia had indeed entered a dark period defined by the loss of basic freedoms, but the worst suffering and indignity was imposed on Jewish families. German authorities took painstaking measures to identify any person of the Jewish faith, often with the aid of Volksdeutsche residents, and forced Jewish residents to identify themselves by wearing a visible patch of the Star of David. All Jewish families were eventually rounded up from their homes and moved to a temporary ghetto set up in town, their lifelong possessions left behind for the Germans. Ian walked in town to take note of the fenced-in ghetto constructed near the train station. Beyond a crudely built fence lay an overcrowded community that nobody was allowed to enter or leave without a permit.

Ian was overjoyed to learn that Mulek was still living across the street upon their return, but that mood was quickly relinquished. Within days of their return, he ventured across the street to visit his friend, where an uncle had joined them. Despite a perversion of darkness that hung in the air, Mulek warmly greeted his lifetime friend. Two things struck Ian as they walked into the living area. First, the home felt barren, a darkness smothering away life and energy all around them. Second, Mulek's Star of David patch stood out as an unwelcome badge of identity. The blue star resembled more an ominous sign than a proud symbol, crudely sewn onto a white band visibly displayed over Mulek's left sleeve.

In an attempt to ignore the darkness suffocating them, they discussed conditions in Bochnia. Mulek shared his knowledge of the Jewish ghetto set up in town. Their stay in the ghetto was to be temporary, as families were ultimately transported by rail to forced labor camps. Ian tried to offer hope, suggesting that his friend leave, hide in the forest, or join the underground movement known to be operating in town. Mulek simply smiled and shrugged it off. He reckoned that members of the underground movement had their own job to do and issues to deal with, and little time for a young Jewish teen in need of help. Besides, he'd be with family, and together they would find the strength and means to overcome any hardships. Ian outwardly shared his optimism and offered words of encouragement, but could not help but feel concern for the yielding family. Within the week, all Jewish families from the neighborhood were rounded up and sent to the ghetto. Following their departure, Ian often ventured to the crude ghetto entrance, wondering if his best friend was still there, how he could reach him, and how he was managing with such dreadful conditions and prospects.

Coupled with the loss of the Jewish families in their neighborhood was the presence of German soldiers. Shortly after the occupation, German officers forcibly moved into the family house for several weeks, relegating their grandfather to a back room. Also on the family property, tents were temporarily set up to house soldiers. One of Ian's friends shared a story of how he would stop and talk with one of the soldiers. One day, the young soldier carelessly left his gun behind, so the friend managed to walk away with his gun. He suspected that the soldier must have gotten into serious trouble for losing his weapon.

Ian was surprised when he came home one afternoon to see a group of German officers seated in the living area, politely engaged in conversation with his parents over a cup of tea. It seemed that they overheard Jozefa speak and detected an Austrian accent, soon learning that she was quite fluent in their German language. They also found her to be quite knowledgeable and articulate in the appreciation of classical German music. His mother grew up in Vienna where classical German composers were quite popular. Excited for the chance to discuss the music and arts of their homeland, the officers invited themselves inside to enjoy a break from their normal routine.

The family also learned of an incident that cost the lives of many of the locals, and very nearly the life of their father. Around Christmas of 1939, four young Polish men decided to attack the police station, killing two German officers. Following their capture, the men were promptly sentenced to death by hanging. To set an example, German authorities decided to leave the men hanging on lampposts in the town square. Ian's father joined the town representatives, requesting to have the bodies removed. But they were left to rot, dangling in the square throughout the Christmas season. Still not satisfied, the German authorities threatened to round up all Polish government officials, line them up, and kill so many of the officials for each of the German officers killed. Because Ian's father was in charge of the county law department, was involved in covert operations, and also quite vocal in the request to remove the bodies, he knew that his life was very much in danger. The International Red Cross and other agencies learned of this planned atrocity and tried to intervene. They managed to convince the Germans to spare the county workers, but their desperate negotiations only went so far. The authorities rounded up fifty townspeople (twenty-five for each German officer killed), most of them young men who were in the jail for petty or trumped-up offenses, and marched them to a park behind the city stadium. There the townspeople were lined up along a deep trench that had been dug out and unceremoniously shot to death. One fortunate soul miraculously survived the gunfire. Wounded, he somehow managed to escape, running for cover in the nearby forest. The man was never found or seen again.

Another change was that the high school was shut down, and German author- ities required every male aged sixteen or over to register for work duty. Henryk was sent out shortly after the death of Stanislaw for work assignment in the Sudeten Mountains. Ian enjoyed school and should have been continuing his high school education, but came to grips that his education would soon be replaced by a manda- tory work assignment.

The Germans viewed education for Poles quite different from what Ian observed under Russian occupation. While in Przemsyl, Ian spoke to some of the local teens, learning about their schooling under Russian rule. The main focus of Russian edu- cation was based upon learning the social and individual merits of Communism, and of loyalty to the party. Lessons about Marx, Lenin, and Tolstoy replaced Polish history. Little time was spent on math or writing. Conversely, Hitler's plan was to have the Polish population provide manual labor under German rule. While the high school was shut down, trade schools were made available. Upon his return, Victor was able to continue work as an apprentice under a local tailor. But the high school was discontinued, and young men hoping to continue their education were instead forced to provide manual labor for their German occupiers. Some families and for- mer teachers did take it upon themselves to continue educating the youth in secret. That education came with great danger and risk. Any family or educator suspected of this practice was immediately arrested and shipped to a concentration camp.

Having just had his sixteenth birthday on 21 February while in Przemysl, Ian was required to report to the authorities and assigned to work on rebuilding a roadway. Despite an earlier arrangement with Russia to divide and conquer Poland, Hitler now expanded his plans for further German dominance. The roadway was being upgraded to provide a main thoroughfare running east and west, allowing for eventual transport of heavy equipment, supplies, and his army to the Russian front. For twelve hours every day, from 6:00 a.m. to 6:00 p.m. and six days a week, in the middle of a hot, sticky summer, Ian was assigned the task of breaking up rocks. For this backbreaking work, he was paid the equivalent of about one dollar each day.

After several months of this grueling work, Ian managed to switch to an easier job digging a drainage ditch in a remote area outside of Bochnia. Roughly one hun- dred men were assigned to this task, all housed in a barracks about ten kilometers from town. This new job was much improved over the highway assignment. Ian now worked eight hours rather than twelve, and the job also included improved food rations. For breakfast, they would stand in line to be treated to a slice of bread and a bowl of coffee. Many of the men used the last drops of coffee for shaving, as they had no access to hot water.

One morning in early December, Ian joined his coworkers on their daily march covering several kilometers from the barracks to the work site. Along the march, the men managed to bear the cold and relieve some of the boredom by singing songs in unison. The pompous commander had no clue that the patriotic-sounding songs were targeting him, as he did not understand Polish. Beginning with each refrain, a different worker chimed in with a catchy phrase that made fun of the commander, and the rest joined in with much enthusiasm and vigor. Not only did the songs keep their spirits up, but also provided entertainment in watching the uniformed German commander proudly lead a march to tunes and vocals that openly mocked him.

Upon reaching the work site, Ian was ordered to cross the ditch by walking on a narrow plank set up as a temporary footbridge. Unfortunately, with his muddy boots and icy conditions of the plank, he slipped and fell into the half-frozen ditch. Before realizing what happened, he was immersed to the waist in freezing water. It took minutes to surface from the fall, and Ian found himself soaking wet and shivering. The commander impatiently waited with a shovel, letting out an angry tirade in German while motioning for him to get back to work. Ian pleaded to go back to the barracks and change into some dry clothes. But the commander refused, more focused on finishing the project.

For four hours, Ian worked shivering in his wet clothes in temperatures hovering around the freezing mark. With lips blue, teeth chattering, and entire body shaking, the commander finally relented. Ian was escorted back to the barracks during their lunch break. There, the doctor wasted no time, immediately sending him to a clinic in town where he was diagnosed with a high fever, likely pneumonia. They kept him overnight and sent him home the following morning. A nurse stopped by to visit the house every day and informed him to stay in bed for one week, time to break the fever and regain some strength.

Although subject to severe discomfort associated with a life-threatening fever, the rest at home did provide a welcome reprieve and quality time with family members. Even with their limited rations, Jozefa managed to make a watery soup that was at least an improvement over what he had tasted in the barracks. Meanwhile, his young siblings took it upon themselves to provide a vigil of sorts, making sure that at least one of them was almost always in his room to provide company.

One afternoon, Krystyna brought in a bowl of soup that her mother had prepared as Jerzy sat on the bed next to his, occasionally reading out loud select passages from the Bible. Before Ian could sit up to taste the soup, Zdislaw entered the suddenly crowded room. He carried with him his wooden soldier and placed it on the bed next to Ian.

"I'm letting you borrow my soldier while you're sick. But you'll have to give him back after you get better." He paused for a moment before continuing. "Marian, are you going to die like Stanislaw?"

"Oh no, Zdislaw, I'm going to be just fine. And now that I have your soldier to watch over me, I'll get better even faster and be back on my feet in no time."

Jerzy smiled and got up from the bed. Pointing to the crucifix hanging on the wall between the two beds, he explained to Zdislaw that both his soldier and Jesus were now watching over and protecting their older brother.

Zdislaw glanced back and forth between the crucifix and the wooden soldier, appearing a bit perplexed. He looked over at Krystyna, perhaps in hopes of receiving further clarification from his big sister, but she only giggled. Finally, after enough contemplation to satisfy his curiosity, he appeared content and turned to leave. Before walking out the door he turned to face Ian, "Now don't forget to give him back after you get better. But you can let him stay here for a while longer if he and Jesus become friends."

Within one week, Ian recovered enough strength to get back on his feet and report for work. Although he missed out on the songs, his coworkers informed him that his fall into the frozen ditch and predictable fever were not forgotten (or forgiven) on their morning marches. His fellow workers chided their unsuspecting commander with harmonious barbs and insults for his foolishness, as he proudly led them on the daily marches to their work site.

Just days after regaining his health and returning to the camp, Ian was sent home again, this time for Christmas. And the lone gift he received that holiday was most appreciated, a certificate stating that he had fulfilled his work duty. Ian was now free to stay home and find work without having to register with the authorities.

Finding himself in a sudden joyous state and wishing to do something special for the family, Ian decided to take a huge risk. In contrast to the previous year when they were refugees in Przemysl, he was determined to make their Christmas of 1940 a joyous one. He did retain one fond memory from the prior Christmas. Typically, the family was required to traverse over harsh cold and heavy snow to attend Midnight Mass on Christmas Eve. However, because their residence in the Przemysl monastery also housed the church, Ian felt somewhat special that they could bypass the cold walk and simply stay indoors to attend the church service. It was the one moment when living as refugees in a monastery carried with it a form of privilege.

On this Christmas Eve, there would be no Midnight Mass. The imposed curfew made sure of that. But the family was together and in their own home, affording another opportunity. Ian fetched an axe and slipped into the nearby forest after dusk and well past the imposed curfew. There he came upon the perfect tree. In the middle of an open area under a starlit night stood a well-rounded spruce, stranding proud in a soft blanket of fresh snow. Ian gauged the tree over two meters in height and just right for the main living area. Expecting to quickly cut down the tree and depart for the safety of their home, the task was much more difficult than anticipated. Hacking and chopping away in the frigid night, desperately hoping nobody would see or hear him, he finally managed to chop down the tree, only to be confronted with the arduous task of dragging the tree back to the house undetected.

Ian followed the forest's shadows, maneuvered up and down heavily wooded terrain in an effort to reach the house undetected. With great relief, he struggled to get the tree inside, where a joyous Krystyna shrieked in delight, squeezing her brother tightly. Jozefa offered her son a subtle smile and gathered the children to create colorful religious decorations from their limited supplies. Hours later, the family sat around the decorated tree in silence. Drawing heavy curtains to conceal their treasure, they simply took in the beauty of the spruce. Little was spoken. Nobody left the room to go to sleep. Candles illuminated their tree in the darkness of night, providing a comfort and warmth that had not been felt since the German invasion of their homeland.

* * *

Back in familiar surroundings, Ian was free to find work in Bochnia without having to report to the authorities. The brickyard and flourmill across the street were likely possibilities, though both were now property of the Germans. He made sure to always carry his certificate with him, showing he had completed his mandatory work order. The document did provide a small sense of security and freedom, but life had taken on a daily grind and monotonous existence built upon survival and hope for the entire community.

Ian's father, Stefan, continued to do his best to lay low, keeping out of view as much as possible to avoid arrest. As the former county official in charge of the law department, he was an easy target to be viewed with much suspicion by the German authorities. If German authorities were to discover his prior role as military head for the district, it would have resulted in immediate arrest.

He cautioned the entire family to be careful and wary of not only Volksdeutsche but also any stranger, even casual acquaintances, to be viewed with skepticism. He reminded them of the unexpected visits from Mr. Ziegler in August 1939, just prior to the German invasion. Mr. Ziegler was a shop owner and bit of a loner in town who

Ian knew as a bachelor and uncle of a classmate. Out of nowhere, Mr. Ziegler took it upon himself to walk up the hill from town, looking to engage Ian's father in conversation. With his heavy German accent and awkward manner, Stefan Sr. immediately recognized that Ziegler was acting as a spy for the Germans. Jozefa warmly offered their visitor biscuits and tea while Mr. Ziegler feigned sudden concern. "What will happen to families if the Germans invade Bochnia? Do we even know if Polish troops will be available to provide protection?"

Ian's father acknowledged the concerns, throwing his hands up in exasperation as if troubled with the same matters. Meanwhile, he freely inundated his guest with boring detail of official matters that had nothing to do with wartime preparation. It became a bit of a game for Stefan to easily deflect Ziegler's clumsy attempts in gathering meaningful intelligence, and he rather enjoyed watching his visitor visibly squirm in frustration over not learning anything of significance. However, the visits also cast a disturbing element, adding to growing speculation that an invasion could occur at any time.

While cautioning the family to avoid conversation that might lead to suspicion or arrest, Stefan made certain to keep the family together and informed despite the obstacles. Since the family's return, they listened to reports from Radio London, but had to do so under extreme caution and coordination with only their trusted neighbors. The Germans banned citizens from listening to the radio, and proof of doing so resulted in arrest. Every night, a German truck containing a listening device drove down their street, looking to identify anyone tuned in to news reports. Neighborhood residents established a relay system to alert one another of the approaching device, thereby avoiding suspicion or arrest.

Despite their efforts to keep the Polish citizens uninformed, no wartime news was kept secret as Polish citizens found the means to covertly share news of the war on a daily basis. Citizens took great measures to avoid communicating news with anyone suspected of conspiring with the Germans, and even developed cryptic expressions through casual conversation to share news events with one another as a means to avoid suspicion.

Most of the news was foreboding. Shortly after the family returned to Bochnia, they all learned that Hitler unleashed his blitzkrieg against France, taking over Dunkirk and areas along the English Channel. The German Army continued their advance southward, and by 14 June 1940, their army entered Paris without resistance. That entire week, Stefan Sr. closely listened to the radio with a look of grave concern. Against a backdrop of scratchy interference, reports came to light that the French government, which had retreated to the southern French city of Bordeaux, had disintegrated. The French resistance to the German invasion ended with the following words from acting government head marshal Philippe Petain: "It is with a heavy heart that I tell you today that we must stop fighting."

His father's thoughts were consumed with images of his son Stefan, who left the house six months earlier on a quest to join the Polish Army in France. "If Stefan is in France, he surely fought the Germans. He would never surrender."

Following Ian's return home, the family remained resolute in their effort to learn of news on the warfront, hoping for a breakthrough, but very little in the way of good news was offered. Further adding to their unrest was the arrest of several former county workers on suspicion of having earlier aided the Polish Army. Ian's father remained wary and kept distance from his former office. He had taken painstaking measures to remove his name from potentially incriminating documents in his law office before leaving Bochnia. However, every night they sat at the dinner table in wonder if an unwelcome German official would knock on their door. Certainly, Zeigler knew of Stefan's position, and suspected his involvement during the town's wartime preparation. To their ongoing relief, the unwelcome visit had not yet occurred. Perhaps it was out of respect, as Ian's father enjoyed a good reputation with business owners in town. He once removed a fine for Ziegler's shop being secretly open on a Sunday, extending only a warning while tearing up the fine. Or perhaps it was conscience, as Ian's parents always received Ziegler warmly on his visits. Whatever the reason, Ziegler had yet to betray Ian's father to the German authorities. The family felt a sense of relief but remained on constant alert that they were likely being watched and exposed to constant danger.

Dreaded news of arrest finally arrived, but it was not the German authorities who delivered the news, and it was not Stefan Sr. who was under arrest. Ian's Aunt Jozefa Lekki entered the home early one frigid morning in a frantic state, informing them that her son Tadeusz was taken away by gestapo personnel the prior evening on suspicion of plotting against the German occupation. Cousin Tadeusz was like a brother to Ian. Several years older, he had graduated from high school just prior to the German invasion. During normal times, the two spent countless hours together, walking home after school on a near-daily basis to join Ian's brothers and Mulek in competitive matches of ping-pong. He was at that time also a regular at the family dinner table. Ian sat stunned as his aunt now informed them all how Tadeusz was arrested with a group of about a dozen young men, an informant (likely a Volksdeutsche resident) alerting the German authorities of their suspected meetings and intentions.

Ian was well aware of not only an organized underground organization near Bochnia but also smaller groups known to plot activities intended to sabotage German operations in and around town. The established underground movement was quite organized and effective. They had managed to establish contact with Polish government officials outside of the country and coordinated an array of well-planned activities to assist the Allies. Word was often relayed to local residents of their successful missions, many of which required complex coordination and timely movement. Following the arrest of important individuals who were of key interest to the gestapo, the underground was sometimes successful in breaking them out of prison, and ultimately Poland. Using established contact with officials in London, they would guide late-night planes to land in desolate fields and pick up relieved escapees, transporting them to safety back in London. Other missions included dynamiting railroad bridges, armored vehicles, and other means of slowing or sabotaging German Army activities in Poland.

While the underground organization was known to be highly secretive and effective, smaller groups that hoped to assist in their efforts faced much difficulty and peril. Ian was not certain how involved Tadeusz was with the group of young men arrested, or how serious or close the group was in actually carrying out any of the alleged activities against the German occupiers. But upon his arrest, Tadeusz and the group had no recourse. There was no trial, no means to visit with family members or friends. Tadeusz was shipped to a concentration camp in Auschwitz. Ian would never see his cousin again.

Tadeusz Lekki was born on 1 August 1920 in the town of Brzeznica, Poland (near Bochnia). He was transported to Auschwitz on 10 January 1941 and assigned the political prisoner number of 9234, identifying him as one of the earlier arrivals in the infamous camp. The only available records about him that were retrieved following the camp's liberation (many records were destroyed in the camp's waning days) reveal that he was admitted to the camp infirmary on 23 July 1941 for x-rays and died on 6 September 1941.

News of Tadeusz's arrest hit Ian and his family with a heavy dose of sobering reality. They had to remain vigilant and on alert, not trusting anyone outside of family or their closest circle. The threat of arrest was not the only tension filling the household. Ian's father once held an important and well-respected position within the community, but now his inability to work coupled with strict rationing caused extreme hardships. The family was relegated to food rationing barely enough to feed a family of two, let alone seven. They were able to purchase bread along with simple basic staples only one day a week, and the bread had a crusty taste that resembled sawdust. There was no availability of sugar or salt, so they were thankful for the hen house, fruit trees, and vegetable garden they had carefully nurtured over the years. But even from their own supplies, they were limited to fruit and produce left over after helping feed less fortunate neighbors. Although German soldiers did not bother with the vegetable garden, they were known to be stealing eggs from the hen house. Apparently, eggs were in short supply of the daily rations served to German troops in Poland.

As a means to help support the family, Ian managed to earn some wages at the flourmill and brickyard across the street, and kept his eyes open for ways to assist the family. One day while working in the flourmill, he seized an opportunity. Upon completion of his work assignment, he spotted a fifty-kilo (110-pound) bag of flour lying by the exit door. Acting as if it was his job, he picked up the sack and confidently carried it outside of the factory. Once outside, he took a deep breath, regained his grip, and walked across the street toward the house with the bulky sack over his shoulder. Nobody stopped him, nobody noticed, and he entered the house where his mother was busily working. A surprised look crossed Jozefa's face, but she asked no questions and hurriedly helped move the sack to a storage area in the kitchen. There, she immediately began the process of preparing delicious food unlike any the family has tasted in years.

On another work assignment, Ian was required to fill railroad cars at the train station with wheat and grain. After several days, he came up with an idea. He took an old pair of loose-fitting trousers and constructed a drawstring to tighten around the ankles. He manufactured his own personal storage unit. While back on his assignment, when nobody was looking, he managed to fill enough wheat inside his trousers to feed the family for weeks. Again, Juzefa asked no questions when he robotically entered the house. But she enthusiastically began the process of creating fluffy loaves of bread to replace the sawdust-tasting bread the family had been forced to purchase since returning to their home.

Toward the end of 1941, the family received an unexpected welcome when Ian's oldest brother Henryk arrived at the house for a brief stay from his work assignment in the Sudeten Mountains. Shortly after his arrival, Henryk went into hiding, moving to a nearby town with relatives of their grandfather, so as not to be sent back to Sudetenland to labor for the Germans.

Historical Perspective

Hitler claimed the Sudeten region from Czechoslovakia in 1938. As part of the Munich Agreement, Hitler convinced nervous leaders wary of another world war to allow him control of the Sudeten region to protect an indigenous German population who were clustered in the mountainous region. Western leaders may have agreed to this seeming minor request in an attempt to pacify the aggressive German ruler. However, this agreement would effectively deprive Czechoslovakia of her natural borders and buffer zone, further weakening the country in the impending invasion and occupation from the German Army.

The family supported Henryk's decision to avoid going back to his work assignment, but that decision did not come without risk. The authorities would soon come looking for Henryk, and their investigation of the missing man could lead to further evidence of Stefan Sr.'s activities in the pre-invasion war preparation. Tadeusz's recent arrest was also a painful reminder of the authority's impatience and intolerance toward Polish citizens breaking their strict laws.

The unwelcome visit came as expected. A local policeman was summoned to the house during the evening, with papers stating that Henryk Bajda had failed to report on time for his mandatory work assignment. Ian noted the police spoke to his father in a tone showing that he indeed took his job quite seriously, as many of the Volksdeutsche police officers were known to do. "If Henryk Bajda fails to report to the local police station, there will be severe repercussions not only for your son but for your entire family."

Stefan simply smiled, not showing much emotion or his real concern. "There is no need for such talk or worry. He is a young man not looking for trouble. No doubt he is simply catching up with old friends, perhaps a young lady. Surely you can understand that. I expect that he will report soon."

The police officer appeared somewhat comforted, but made a point to once again exert his authority before leaving. "I will be back if he fails to report. And as I warned you, there will be severe repercussion for the entire family."

Ian awoke early the following morning to meet up with his brother and alert him of the visit. Not wanting to cause problems for the family, Henryk decided to turn himself in to the authorities.

Several days later, Ian stopped to visit his brother who was being detained at the town jail. A local police officer casually allowed him inside, where he spotted Henryk joined with a group of young men, all in reasonably good spirits considering their predicament. Several of the men sat around a small table playing cards, while Henryk and others openly talked of work assignments and latest gossip of people and activities in town. Henryk got up to greet his brother alongside the barred wall.

"Henryk, what will happen to you now?"

"One cannot say for sure. They're trying to figure out where to send us next, based upon where the work is needed. How are Mother and Father and the family?"

"Everyone if fine. There have been no more visits from the police. Are you managing okay?"

"Sure, I'm fine. But do you know what the worst thing is besides not being with family? The worst is that I can't practice my hobbies. No model airplanes. No chance to take photos. And let me tell you, I could have taken some wonderful photos on my last assignment if I had a camera and they'd let me get away for just a few hours."

Ian felt sad for his brother. Henryk loved his hobbies, spending all his free time making model airplanes and hiking into the countryside, shooting and developing photos from his prized cameras. Ian contemplated how he might be able to deliver one of the cameras undetected to his brother. Sensing his brother's concern, Henryk picked the conversation back up in an attempt to lighten the mood. "I'll be out of here in no time, and soon they will send me on my next holiday. They would prefer to have us working rather than playing cards in a jail cell."

"I have this feeling that I too may be sent away before long. Perhaps I can find a way to work in the same location where you'll be sent."

Within the week, Henryk was transported to Austria in a small village near Vienna. It was a move that would prove pivotal for Ian in the course of events that were to unfold.

Not every encounter with the German authorities proved to be harsh. There were moments of sincere friendship and appreciation. On one assignment, Ian and several others were sent to the residence of a German officer. They were ordered to remove piles of sawdust that had accumulated on the property, as well as complete a number of tasks that required several people to manage in and around the household. Working diligently under the direction of the friendly officer, the workers completed the entire job in one day. The smiling officer clapped in delight, commending the men for a job well done. Thinking they were done for the day, he instead took them to a nearby cafeteria where he treated them all to a hot meal of their choice. Ian appreciated the relaxed manner of the officer, and for one of the few times looked at a German as a regular and genuine person, and not as a superior who thought of himself better than the Polish residents.

Back at the house, the family continued seeking and learning of news on the warfront. Germany continued their aggression throughout 1941, their troops now extending east in a move to control and occupy the Soviet Union. Japan joined the Axis in December 1941, meaning the war was now spread across Europe, the Soviet Union, Northern Africa, and the Pacific. However, despite unprecedented growing aggression of their enemies, Stefan Sr. saw a silver lining. On the morning of 7 December 1941, Japan attacked a US Naval base at Pearl Harbor. The next day, President Franklyn Roosevelt declared war on Japan.

"I believe it is only a matter of time before the United States military will increase their support by sending troops into battle. They do not want this war to encroach their territory."

His father's words would prove prophetic. Radio London finally provided a hint of promising news in the third year of the war, 1942. US troops joined Allied forces in battles across the Pacific, Northern Africa, and Italy. German advances appeared to slow. Meanwhile, Ian grew increasingly restless. He had been back at home under German occupation for two years, his two older brothers were away from home, and he felt helpless in the course of events that were shaping the world.

Ian would turn eighteen years old on 21 February 1942. He was searching for answers. Should he run? Join the underground? Stay with his family? Await fate? Throughout his life, there was one place where he could always go to find peace and answers.

The Polish custom is to observe Names Day rather than one's birth date. With his full name Marian being close to the Virgin Mary's, he paid a visit to St. Michal's church on 2 February for prayer and reflection. Perhaps the woman he looked up to so often for guidance would provide answers or direction.

Entering the iconic basilica for Sunday service always gave him chills. Graceful arched ceilings reaching for the sky coupled with rich woodwork, ornate statues, and colorful stained glass windows cast an out-of-this-world feeling. But now easing inside the impressive empty edifice brought about an even higher sense of mystique and wonderment. With a virtuoso of sounds echoing off the high ceiling from his slightest movement, he sat down at a pew toward the back of the church and soaked in the spiritual beauty before him. An organ player practicing in the upstairs choir loft produced intermittent moments of rich, reverberating sounds that suddenly came to an abrupt stop. Immersed in total silence, Ian's acute senses picked up the echo of departing footsteps bounce off the walls before the church once again faded into echoed silence. It took several minutes to recover from his heightened senses before Ian was able to reflect on his thoughts.

Kneeling upright on the kneeler before him, he slowly made a sign of the cross while intently studying his favorite statue near the main altar. A life-sized figure of Jesus nailed to a cross revealed pain and bravery, his compassionate face bearing a suffering that will enable mankind to be saved. Close by stood a statue of the Virgin Mary. Adorned in a flowing blue gown, staring lovingly at the baby Jesus held in her arms.

Ian's thoughts and emotions eased out like water spilling through a fractured dam. Eyes moistened, he prayed for the soul of his little brother Stanislaw. He prayed for Stefan in the hope that he was somewhere safe and alive. He prayed for Henryk, that he could return home and once again freely enjoy his beloved hobbies without fear of arrest. He prayed for his parents, Stefan and Jozefa, that they could once again be happy and free of worry for their family. He prayed for his sister and younger brothers, that they could once again openly laugh and play with their neighborhood friends. He voiced a prayer for his cousin Tadeusz and best friend Mulek, and made an impassioned plea that they and other families were somehow spared from unthinkable atrocities rumored to be occurring in the dreaded camps.

Staring at the statue, he openly asked, "What do I do?"

Silence. Capturing the Virgin Mary's downcast eyes directed toward him, the world appeared still. Tears flowed freely, a whirlwind of emotions unleashed. For the first time since they left the house on the horse-drawn carriage to escape the German invasion, Ian allowed his emotions to release, and he openly cried. He pleaded for forgiveness. He apologized for his misgivings, and prayed for strength and guidance. He prayed for the strength to overcome any hardship that he would be asked to endure, and for the bravery to find his way in becoming a benevolent soldier in the liberation and freedom of his beloved Poland.

CHAPTER 6

Amnesty Leads to Liberator

Siberia, Russia
Spring 1940 – Late 1941

Stefan's quest to join the Polish Army in France had taken a most unexpected twist. Following his capture by the Russians in Romania, he managed to survive tortuous interrogations, the oppressive march from Kiev to Moscow, the notorious and over-crowded Lubyanka prison, and hard, forced labor in the extreme conditions of a Siberian labor camp. Before the end of 1941, Stefan had lost considerable weight, his ribs visibly protruding through his skin, and was slowly starving to death. But before the year was over, an Allied agreement and a fortuitous illness mixed with a series of world events that were about to change his fortunes.

Prior to that illness, Stefan was subjected to the most extreme conditions in northern Siberia, and facing a likely outcome that was bleak at best. Many of Stefan's fellow prisoners who managed to survive the forced march from Kiev to Moscow (and suffocating train passage from Moscow to Siberia) died within the first few months at the camp. Shortly after his arrival, a shadowy moribund prisoner who had already spent time at the camp candidly informed Stefan of his likely fate. "Welcome to your death sentence. In the unlikely event that you survive, they will simply extend your time and keep you here until you die." Stefan was determined not to accept that fate, despite the backbreaking work and morbid outlook.

Prisoners were housed in barracks that provided no insulation from the long, harsh Siberian winters, and medical supplies consisted of simple bandages and the most rudimentary aids. The outlook in the camps was so bleak that even the guards were considered prisoners. Russian soldiers receiving punishment for some form of offense were sent to Siberia, serving their sentence as guards in the dismal gulag system. Facing such harsh penalties, the guards were locked in bitter moods and with little to zero tolerance for the prisoners.

The camp was located somewhere in the dense forests of Northern Siberia, where prisoners were assigned the task of logging, cutting down trees that would form the foundation for an upgraded roadway. Extreme Siberian winters created conditions that caused difficulty in roadway construction, the tundra being too soft for a solid foundation. So after cutting down hardwood trees, prisoners were required to carry giant timber to a roadway site, splitting and laying the logs side by side to build a foundation for the road. Having access to only the most primitive tools, an already difficult task was made tortuous.

A quota system was set up for the work groups in an attempt to increase production. Workers were required to cut down so many trees and lay so many logs for the privilege of receiving increased levels of food rations. Not surprisingly, the quota system had just the opposite of the program's desired effect. With some winter days reaching as low as minus 60 degrees F in blizzard conditions, workers struggled merely to survive the brutal conditions. Most work groups were unable to keep up with the required quotas, and a number of prisoners perished or fell ill in their desperate attempts to keep up. Stefan and his crew quickly assessed the impossibility in keeping up with the maddening scale, so they devised a scheme to meet their required quota. Using a deceptive means of carrying and loading logs, they were able to fool their administrator, distracted from the brutal conditions, in their work effort. They managed to report numbers that met the group's required quota, but the extra rations were barely enough to improve their conditions. Somewhere around the latter part of 1941, Stefan fell ill and was too weak to continue. He was taken to the infirmary. With the timing of world events that were about to unfold, the visit to the ill-equipped infirmary most likely saved his life.

They say that war sometimes makes for strange bedfellows. Despite an initial clandestine agreement between Russia and Germany to divide and occupy Poland, the two countries were now at war, each harboring their own secret plans for continued aggression and control of Poland. Russia's war with Germany now aligned them with the Allies. However, that alliance came with conditions. Behind the leadership of Winston Churchill, England and the United States demanded that Joseph Stalin release all political and war prisoners being held in Russia. Stalin agreed to the amnesty program not only to receive the support of Allied nations in his war against Germany but also to enable recruitment of Polish prisoners to fight for his Red Army.

Finally the recipient of some good fortune, Stefan was sent to the infirmary just weeks prior to an agreed-upon amnesty program which released prisoners being held in Russian camps. The combination of rest and shelter allowed him to regain some strength while in the infirmary. Had he not been sent to the camp infirmary when he was, Stefan might not have survived the brutal conditions even long enough to be amnestied. He was losing hope, but there appeared a way out. The reprieve and improved health, although marginal, were also needed to navigate the broad Russian landscape following his release.

Siberia, Kazakhstan, Persia, and Palestine
Late 1941 – Summer 1943 (and beyond)

After serving over eighteen months as a prisoner under the most grueling conditions, Stefan was miraculously classified a free man. Despite this unexpected turn of events, Stefan was still not out of the woods as he and his fellow countrymen faced many perils in Russia. They were not provided money or supplies, leaving with only the rags on their backs in hopes of reaching recruitment camps set up far to the south. Many men lacked even boots to make the journey, wrapping their feet in rags to traverse the broad landscape.

Red Army posters were visible all along the journey:

Nie matura lecz hec szczera
zrobi z ciere officera.

Which translates in English loosely to:

Not a high school education is required
But desire will make you an officer.

Stefan and his fellow travelers were more than eager to join the Army. Unfortunately, many did not survive the treacherous journey given their poor health and numerous roadblocks along the way. After finally locating a train station, trains were so overcrowded that much or their journey remained on foot. Poles were required to continually show documents to the authorities. Many of the amnestied prisoners were detained and sent back to the camps for an endless array of trumped up or petty offenses, including taking food from open fields as a means of survival. It was widely believed that the arrests were made simply to enable the camp commandants to bring back more prisoners to meet their required quotas.

Following weeks of travel, he reached a recruitment camp in Kazakhstan, where a Polish Army was formed and training under command of the Red Army. Their mission was to fight alongside Russian troops in defense of the German Army's blitz-krieg into Russia. Stefan joined up and took part in the training, but he and the new arrivals quickly grew disenchanted. The food rations were not enough to regain their strength, and training bordered on comical. With a shortage of supplies and proper instruction, sticks and brooms replaced guns and rifles. Meanwhile, drills and marches resulted in chaos and bodily collisions rather than military precision.

Historical Perspective

Even after German and Russian occupation of Poland, the government remained active and alive throughout the war. It was a government-in-exile. Elusive Polish government officials managed to escape from Warsaw to Romania during the German invasion, before successfully setting up operations in France. During and after the French surrender, these same officials managed to escape and operate out of London. With experienced officials in place, an intelligence service and armed forces were effectively established and operating outside of Poland, making significant contributions to the Allied effort. Despite a government-in-exile and armed forces operating without an actual home base, the Polish Army made up the fourth largest fighting force among all Allied troops, with only the Soviet Union, the United States, and Britain fielding larger armies.

A Polish Army on Soviet soil was created following Germany's invasion of the Soviet Union in 1941. Stalin declared all previous pacts with Germany null and void, releasing tens of thousands of Polish prisoners of war held in Soviet prisons and gulags. Included among those released was the charismatic Wladyslaw Anders, who was a cavalry commander at the outbreak of World War II, wounded in battle against the German Wehrmacht, and taken prisoner by Soviet forces after he retreated east. He was held and tortured at the infamous Lubyanka prison in Moscow (this brutal imprisonment did spare him from the bloody massacre of Polish officers in the Katyn forest).

The Polish government-in-exile nominated Anders as leader of a Polish Army to be formed on Soviet soil. Anders was soon met with several surprises. The camps were filling much quicker than anticipated, with scores of both amnestied soldiers and civilians arriving by the day. However, there was mystery surrounding the whereabouts of an estimated 15,000 Polish officers. Virtually none of them made it to the camps, and Anders attempts to learn of their whereabouts were met with skepticism or denial. Well aware of the Katyn murders, Stalin insisted that the officers must have escaped to Manchuria.

By early 1942, over 70,000 malnourished POW's had arrived at the camps. Meanwhile, tensions were mounting between Anders and Stalin. Not only did the officers remain unaccounted for, but rations and supplies were in short supply for Anders' growing army. Further, Stalin insisted that Polish troops be sent to the Russian Front. Anders refused to the demand, stating that his troops had not received proper training or required rations.

Few could have predicted that this rag-tag band of troops would go on to become a formidable fighting force. Certainly not Stalin. By spring of 1942, unable to feed the growing Polish Army, he allowed Anders to transfer his army away from Russian soil and into Persia. General Anders was free from Russian authority, his forces to be trained under the command of British General Bernard Montgomery's Eighth Army. An estimated 75,000 Polish troops and 40,000 civilians were shipped over the Caspian Sea to Persia. Unfortunately, hundreds of thousands of Poles never reached the recruitment camps, left behind to survive the broad dangerous Soviet landscape.

For the second time within a matter of months, Stefan and his surviving peers were recipients of the most welcome and unexpected news. An alternative to fighting under the Red Army surfaced. Stefan's entire Third Division of the Polish Corps, along with other Polish troops, boarded overflowing ships for transfer to Persia. There, they observed an energized General Wladsyslaw Anders, whose army now served under the command of British General Bernard Montgomery's Eighth Army.

In stark contrast to training received in Kazakhstan, Polish troops were provided with crisp uniforms, nutritious meals, and professional military training. Stefan and his fellow Poles were able to enjoy a real meal for the first time in years. From Persia, he was transferred to Palestine for yet more training. In May of 1943, Allied forces were victorious against the German Desert Fox, General Erwin Rommel, which proved to be a pivotal point in the war.

Allied control of North Africa blocked German access to the strategic oil fields of the Middle East, allowing victorious Allied forces to shift their attention to the European continent. The liberation of Italy would begin for Stefan that July on the island of Sicily. In order to get there, he and fellow Polish troops joined Allied Forces en masse for transfer across the Mediterranean Sea, an impressive collection of victorious armed forces travelling on the sea and in the air. For Stefan, the journey must have been most memorable.

Glider planes were used to transport large numbers of the troops. Up to thirteen men fit comfortably inside each glider, connected to an airplane before being released and freely gliding to their destination. In the air, Stefan could hear the distant hum of airplanes carrying troops and supplies. The comforting hum was gradually replaced by total silence as they glided over sparkling blue waters. In that peaceful serenity he counted his blessings, recycling the turn of events that brought him to that moment.

After the attack on the home at Podwoloczysko, Stefan was determined to join the Polish Army. And join the army he did, but in a most circuitous route—captured in Romania, subjected to torturous interrogations, the grueling march from Kiev to Moscow, the labor camp in Siberia. How fortunate to fall ill when he did. Then the amnesty brought hope. How different would his fate have been had he remained in Kazakhstan and sent to the Russian front, ill equipped and poorly trained. Although unaware at the time that he would not only be part of the liberation of Sicily but also Monte Cassino, Ancona, and Bologna, he was comforted to be joined by Allied brothers, all well equipped and professionally prepared for the upcoming battles.

With views of remote islands in the distant horizon, thoughts turned to his family. What has become of them, his parents, brothers, and little sister? When he left his father and grandfather in Bochnia, the rest of the family remained refugees under Russian occupation, determined to make it safely back home. Such a large travel party, confronted with peril and danger all around them. Stefan was able to send a message to them after his release from Siberia but had no idea if the message was received. To be safe and for protection of the family, he left out details of his situation. He simply let them know that he was alive and well.

As the glider continued its slow descent and slowly approached land, little could Stefan have been aware of the good fortunes waiting to greet him. A spirited and attractive young lady from Rome will enter his life. His quest to join the Polish Army will indeed continue to prove eventful. Following the liberation of Sicily and Italy, his valued service and bright potential will result in a recommendation to attend officer school. And on the platform at a train station in Fermo, Italy, waiting to board a train that will take him to officer school in Matera, another one of his prayers will be answered.

CHAPTER 7

Work Duty and Escape from Austria

Weikendorf and Vienna, Austria
December 1942 – July 1944

During foreign occupation at a time of war, a capable young man does not go undetected by the authorities for very long. Things were not going well in Germany. Their people and economy were suffering. Help was needed to restore the Deutschland and do whatever was necessary to ensure victory for the Third Reich. Ian was again required to report to the authorities, only this time to be assigned for work duty at a location in Germany. Knowing that Henryk was sent to German-controlled Austria after turning himself in to the authorities, Ian applied his resourcefulness in hopes of arranging an assignment that would reunite them. It worked. The official in charge of work duties was impressed with Ian's ability to articulate a request in his native German tongue, and the request was surprisingly carried out quite well. The German official assigned Ian to the village of Weikendorf, about forty kilometers east of Vienna, the birthplace of Ian's mother Jozefa. Henryk and Ian were to be reunited.

It was early morning when Ian took in the surroundings from his coach seat on the near-empty train from Vienna to Weikendorf, feeling relief in the welcome separation from the previous day's mass of passengers. One day earlier, he began his journey by taking the train from Bochnia to Cracow with papers in hand for his latest work assignment. Beyond the papers, he packed only whatever he could carry in the pockets of his trousers and layered jackets—extra underwear, socks, a few personal items, and a toothbrush. After reaching Cracow, he reported to a holding area near the train station where hundreds of young men like himself were assembled for assignment to various locations throughout Germany.

Ian was directed to board the train for Vienna, which quickly filled with passengers. The entire train made up of young men under the watchful eyes of armed German soldiers. The trip was largely uneventful save for one unlikely occurrence. There was no food made available for the crowded passengers, but a young Ukrainian man sitting across from Ian managed to enjoy his own meal. Pulling out a loaf of bread from a paper bag was surprise enough, but also included in the bag was a slab of butter which he generously spread over thick slices. Ian looked on in amazement; he had not seen butter in such abundance since the beginning of the war. Yet the man across from him enjoyed his bread and butter alone as if oblivious to everything and everyone around him. Despite his hunger, Ian couldn't help but feel more wonder, if not humor, than envy. How was this young Ukrainian man able to secure such a prized possession as butter, and carry on as if it was the most natural act to enjoy such a precious commodity among hungry passengers under watch on the crowded train?

They arrived in Vienna late in the night and were directed to a prison-like building where they bunked for the evening. Ian lay on the hard cot, painfully aware that he was in the city of his mother's birthplace, knowing he would soon have to leave the city that he had heard so much about as a child. It hurt much more than the hunger he was feeling to know that he was more a prisoner than a guest in the city of his ancestry.

Another surprise greeted Ian when he awoke the following morning. He was given instructions to report to the family business of a butcher, Mr. Otto Schuster, in the village of Weikendorf. That he was assigned to work in Weikendorf was expected, but reporting to that destination on his own was not expected. The urge to escape was the first thing to cross his mind. But difficulty in maneuvering safely in enemy territory, coupled with the expected consequences that his family would face if he were to escape, kept him on track to reach his assigned destination.

As the train slowed to a stop at Weikendorf's small station, Ian felt the anticipation of reuniting once again with his brother. Soft flakes of snow contrasted against the wintry morning sky as Ian sought out Marktstrabe Street from the village train station. He was guided forward by the distant presence of a church spire, and felt a sense of calmness and comfort as he reached the landmark, a smart-looking yellow-colored church pointing to the street of his destination. Turning right onto Marktstrabe, the number 10 above a door revealed the address of the butcher shop, connected to and just one building past where Henryk was assigned. Ian took note of the neighbor's large open entrance, where Henryk cared for the owner's horses and drove a wagon for the business. Ian wondered just what work assignment was required for a butcher.

Entering the shop's front door, a woman working behind a counter warmly greeted him and offered a brief tour of the area. Connected to the butcher shop was the owner's household, where Mr. Otto Schuster lived comfortably with his wife, young daughter, and a large spotted dog. Also on the premise was a shared dining area and living quarters provided for the workers. Behind the butcher's shop and home was a barn, open fields for the grazing livestock, a sugar beet field, and neat rows of vineyards. The property also included a separate household, occupied by the butcher's father-in-law, who supervised the farm.

While workers on the farm went about their business, Ian was escorted to the living quarters that he would be sharing with three fellow workers, and told to await further instruction from the farm's supervisor. Conducting an inspection, Ian considered the arrangement as not so bad. The room was cramped and drafty, two bunk beds took up most of the available space, and there was no electricity. But the prospect of working outdoors on the tidy grounds was appealing, and knowing that Henryk was next door was quite comforting.

Ian reunited with Henryk the next morning, and it was as if the two had never been separated. There was also plenty of company and familiarity within the butcher's household. Working on the farm with Ian were three fellow Poles, a Ukrainian maid, two Austrian apprentices, and a young Ukrainian man about Ian's age who was brought in every day from a nearby camp holding a large number of Russian prisoners. In addition, the owner brought in workers from Slovakia every spring and summer to help out in the sugar beet operation.

Surrounded by a medley of nationalities and languages, Ian enjoyed the opportunity to communicate with a variety of staff members and workers on the farm. Learning Russian, Ukrainian, and Slovak came quite easy as he had experienced the languages, and they all shared a Slavic origin with Polish. German was more difficult, but he had a good base and soon mastered the language, becoming quite fluent and able to converse with the locals.

Ian's job on the farm was to clean the stables and feed the livestock in preparation for their slaughter, tasks that required hard work but allowed a generous measure of freedom in the outdoor air. In addition, he soon came upon new opportunities while working on the farm. He initially shared a cramped room with the three other Poles, built as an addition toward the back of the household. Although the addition was connected to the main household, they had no electricity, relying on kerosene for light. Observing an electric box in the hallway, Ian devised an idea. Scrounging some spare electrical wire from the attic, he managed to connect the wire from the box to the room, bringing electricity into their quarters. The supervisor was surprised when walking into their room one evening, observing the workers reading and enjoying brightness from a spare lamp. He asked incredulously, how did you manage this? Ian simply shrugged, offering that he was always interested in the workings of electricity so decided to read a book on it one day as a schoolboy in Poland.

As an added enhancement for the boarders, wine was readily available from an oak barrel filled with homemade wine right outside their quarters. Adding to his fortunes, one of the butcher's apprentices was drafted into the German Army shortly after his arrival. Their supervisor assigned Ian to the vacated room. He now enjoyed his own private boarding on the farm.

Working for a butcher had other advantages as well. Henryk and other workers in town had limited opportunities for good meals, so Ian arranged to provide them with samples of the farm's nutritious and tasty meat. He managed this through a friendship that he developed with the Ukrainian maid Zofia. She worked and also lived in the owner's house, enjoying access to the kitchen and other areas in the house. Zofia had a stocky build with a warm personality and friendly smile, reminding Ian of the farm girls he sometimes viewed toiling in the Polish countryside. She occasionally shared deserts or extra food from the kitchen with Ian, who was more than happy to accept the offerings.

The butcher, Mr. Schuster, visibly supported the Nazi party, so Ian was cautious in what he said when around him. His father's warnings and prior experience had taught him well regarding the need to be cautious and vigilant when it came to words and actions around Nazi members or sympathizers. Ian felt different around the butcher's father-in-law, who supervised the farm. The father-in-law made it a point to treat the workers with kindness and respect. He listened to their concerns and made sure they all attended Sunday church services. He was well liked by the workers, and all believed him to be trustworthy. Early one morning, Ian was surprised to learn just how much the father-in-law returned that trust. Sending Ian out to purchase some basic supplies in the village, he stopped to ponder a thought. Opening the office desk drawer, he pulled out a blank sheet of stationery paper containing the official business name and emblem. Scribbling a quick note on the stationary, he handed it over with a wink and a nod, informing Ian that he was free to travel to Vienna. "Enjoy the sights of our beautiful city." He smiled. "Just be sure to get some good deals, stay out of trouble, and get back here in good time."

Ian could not stop smiling, could not believe his luck. Vienna! His entire life he'd yearned to visit Vienna, having heard all about the beauty and wonders of the city from his mother. What days ago seemed impossible was now reality. He was free to travel by train without fear of capture, to spend an entire day in a city famous around the world for its elegant architecture and rich culture.

Changing into something reasonably respectable and shining his work boots as best he could, Ian soared more than walked to the village train station. He never felt the ground below him. Glued to the window from his coach seat, the landscape transformed from farmland to views of the Danube to a bustling downtown station. For the first time since the outbreak of war, he confidently walked past black uniformed gestapo personnel and police officers, not even stopped or questioned. Striding outside the station and onto the busy street, he stopped to view a canvas of electricity weaved together by fashion, streetcars, lively colors, and rich architecture. Ian stepped into the painting.

Feeling confident with the official pass tucked securely inside a breast pocket, Ian had no qualms about becoming a wide-eyed tourist. He gathered information about the city and jumped on the trolley, making stops at various points of interest. He stepped out to circle and view the expansive presidential palace, visited an inviting café for lunch where he sat outside and enjoyed watching the cornucopia of people. Fully aware of his need to make one mandatory visit while in Vienna, he hustled back to the trolley. His next stop was St. Stephens Cathedral.

The iconic cathedral was beyond anything he had imagined, appearing as a jewel majestically reaching for the heavens. As breathtaking as the exterior was, Ian was not prepared for the interior setting that awaited him. Walking past heavy doors, he stopped to view the scene before him; his breathing momentarily stopped. He stared in silence and awe, an ornate and elaborate interior design that guided all senses toward a majestic altar decorating the front of the church. Drifting down a wide middle aisle toward the main altar with little thought of his motions, he finally eased to his right onto a rich wooden bench within several rows of the decorated altar.

Ian imagined his mother as a girl visiting the cathedral, maybe seated in the same area he now occupied. His thoughts turned to Jozefa, strong and proud, the matriarch of their family, providing guidance and love to him and his siblings. He thought of her on the family's journey to escape the Nazi blitzkrieg, offering encouragement that kept all their spirits up, even in the most difficult of times. He admired her resourcefulness, always finding ways to keep the family fed and safe. Seated alone in the massive cathedral, he became fixated in thought and lost all track of time.

The supplies! Ian snapped out of his daydream, realizing that he was sent to Vienna to purchase supplies for the farm. Genuflecting, he hurriedly exited the cathedral in search of shops to purchase the required supplies. Although not having the time to bargain for the best deals, he did have time to make the required purchases and get back to Weikendorf right around nightfall. Ian was thankful for his blessings. It was a most memorable day.

Although his job on the farm was largely carried out in isolation, Ian enjoyed the variety of acquaintances with his coworkers. Even within the household, the butcher's young daughter Anna was always visible with a friendly demeanor, unable to hide her curiosity and interest in the presence and actions of Ian and his fellow workers.

A photo of Anna Schuster, her father Otto, and the family
dogs, taken some time before the beginning of the war

Of the workers on the farm, the person he grew closest to was the Ukrainian prisoner, named Michal, who was brought to the farm every day from the nearby camp. Ian and Michal quickly become friends, both sharing an easy manner and sense for adventure. Although locked up at night in the Russian camp, Michal became quite adept at sneaking out and reentering his quarters without being caught.

Following the workday, the two often met up for long walks late into the evening, sharing stories of their homeland and dreams of reuniting with their families. Ian soon learned that Michal also shared his distrust of Stalin's political interests and disdain for communist principles. Having both seen and experienced first-hand the political arrests and removal of basic freedoms, the young men were further united in brotherhood.

During one of their conversations, Michal excitedly spoke of the young Slovakian woman who was now working alongside him in the sugar beet field. Ian was quite interested in hearing about Brigita. With striking, attractive features and slender build, her presence caused quite a stir around the farm since arriving with her brother for the summer. Michal beamed when he spoke of her. He appeared to be walking on a cloud. Ian smiled as Michal glowed. He felt joy for his friend, and just a touch of envy.

In addition to friendships, the job also provided a variety of chores outside of cleaning stalls and feeding the animals. As he gained more experience on the farm, Ian was requested to assist in the slaughtering process. He learned that the cows and pigs did not get fed the day before slaughter. On the fateful day, Ian was instructed to help hold up each cow as a specialized gun was put to their head. A worker fired the gun, which unleashed a rod between the eyes and through the brain. As the rod retracted back into the gun, the cow was pushed over, always on its right side. The butcher then began the process of cleansing and butchering the animal.

Some evenings even provided an opportunity for relaxation and entertainment. The privileged workers not locked up sometimes ventured out to socialize and drink beer at the nearby tavern. One night, Ian and his fellow Polish workers went out after a long day of work. By their second beer, they observed that an upstairs room was used to house several dozen Belgian prisoners. Although the prisoners were not allowed to drink or socialize in the tavern, several would be seen throughout the evening stopping downstairs to fill up a large pitcher with dark draft beer.

With so many shortages caused by the war, business for Mr. Schuster proved to be quite robust. He often found the farm in need of help, so one day arranged to bring in one of the Belgian prisoners and have him stay on the farm, where he shared the room with Ian. The two young men enjoyed working together and quickly developed a friendship. During the evenings, the Belgian taught Ian French, and they found ways to communicate and share stories of their homeland, dreams for their futures. The young man stayed on the farm for about a week. Before leaving he presented Ian with a gift, offering him his smart Belgian-made tailored jacket.

One evening, Ian and Michal discussed the idea of breaking away, leaving the farm. Michal expresses frustration in being locked up and having to sneak out, and was growing increasingly concerned of the consequence if caught. He talked of his family and friends back home, worried for their safety and well-being. Before heading back to his camp, he further confided that Brigita no longer seemed so interested in him. A new worker had come to join them, and she now seemed more interested in the new arrival. Watching Michal carefully slip back to his quarters, Ian felt sad for his friend. Just a few weeks ago he was full of life, but now appeared out of sorts. He knew that Michal was feeling down and homesick, and came up with an idea.

Ian sought out Zofia to request a favor following his work shift the next day. He asked if she could secure for him several blank sheets of official stationery from the main office desk. Upon explaining his need for the paper, Zofia smiled and assured him that it would be no problem. "I'll have them for you tomorrow."

How difficult can it be to forge a document? Ian held on to the original document with the scribbled note and signature, and carefully recreated a new note, adding Michal's name while dating the note with the coming Sunday's date. Ian arranged for Michal to meet him on Sunday morning, telling him he had a surprise and to wear his finest clothing. When Michal showed up on Sunday, Ian held up the document and stated, "Surprise, Michal! We're spending the day in Vienna." His friend was incredulous. "But how? And I can't go looking like this." Ian assured him it's real and informed him he had just the accessory to complete the required look.

"The first thing you need to do is take that unsightly patch off identifying to the world you're a Soviet. I haven't worn my P patch since the day I arrived. Next, I have a surprise." They were roughly the same size, so Ian pulled out his Belgian jacket and handed it over. Michal tried it on and beamed with pride. "Wow! This fits perfect and feels wonderful." Vienna was inching closer.

Because it was Sunday and a free day, the pair managed to leave the farm without raising suspicion. They walked in the direction of the train station as if simply going for a stroll. After getting over his initial excitement, Michal grew increasingly nervous.

"How do we pull this off? How do we manage to spend a day in Vienna without getting caught?"

Ian assured him it was no problem. He'd done it before. The note would ensure their safety. The only obstacles they'd likely face were gestapo personnel at the train station. That comment did little to settle Michal, so Ian tried to reassure him. "You look like an educated Wiener in that jacket. Just look relaxed, confident, like you belong. If we get stopped, I'll do the talking. My German is good. Just don't let them hear your accent."

The train rolled to a stop at a busy station inside Vienna. Nudging Michal to depart the train, they immediately spotted the intimidating black uniforms of several gestapo, the officers peering intently over the hurried passengers as if looking for someone or something in particular. Michal felt certain they were being watched. Sensing his unease, Ian chatted to his friend in a casual manner, employing a familiar-sounding soft Austrian accent to explain in German their plans for the day. The two worked to blend in with the crowd, walking toward an exit that spilled out onto the busy streets. Passing the officers without incident, they quickened their pace to view the city from outside the station. Michal glowed in excitement, a look of awe and disbelief. "I can't believe it. We made it! This is amazing!"

Ian was already walking ahead. "Come on, Michal, we have a busy day planned in Vienna." Michal rushed to catch up with his friend, still not exactly sure how they were pulling this off.

By summer of 1944, a sudden change occurred within the household. The owner, Mr. Schuster, had unexpectedly passed away. His wife and the father-in-law were now responsible for the business operations. Ian felt a sense of sadness for the family, particularly the young daughter Anna, who often appeared quite alone as she continued to follow Ian and not so secretly observe the actions of workers on the farm.

Ian had now been working on the farm for over a year. Memories of home and a determination to liberate his country were always on his mind. He and Michal continued discussion of escape, sharing a desire to leave the farm and return to their homeland. They also recognized and bemoaned that their labor on the farm enabled young Austrian men to leave and fight for the German Army. The two agreed to make a break and escape the farm.

Shortly before their scheduled departure, Michal threw out an idea that caught Ian by surprise. The Polish worker, the one who captured Brigita's attention away from Michal, openly talked of reuniting with her in Slovakia. She and her brother had returned home, and the young man could not stop talking about her since their departure. When Michal confided to his coworker that he and Ian were contemplating escape, the young man pleaded to join them. Michal reasoned with Ian that it might be beneficial to know someone inside Slovakia who could provide aid and information. Ian met with the Polish worker, who could not contain his excitement.

"When do we leave? I can be ready anytime, even today if necessary."

"That's good, and we all need to be ready, but we must put some thought into this. Michal is under watch and locked up at night, so we'll have to leave well after his roll call, when everyone is asleep, and he is able to sneak out. And we want to leave when the business owners are least likely to search for us. If I'm not mistaken, this coming weekend is when they have their monthly meeting in a wine cellar. They will surely not want to be bothered."

Ian had observed the wine cellars early during his stay at the farm. In an open area outside of the village, he noticed a group of small flat-roofed sheds clustered near one another. Each shed looked barely big enough to house a small room, so he was puzzled by their purpose. He asked around and soon learned that the sheds merely covered steps leading down into a wine cellar. Even though he never stepped inside, he was told that each cellar had a wide alley running lengthwise with wine barrels stacked on both sides. Once a month, a group of landowners met up in one of the cellars, where they camped out for the weekend. It was a chance to get away from their normal routine, converse, smoke, dine on meals brought to them, and sample the many local wines. Once they entered a cellar for the weekend, the men were typically not seen for days.

All agreed to time their escape after the group had spent sufficient time in the cellar. Their fate now sealed, the three young men fine-tuned their escape plans in wait for the opportune moment.

Austrian Border, Slovakia, and Bochnia
July 1944

From their limited knowledge of the countryside, the three estimated they would reach the Slovakian border by foot sometime before daylight. As expected, the group of landowners congregated on a Friday afternoon to visit one of the cellars. As planned, the escapees met up at a designated spot right around midnight. Satisfied that they had all arrived without being seen or heard, they set off in a NE direction, guided by a narrow creek. It was a most pleasant balmy summer evening with a full moon providing clear visibility across the open farm country. The three never once came across a person or village. They reached the border much sooner than expected, realizing they had plenty of time before daybreak. Taking cover in an elevated wheat field, they peered from behind a vertical wheat stack to shield their appearance from the moonlight. From there, they assessed their situation.

A flowing river roughly thirty meters wide separated Austria from Slovakia. Along the river on the Austrian side was a mound built up as a floodwall, stretching as far as they could see. Along the top of the mound was a worn path where they spotted an armed border guard walking in a casual stride while looking around with a rifle slung over his shoulder.

In silence, they moved to the nearest wheat stack and closely observed the guard for a good half hour, timing his pace and direction. Then on cue, as the guard made his predictable turn and passed to their left, they moved one at a time, quietly climbing over the mound and sprinting toward a cluster of trees along the river's edge. There, they regrouped, hidden by thick reeds jutting from the bank, and removed their clothes in preparation to cross the river. Upon closer inspection, they observed that the river appeared quite treacherous, a steady noise from the swift current raising their apprehension. Ian and Michal were both accomplished swimmers and ready to cross. However, they were abruptly stopped when their travel companion nervously informed them that he was unable to swim and afraid to cross. A bluish orange hue blending into the eastern sky revealed they had barely one hour before daybreak. The men decided to attempt sleep and come up with another plan when they awake.

* * *

The current gained speed and strength. Unable to breathe, Ian struggled to lift his head above water in a desperate attempt to gasp for air. He was fighting for his life. There was no visible sign of either Michal or their travel companion, but he could not be certain if they were indeed separated. His peripheral vision was impaired from a combination of rushed panic and the angry waters that engulfed him. In this state of disarray, he felt a hand from below the surface. He grabbed the outstretched reach with his own, securing a tight clasp. At first the hand dragged him deeper into darkness, but as the current swept them downriver a light appeared from above the depths of the river. It brightened as they struggled to reach the surface. He could feel its warmth.

Their heads bobbed above the surface for a brief moment. Still grasping on to the hand, Ian could not immediately make out who it was but could feel his grip slipping. The current tugged the person away as Ian was suddenly frozen in movement and space. From a clenched grasp to four fingers, three, two, the hand was slipping away. Ian tried desperately to hold on, but it was no use. Their grasp was broken as he helplessly watched the body swept downstream by the angry current. The face became clear. Expecting to see Michal, his heart raced as he recognized familiar eyes burn into his consciousness. Stefan's eyes locked into his soul.

"Ian! Ian, you have to free yourself!"

Unable to move with arms and legs paralyzed, Ian was stricken with panic as Stefan's voice faded, barely audible from the current's vicious roar. He tried in vain to break from the paralysis but grew increasingly frustrated as all bodily movement failed him.

"Stefan, hold on! I'm not going to let you go. I'm going to find you."

"Ian! Ian!" His body jostled from its paralyzed state, Ian shot his eyes open to see Michal's face right next to his own. He could barely make out Michal's stern but restrained voice above the sound of rushing water. "Ian, you're having a nightmare. Stefan's not here, everything's okay. You've got to wake up and keep your voice down. The guard may be nearby, and they're probably looking for us."

Sitting up, Ian fought to collect his bearings. Their travel companion slowly stirred from his own slumber, a rising sunshine waking him; he stretched and wiped the sleep from his eyes. Ian breathed a sigh of relief that the paralysis was merely a dream but remained shaken as he took note of the dream and examined its meaning. After allowing time to sufficiently awake, the three huddled together to discuss their predicament and prepare a plan that would enable them to safely cross the river.

Taking inventory, they possessed a pocketknife and some string that would be their tools to construct a makeshift raft. So they quietly set to work. Ian proposed a sturdy design, suggesting a rectangular wooden frame by notching and tying together properly fitted twigs and branches, the frame to be reinforced by two connecting branches, making up three sections for a raft wide enough to hold one man. The three carefully cut down or sought out fallen twigs and branches, allowing Ian to construct a solid frame. While Ian worked on the frame, the other two removed thick reeds along the bank to provide a secluded clearing where they could complete the project. With the frame completed to his satisfaction, Ian instructed their travel companion to further cut the reeds into smaller lengths of equal size, while he and Michal began the painstaking process of tightly weaving the reeds to fill in each of the three sections.

Working cautiously and remaining under cover to avoid detection, the project took most of the day. Battling fatigue and hunger, they worked diligently until completion of the raft. When the final reed was weaved in place to the point that every possible opening was covered, they paused to admire their finished product. Now there was nothing to do but rest and wait once again for the cover of darkness.

Daylight lingered for what seemed an eternity, but nighttime crept upon them under glow of a bright moon peeking in and out of intermittent clouds. The effect was haunting. Observing throughout the day that there appeared to be no guards across the river, their focus remained on the guard behind them. Once again they stripped to their underwear, tied their clothes in a bundle, and quietly set off with their companion atop the raft. Ian moved to the front, pulling the raft while Michal pushed from behind, the swimmers guiding the raft with speed and ease. Then the unthinkable happened. Well beyond the halfway point, the river's current gained strength and they were swept downriver, thrown into the throes of a fierce rapid. To make matters worse, the raft was not holding so well, and all three found themselves in a desperate struggle to stay above water. Once again, Ian struggled to gasp for air while attempting to hold up their travel companion, who was barely holding on to a raft that now provided only marginal support. This time, he was convinced it was no dream.

The current drove them farther downriver at a dizzying pace. The three continued fighting to stay above the surface, the tattered raft now visibly bobbing beyond their reach. Since their clothes were tied to the raft, Ian swam to retrieve it as Michal held on to their companion, steadily moving downriver. Working to move closer to the shore, they tried in vain but were unable to grab a branch or anything to hold on to. Ian had no idea how far they travelled or how long they struggled. It might have been five minutes or much more, but there appeared no escape from the angry waters that swallowed and spun them. Even with the occasional reprieve of calmer water, they fought fatigue while treading in the deeper river water. Their battle was further hindered by the need to hold the raft and support their panic-stricken travel companion, who struggled to remain afloat in the dark and treacherous waters. They all fought to edge closer to land. Michal finally managed to retain his grip on a rock close to the shore. From there, they created a chain to pull one another to a rocky cliff hugging the opposite bank.

Fatigued and chilled, bloody fingers scaled jagged slippery rocks that pointed like protruding attackers in the caliginous night. Exerting every ounce of strength in their possession, they reached the top of the cliff and viewed their surroundings with great relief. A thick forest's shadowy outline was their welcome to Slovakia. Finding the strength to crawl over the edge, they walked far enough into the forest to ensure safety. Settling on a small clearing that provided even space under a canopy of trees, they dropped their fatigued bodies to the ground and covered themselves with wet clothes. The three slept for the remainder of the night.

Ian awoke unsure if he was once again dreaming, but it was no dream. The sound of birdsong stirred his senses. His body felt welcome warmth from early morning rays that filtered through thick foliage, angled rays visible as if a hand touching them from above. Sitting up, he watched his fellow escapees awake with similar motions of relief and exhilaration. Even though hungry, they felt a freedom in the Slovakian forest, safe from capture. Their companion grew particularly exuberant; he could not stop talking about the prospects of reuniting with Brigita. The three casually got up to find an open area where they laid out wet clothes on dry rocks, doing their best to smooth out the wrinkles. If they were going to make it safely travelling through Slovakia without raising suspicion, they would need to make themselves appear presentable. It didn't take long before they were satisfied enough to get dressed and continued their journey.

By afternoon, they made it to a small village outside of Bratislava where Brigita lived with her family. To their relief, the locals proved quite friendly and provided directions, but there remained some apprehension as to how they would be received by Brigita's family. Their concern was unwarranted. Her family warmly received them, providing a much welcomed meal and comfortable lodging for the night.

Ian slept well into the next day. When he awoke to join his guests, they were all sitting around an outdoor area engaged in conversation. Brigita's father joined them as he diligently worked on a task of wrapping string in tight knots to create thick ropes. Showing an interest in the process, Ian asked if they could help out. After receiving instructions and materials, he and Michal spent the day in conversation discussing their experience in Austria and hearing updates on the war, all the while helping the father with his rope-making task. Their friend appeared more interested in spending time with Brigita, and understandably so. She was indeed a fine-looking woman. They stayed with the family a second night before leaving their love-struck friend behind and continued their trek to Poland. Ian couldn't help but suspect that Michal was probably thinking that could have been him staying behind with the attractive Slovakian woman.

The two walked to the town train station, where they used some of what little money they possessed to take a train heading north in the direction of Poland. Departing in a small village no more than thirty minutes from Bratislava, they embarked on a journey that would cover hundreds of kilometers across rugged mountainous terrain to reach the Polish border. In contrast to the peril they faced in entering the country, travel through Slovakia proved to be an enjoyable experience that captured the country's charm. Ian and Michal hiked northeast along a scenic river valley that flowed alongside a road and railroad tracks, accented by hills and mountains on both sides. Throughout their journey, the locals continued to be friendly and hospitable. Most nights they slept under the stars, but some nights they stopped at a house to ask for food and travel information. More often than not, they were invited inside for dinner and a place to sleep. In the morning they were always provided a breakfast and typically a package containing bread and snacks for the journey. Once on the trail, fruit trees were plentiful and the season just right for yet more delicious treats.

Even the one time they were stopped by a policeman, it turned out to be uneventful. Escorted to the station, Ian and Michal passionately pleaded they had done nothing wrong and were simply hiking back to their home in Poland. The policeman, not seeming to know what to make of the drifters, finally threw his hands up in exasperation and simply said, "Oh, just go home!"

Guided by the path of the river valley, they closed in on the Polish border, remaining west of the Tatry Mountain's higher elevations. It was not until they reached a rocky summit early one morning that nondescript border markers finally indicated their entrance into Poland. They cautiously surveyed the area, on the look-out for border guards who might stop and question them. Satisfied that nobody was in the area, they continued moving northeast in search of a farmhouse or local village. Ian took in the rugged beauty of the mountainous region, but hunger and fatigue was overtaking them.

Civilization finally arrived in the form of Polish Highlanders. Ian had always been fascinated with their culture and colorful lifestyle, and now they spotted a group of the clan digging for turf. The rich organic soil a source for fuel in much of the region, and it was obvious from its jet-black appearance that this bog produced prized and ample offerings. The head worker offered water and provided them each with a shovel. "Please feel free to join us. We can finish this task much sooner, and I'll provide a place where you can stay for the evening."

The Highlander was true to his word. Finishing their day's work, he took them to his home and had his wife prepare a meal for the hungry travelers. Ian felt energized and right at home in the Highlander's log cabin. Polished yellow pine accented the rustic interior. Ian was fascinated by the attention to detail in every facet of the house built by their host. Everything from intricate carvings on the stairwell to personalized touches on the home-made furniture. He enjoyed the masculine look and feel of random knots spread over wide pine planks. Scenic vista views defined with green foliage were visible from well-placed window openings, complemented by wood panels and colorful artwork representative of the region. The cabin blended perfectly with the dense forest in their mountainous setting.

Seated in front of an elaborate fireplace following dinner, they all engaged in conversation over drinks of vodka produced from sugar beets. Ian was fascinated to learn every detail and technique used to construct such a perfect setting within the mountains. Smoking flavored tobacco from a pipe offered by their host, Ian imagined himself a local Highlander living in the mountain forest under a roof of his own.

The next morning, they were each treated to a full breakfast—bits of sausage mixed with scrambled eggs, sliced tomatoes and beets, bread with jam, grits sprinkled with a dab of cinnamon, and herbal tea. Ian and Michal had just enough money left over to purchase train tickets, so their host took them on his horse-drawn carriage to the nearest village where they purchased tickets to Cracow. Once there, reaching Bochnia would be easy. After coming this far, the final forty kilometers to reach Bochnia on foot would be little problem. If stopped and questioned, they had their stories corroborated. They were sent home to report for further work duty after spending the past few years in Austria. Ian decided that after the war, he's like to settle and build a place of his own in the mountains. The thought consumed him, but first there were other matters to take care of.

As expected, their final leg to reach home proved uneventful. Nobody stopped or questioned them on the road from Cracow to Bochnia, where they quietly slipped into the yellow stucco home. Ian was happy to be home and reunited with his family, but because they escaped from their last work assignment and thus unwilling to report to the authorities, their situation was very precarious. If discovered, they would be identified as escapees and sent to jail, the threat of a concentration camp always a haunting thought. To remain out of view, Ian shared a room with Michal in the attic, where they planned their next moves.

Michal was not sure which way to turn; he longed to find and reunite with his family, but had no intention of reentering Russian territory. Rumors swirled that any Ukrainian born in Russian territory and known to be captured by the Germans were not treated well by Russian soldiers who were taking back their territory. Russian liberators viewed them as traitors who failed to defend their country. As such, they remained prisoners, simply transferred from German hands to labor camps spread across Russia.

Michal left the house a few days later, still not sure of his destination. Bidding his friend well wishes and watching him leave in search of his destiny, Ian contemplated just how much his friend had lost and how much he deserved to land safely. He also felt a strong sense that he would one day learn of Michal's outcome.

With his friend gone, Ian carefully avoided detection from the German authorities while learning what he could from various sources within the community. He was now twenty years old, young and restless, thirsty for change, and yearned to see his homeland liberated from foreign occupiers. Though he said nothing to his family, he lamented that he was tired, tired of laboring for the Germans, tired of hiding from foreign occupiers, tired of the indignity of arrest if found in his own home. A home once filled with so much joy and happiness, with neighbors who would share their happy times. Bochnia was once a vibrant town where people got along, where jobs and food were plentiful. Now they were bereft of even the most basic freedoms. He reflected on the unnecessary loss of his brother Stanislaw. Of Henryk, so talented and passionate for his hobbies yet still in Austria and forced to labor for the Germans.

And of Tadeusz, shipped to a concentration camp where rumors of unthinkable atrocities were growing by the day.

His thoughts again turned to Stefan. Memories of the dream remained vivid. The family received word that Stefan was alive, and knowing his brother, Ian sensed that he was probably fighting right now to restore their independence and way of life. Ian was determined to find his brother, to join him in restoring basic freedom and happiness and be a part of the liberation of Poland. He longed to see his family reunited and happy once again.

One of the young men he met up with while in Bochnia was an old friend from school named Artur Wlosek. Artur was spending time in the neighborhood, seeing the aunt of a former classmate from the neighborhood. Ian's former classmate lived across the street with his mother, aunt, and grandfather (who was now director at the brick factory). The aunt was actually a year younger than Ian and Artur, the youngest of three daughters. As soon as Artur learned that Ian was back in Bochnia, he arranged to meet with his old schoolmate. They had much to share, and soon learned, much in common.

Artur came from a military family and had a military background. His father served as an officer in the Polish Army, and Artur himself, whose lifelong dream was to be a pilot in the Polish Air Force, received homeschooling required of a young man destined for a military career. His family risked arrest to secretly educate their son on a variety of subjects, including Latin, in which he was quite accomplished.

Ian welcomed his friend as they walked up to the stuffy attic to catch up on events that had now brought them together. Artur possessed a quiet cool and confident aura, with broad shoulders, lean muscular build, and close-cropped hair. Physically, he certainly struck the pose of a soldier.

After a brief exchange of initial pleasantries and talk of happenings in the community, Artur got right down to the purpose of his visit. "Marian, have you heard the news of General Anders and what his Polish Corps are doing in Italy?"

Ian was well aware. Despite the German's continual efforts to block all war front news from the Polish residents, their efforts were fruitless as news managed to travel with both speed and accuracy. Most residents unconditionally accepted risk of capture and imprisonment just to gain knowledge and information about the war. And now in the fifth year of war, that news filtering through was growing increasingly positive. The Polish Second Corps, under General Wladyslaw Anders, stood out as a leading fighting unit in a broad coalition of Allied forces liberating Italy. This same corps, a growing army whose soldiers included men brutally imprisoned by the Russians and later amnestied following German invasion of Russia, were quickly gaining the reputation of a fierce fighting force well-respected by the German Army. The reputation and exploits of the Polish Corps were becoming so well known that they were becoming known as simply Anders' Army.

"Oh yes, I'm well aware of Anders and his Second Corp. I heard that his army were the ones to finally seize the Monte Cassino Abbey following months of bloody battles. No other Allied army was able to take it."

"That's correct. And seizing Monte Cassino enabled the Allies to liberate Rome. Now they're advancing north to liberate all of Italy. Once Italy is liberated, their advance will surely move north to Poland."

"You know, Artur, my driving force to leave Austria was to do something to liberate Poland from the Germans. The more I hear of Anders, the more I want to find a way to join his army. But to do that, I need to get to Italy, and that's not going to be easy."

"Exactly, but I've got the best route to do it. I've discussed it with my family. Palestine! If you're interested in joining me, we travel south. Stay low to avoid hostilities, Northern Africa is now safe, and the Brits will aid us in reaching Palestine. They'll provide safe passage by sea to Italy. Once there, we join Anders' Army."

"Artur, the battle of Monte Cassino, I understand it was long and bloody. Do you know how many Polish soldiers lost their lives there?"

"No, I don't know the exact number, Marian, but I know it was a lot. The poppies on Monte Cassino were drinking Polish blood."

After some pause, Ian pondered the plan laid out to him. It had promise. The route long and indirect but sounded feasible. Once they made it beyond Turkey they should find clear passage to Palestine. If the Brits could indeed provide transport by sea, it seemed the safest route. Further, he always viewed Artur as a trusted friend who possessed both a keen intellect and an outgoing but thoughtful demeanor. Together, they just might make a formidable team who could actually pull this off.

The dream came back, every detail vivid in his mind. Ian felt sure that his brother was there, but refused to believe that family blood fed the poppies on Monte Cassino. Stefan's voice rang in his mind: "Ian, you have to free yourself!"

"All right, Artur, I'm in. But promise me, please do not discuss or mention this to anyone. We can't afford to have anyone suspect or know of our plans, or for some to even know I'm here. If others know, they may say something that could alert the wrong person, and the less anyone knows, the better it is in the event that they are ever questioned."

Artur showed delight in his friend's decision to join him. "Consider your wish granted. Now let's get down to work. We have much planning to do."

Historical Perspective

The battle of Monte Cassino marked one of the longest and bloodiest engagements of the Italian campaign during World War II. A historic abbey sat strategically in rugged terrain atop a cliff that provided protection in Germany's defense of the Gustav Line. Penetration through that line was viewed imperative for the Allied offensive to advance to Rome and beyond, a concentrated effort to liberate Italy from the Germans. The offensive also forced the German Army to commit maximum numbers of divisions in Italy at a time when the Allies were planning to launch a cross-channel invasion in northern Europe.

From January through March off 1944, the Allies made three unsuccessful attempts to capture Monte Cassino, resulting in tremendous loss of lives and destruction of the abbey. It was not until the fourth battle, with Allied troops maneuvered into position over weeks of nighttime movement across dangerous terrain, that the Allies successfully penetrated Monte Cassino. On 18 May, a band of surviving Polish soldiers from Anders Cavalry Regiment were the ones to finally to raise a Polish flag over the abbey ruins, opening the road to Rome.

On the eve and day of this historic battle, a striking transformation occurred. A sea of red poppies arose in full bloom in stark contrast to the tenebrous surroundings, casting a symbolic backdrop of bravery and death on the fabled battlefield. In this setting, two Polish soldiers, garrisoned in the shadow of Monte Cassino, wrote the melody and lyrics to a song that would become a beloved Military Polish song of World War II. The first two stanzas were written during those bloody days, a third added a few days later, and a final stanza would be added a quarter century later to commemorate the battle's anniversary.

On the evening of 18 May, before smoke had cleared from ghostly rubble on the battlefield, General Anders sat down in his headquarters to hear the very first performance of the song, Czerwone maki na Monte Cassino (The Red Poppies on Monte Cassino). Moving lyrics capture the fierce determination and bravery of his soldiers who fought in the battle. And the song's refrain reveals that the poppies on Monte Cassino will be forever redder, because rather than drinking dew, they drank from Polish blood.

Part 2

CHAPTER 8

The View from the North

Millom, England
Spring 1944

Seated on a woolen blanket at her favorite spot, Iris soaked in the view from atop a bluff overlooking the Irish Sea. Puffy clouds blended into a shadowy outline that revealed the Isle of Man far in the distance. Sea, land, and sky merged together, a vast horizon painted on a clear blue canvas. Viewing her cousins Pauline and Ethel gingerly walk along the rocky shore, she pondered if one could actually walk directly across the bay to reach Barrow-in-Furness from here at low tide. It certainly appeared doable on this day and from this vantage. Her two cousins' laughter could barely be heard above the brisk wind that swirled around her. The salt sea air was invigorating, and Iris realized just how fortunate she was to be with her cousins in the quaint seaside town of Millom.

There still was not a day that went by where she didn't think about the loss of her mother and Grandma. Still, there was nobody else she'd rather be with than Pauline and Ethel. When the war first broke out, they were sent off to work at the Tannery in Havrick. Iris was overjoyed now that they were back, the house once again filled with sisterhood and laughter, though often at the consternation of Uncle Will. Iris had no memories of her own father, who died before she was a toddler, so it was certainly an adjustment to have a strict male figure in the house. But Uncle Will probably couldn't be totally blamed for his strict ways. Since the sudden loss of both his wife and sister-in-law, he had little choice but to take responsibility for a household filled with four young ladies and his son Frank. As soon as war broke out, Frank had joined the Royal Navy, but now Iris was happy that he was currently back at the house, home on leave.

Iris idolized her cousins Pauline and Ethel. Both stood tall and graceful, so different from herself, who was always not only the youngest but also the smallest in the family. The three shared a love of life and a light sense of humor that had them laughing almost on cue at the slightest interruption of their daily lives. Pauline was closest in age to her and had a genuine personality to go along with a penchant for saying the first thing that came to her mind. And it was those comments that so often set them all off into unending laughter. Ethel, on the other hand, had a keen wit and a smart sense for fashion, loved to wear hats, and always attracted attention, especially from the opposite sex. Their sister Mary was more reserved and matronly in appearance, and typically stayed at home taking care of the house. Although Mary could be considered aloof and Iris never felt close to her, she appreciated that Mary was kinder and warmer to her when Pauline and Ethel were both away working at the Tannery in Havrick.

Iris with her cousin Ethel

Gazing back toward Barrow-in-Furness, a rising tide answered her question that attempting to walk across the bay was certainly not a wise idea. Iris contemplated if there truly were German U-boats lurking below. Peering intently, she spotted no sign of periscopes. Off in the distance, across the bay stood the shipyards. She sighed in wonder if the bombings would occur again. Those feared bombings were one of the few visible signs of war in this northern England town. Virtually every night over several months, they were awakened to the dreadful sound of air-raid sirens. Uncle Will would dutifully collect everyone and lead the household downstairs to wait by the fireplace, in lieu of the shelter that was set up in town. They all huddled tightly, the sound of distant bombing audible from across the bay, praying for the noise to cease and not get any closer. One fateful evening, a German plane dropped a lone bomb just outside of Millom as the fleet of planes departed their mission to destroy the shipyards. Perhaps it was accident, or perhaps intended, but to the dismay of locals the bomb landed squarely on a cottage just outside of town. Iris knew the girl who lived in the house, who died along with her entire family. Although the bombings had not occurred for some time, they all continued closing each day with the following exchange:

Good night.   *Sleep tight.*
Got your gas mask?   *Right.*
Got your torch light?   *Right.*
Good night.   *Good night.*

Another reality of war was that her brother Wilf and sister Jean were no longer in Millom. Just before the war, Wilf had officially joined the Royal Navy and Jean the WAAFs. Even though he could be such a troublemaker, Iris dearly missed her brother. Would he be coming back home on leave anytime soon? Of course, if and when he did come home, she wouldn't see much of him. Wilf would appear out from the train station with his easy smile and casual stride, and it seemed all of Millom was there to greet him. He wouldn't be in the house long before he'd be off to the pubs, where the stories and drinking and smoking and gambling occurred long into the night.

In truth, Iris couldn't help but feel some sadness for her brother, and she really couldn't blame him for not spending more time with her. He certainly was not made very welcome or comfortable in the house on Oxford Street, and it clearly wasn't the same as when they were all together with Mum. During his last visit, the two were together in the kitchen where Wilf loudly opened pantry drawers and doors before asking out loud, "Where do they keep the bloody food in this house?"

Wilf Graham home on leave in Millom, posing
with his sister Iris and cousin Mary.

In a hushed tone Iris responded, "Wilf, please keep it down! Mary will be coming back any minute, and you don't want to have her or Uncle hear you and see you poking around like this."

Wilf Graham posing on a battleship with an officer in the Royal Navy.

Iris consternated how the war was separating so many families. All too frequently, news of a young man from Millom dying or wounded in battle shook the
community. But at least they were no longer subject to the air-raid sirens. She wondered how the little girl staying with Mrs. Pill was doing. Millom was involved in
a program that hosted young children being evacuated from London, where heavy
bombing had occurred. Iris met the wide-eyed seven-year-old at the train station,
taking her by the hand and explaining how lucky she was to be staying with the
friendly Mrs. Pill. Hopefully, Mrs. Pill was not spoiling the young girl the way her
Aunt Anne was. Auntie Anne made such a fuss over the young girl she was hosting.
Maybe with three sons she always wished for a girl.

Despite the hardships and uncertainty caused by war, there was also a sense of
change in the air around Millom. The newsreels were finally providing some positive

images of the warfront, and things were slowly looking brighter. Even the shortages caused by the war didn't seem such a hindrance. Many items such as meat and sugar were being rationed, and you needed a coupon to purchase these and other staples. But Iris had a friend who worked at the local market, and she was sometimes invited inside to purchase the rationed groceries and other items without having to wait in the long queues.

Iris reflected that the closest she came to actually seeing anyone resembling the enemy was the incident with a young lady named Annie. She really wasn't friendly with Annie, who didn't have a very good reputation in town. So it was surprising when Annie asked Iris to join her on a walk to a farm just outside of Millom. Annie was a few years older and a newlywed whose husband was serving in the British Army. They walked up to a gate on the farm, where a group of men could be seen working in a field under close supervision of armed guards. Upon their arrival, one of the workers walked up to the gate and carried on a short conversation with Annie. He was medium height with lean build, olive skin, and curly dark hair, and spoke broken English with a heavy Italian accent. Before being ordered to get back to his work, she slipped him a carton of cigarettes, which were actually given to her as a gift by her husband when he was home on leave. When Iris shared this with Pauline and Ethel, Ethel was furious, scolding her. "Don't you ever hang around that Annie again, she's nothing but trouble."

And now it was Ethel's voice she heard once again, snapping her out of the daydream. "Pet! PET! Are you coming? We're off to see a picture!" The young ladies walked arm in arm the short distance into Millom, an active seaside town in the English Lake District. They stopped in a shop to purchase some sweets, seemingly unable to go more than ten steps without running into someone who stopped them in conversation.

"One of a kind that one, your mum was truly one of a kind."

"They just don't make families like the Mitchells anymore. Ma and Da is what we'd all call your grandparents. She was such a beautiful soul."

"Tell your brother he'd best look me up when he's back home on leave. The bugger owes me ten pounds and a pack of fags."

Settling into seats in the darkened movie theater raised yet more commotion. The ladies were barely seated before looking around to observe who was there and with whom. The theater suddenly turned quiet as a distinctive and enthusiastic male voice emanated from the screen, accompanying the scratchy newsreel with a background of spirited music. Allied forces preparing for battle were visible on the big screen. It seems that something big was being planned. Moviegoers cheered smiling

British soldiers who were seen with American and other Allied forces in seeming good spirits. An impressive fleet of navy ships prompted a nudge from Pauline, who looked at Iris with shared pride that Wilf was among the ship's sailors. Iris felt empathy for orphaned children shown in their misery, and compassion for war-torn families and refugees shown in their suffering.

Suddenly Pauline nudged her again. "Look, there's Annie!" Iris whirled around and remarked in a dismissive tone, "Well, I certainly hope she's *not* with that dreadful Italian bloke'" Pauline set off laughing. Ethel impatiently tried to quiet them, but it was no use, and before long the three were chatting away while attempting to keep the laughter down.

When they finally arrived at the house, it was dark. Uncle Will stormed downstairs and immediately set off. How dare they be so inconsiderate to come home at this hour of the night and keep him awake and worrying about their doings! Ethel had enough. She gave it right back. "This is a disgrace! It's embarrassing how you treat us. People must be laughing, who ever heard of someone acting in such a way…"

Uncle Will appeared stunned, but they continued their argument as Ethel refused to back down.

Iris and Pauline stepped back and intently observed from a corner of the room, not wanting to stir the pot or cause more problems. And besides, it appeared that Ethel was articulating quite well exactly what had been on their collective minds for some time. Hearing the commotion, Frank sleepily appeared and gave a knowing nod to his sister and cousin. He walked up to Iris with a reassuring smile and said quietly, "Remember what I've always told you, Pet, one day I'm going to get married and you can come live with us."

Iris was touched by his thoughtfulness and kindness, and smiled in return. But it was not what a young lady searching for her place in life was aspiring for. Frank was truly a kind soul, his intentions always so good. But she suddenly felt small and alone. If only Grandma were here. Grandma always had a way of talking things through, of helping her sort out her thoughts, comforting her and providing direction.

The argument wound down, and Uncle Will stomped back upstairs. Iris glanced at Ethel who stood proud and defiant. She turned to Pauline who was now bent over and covering her mouth to stifle laughter. Ethel shot a cold glare at Pauline before a smile slowly softened her attractive features. Now Iris couldn't help but join them as the three were once again bound in shared thoughts and actions. Frank scratched his disheveled head and sleepily trudged back up to bed.

CHAPTER 9

The Quest Begins

Poland, Slovakia, and Hungary
August 1944 – September 1944

The moment had arrived. Ian eased out of his bed in the upstairs attic, well aware that his life was likely to change in ways that even he could not possibly imagine. Moving quietly to avoid stirring anyone in the house, he dressed in comfortable trousers, a long-sleeved shirt, a light jacket with multiple pockets, and a pair of sturdy leather-soled shoes. He packed some food and only enough small items to fit inside his pockets. Included among the items were jewelry and watches.

The time was nearing 5:00 a.m., so he knew that Artur would be expecting him any minute. Before slipping out the front door, Ian peeked inside the home's two bedrooms. His sister Krystyna shared the room with her parents, all fast asleep. Jerzy and Zdislaw now had the second room all to themselves, a room once shared by four brothers. Also fast asleep. His grandfather could be heard snoring from the back room, where he bunked since his arrival at the house in August 1939. With nothing left to do, he left a brief handwritten note on the kitchen table and stepped out into the crisp morning air.

Before walking down the hill, Ian stood by the flower garden, reflecting on their decision. Several days had passed since the first meeting with Artur, and the two continued meeting each day, scouring maps and gathering intelligence to fine-tune their plan. The plan was to trek south, cross Turkey, and travel across the desert to reach Palestine. Ian was well aware that their task was a daunting one. Between them and their destiny lay rugged mountains and unforgiving desert across two war-torn continents. Yet there was a calmness, a belief that they were doing the right thing, along with a sense of wonder and intrigue in the unknown adventures awaiting them.

With one final glance that would have a lasting effect, Ian stepped from the yellow stucco house to begin his journey, walking down the hill to reach Artur's house a short distance down the street. Approaching the house, Artur merged on the street to join him. Ian never broke stride. The two said nothing, simply acknowledged one another as if to suggest, "This is it." Turning back to take one final look up the hill in the misty morning, Ian took a deep breath, and the pair headed south to commence their journey. With enough food to last for several days, they walked past the sleeping town of Bochnia before reaching less-travelled roads leading through the Carpathian foothills, finding occasional shelter and refuge in the many forests along the way. Between the two they carried no travel gear or maps, relying solely on their knowledge of the countryside in order to avoid attention and appear innocuous in the event they were stopped and questioned.

Fueled with energy and adrenaline, they moved swiftly and before nightfall captured distant views of majestic mountains blending into the darkening sky. The uneven terrain did cause difficulty in settling on ground for comfortable sleep. Ian surprisingly woke up the next morning having rolled downhill several meters from where he thought he had fallen asleep. Somehow, Artur managed to stay in one spot throughout the night. Undaunted, they picked up and moved on to continue their journey. By late afternoon they scaled desolate peaks and before nighttime managed to sneak across border markers that indicated entry into Slovakia. They estimated their location to be about thirty kilometers east of Zakopane, Poland. This entry was more passable than through the rocky peaks of the Tatra Mountains. The rugged terrain of the Carpathian Mountains was not their only obstacle. They remained on the lookout for border guards, who were occasionally spotted far in the distance, appearing as haunting figures adorned in long capes, stooped over to brave the wind and cold. Causing distraction for the guards, the bitter weather conditions proved more an ally than a hindrance.

They continued their journey on foot, travelling southeast. Once getting past the highest mountain range, their plan was to locate a small town that would enable them to board a train. However, they were running low on rations, and Ian searched in vain for any sign of a town beyond each approaching peak and valley. As they gathered the strength and energy to climb atop strategic points to assess their surroundings, there was no sign of civilization, only continual stretches of distant peaks and valleys.

On the fourth day of travel, they confronted potential danger. Emerging from a thick forest where they took refuge for the night, they walked out into a clearing and found themselves staring directly at a band of teenagers who appeared from out of nowhere as if ghosts rising above the morning mist. The two groups froze, assessing the situation now facing them; were these friends or enemies? After brief pause, the group of teens exhibited mannerism that expressed more joy than fear. The teens engaged them in conversation, and after confirming the pair of travelers were Poles, their enthusiasm visibly grew. The young men were part of a planned uprising against Slovakia's German occupiers, and were expecting aid and assistance from the Polish underground at a planned rendezvous in the same general location.

"Where are your weapons?" they finally asked. Ian and Artur explained they were not part of the underground but on their own trek to reach Palestine, from where they would board a ship and join Anders' Army in Italy. Conveying disappointment that the Polish travelers were not who they expected to meet, they nonetheless offered what support they could to the pair. Walking together toward a higher elevation, the Slovakian teens shared their limited rations and pointed in the direction of Presow. From Presow, they could safely reach the border near Kosice by train. Once there, they weren't too certain about passage into Hungary, suggesting that it would be wise to gain further intelligence before relying solely on train travel.

The group reached a summit from where they would go their separate ways, and exchanged good wishes and luck in their respective endeavors. Ian and Artur did learn sometime later that the young men's fortunes would not be much improved from their disappointment in failing to meet with the underground. The Germans managed to squash the uprising, and Slovakia continued to remain part of the Axis under German control.

The intelligence provided by the Slovakian teens did prove to be both accurate and helpful. Within one day they reached Presow where they managed to board a train that drove them farther south, close to the border town of Kosice, which at the time was part of Hungary. Departing the train, they continued their journey south on foot and easily slipped into Hungary, steering far from the main roads to avoid being seen by border guards.

Foot travel through Hungary was relatively fast and easy. The terrain was flat with few towns or villages on the road to Miskolc where they planned to board a train that would take them near the Romanian border. For food, they purchased loaves of bread in the villages along the road, before wandering into the surrounding countryside to complete their meal preparation. Fresh vegetables were plentiful all along the roadway. Ian found the Hungarian tomatoes especially ripe and tasty, larger than any he had ever experienced. With bread and fresh vegetables on the menu, they dined under shady trees out of view from the roadside, feasting on juicy tomato slices over fresh bread.

After several days of travel in Hungary, their trek was slowed by an unexpected encounter. The day was hot, and the road grew dusty when they walked into what surfaced as a dream. The village they stumbled upon was unlike any that Ian had ever seen. Slowing to a halt, they found themselves in what could be best described as an ancient civilization resembling a remote village deep in the bush of Africa. Mud huts circled the area; smoke wafting from cone shape roofs cast a wildly contrasting image from the typical European village. Scantily clad children ran freely on the road while a handful of women were visible nearby. They could not help but sense they were being watched. Ian immediately realized they had encroached a Gypsy village.

Ian had never seen a Gypsy village but was well aware of their fables and reputation. Gypsies came to Bochnia every summer. They camped just outside of town at night and populated the square during the day, selling pots and pans made from tin. The area would come alive with their Chardash music, lively vocals mixed with cheerful sounds emanating from decorative fiddles. Adding yet more life to the square, colorful outfits accented the Gypsy's dark features and jet-black hair. Ian thought them to be an attractive-looking people. Older women would visit homes with offers to tell fortunes, always insisting that a gold coin be placed on the table before fortunes could be revealed.

But there was also a dark side to their reputation, not all of which Ian readily believed. What was known was that a partner typically accompanied the fortune-tellers, and these partners were known to steal items throughout the house. As the fortune-teller mesmerized her customer with an astounding glimpse into the future, her young accomplice deftly pocketed items from within the household. There were also tales of Gypsies snatching and selling young children, though Ian suspected those were more folklore than reality. Nevertheless, the Gypsies possessed a dark reputation, and the townsfolk breathed more easily after the wanderers packed up and moved on to the next town.

As Ian and Artur stood out as foreign figures in the middle of the dusty road, engulfed by the strange-looking village before them, they sensed it best not to tempt fate. Slowly retracting their steps, they made a wide berth around the village before reentering the road to resume their journey to Miskolc.

They reached a town just north of Miskolc without further incident and purchased train tickets to Cluj, the last Hungarian city near the Romanian border. Settling into his coach seat, Ian scribbled notes on a pad of paper as he reflected on the journey that he and Artur had undertaken. Since the first night in the mountains of Poland, Ian took it upon himself to write a journal of sorts, documenting places and events the two had encountered. It seemed a good idea at the time, perhaps rekindling memories to be included in a memoir of their journey. Ian would soon come to regret that decision.

Artur sat across from him in his own coach seat, comfortably observing the countryside unfolding before him in the waning daylight. Everything considered, things were going quite well. Foot travel brought about a few unexpected twists and turns, most notably the Slovakian teens and the Gypsy village. But the teens were in fact quite helpful, potential confrontation in the Gypsy village was avoided, and train travel proved to be quite comfortable. Ian took pride that he and Artur were becoming quite adept at slipping across borders; both the Slovakian and Hungarian borders posed little difficulty. Once they traveled through Romania, Bulgaria was a relatively short distance before reaching Turkey, their gateway to the Middle East and Palestine. He looked over at Artur, who was now fast asleep. The coach grew dark and silent as Ian sensed the need to catch up on much-needed sleep himself before their early morning arrival. His confidence grew that they would safely reach Palestine and ultimately achieve their dream of joining Anders' Army in Italy. Jotting down a few final thoughts, he tucked the notepad away and fell into a deep sleep.

The pair of travelers awoke to a rustling of passengers stirring with the brightening predawn sky. It wasn't long before the train rolled to a stop, the city name CLUJ greeting them on the platform of the border city. Ian sensed no imminent danger as they walked out onto the platform. In fact they found help and support from a most unexpected source. Venturing out from the station, they struck a conversation with a friendly Hungarian military officer. He had also been on the train, and joined them in casual conversation, the three speaking a language of common understanding, German. Although the Hungarian Army was fighting alongside the Germans, the uniformed officer asked no absorbing questions. He seemed sincere in providing support for the young Poles, so he took them to his home and provided the hungry travelers with a much-appreciated early lunch.

They continued lighthearted conversation, avoiding details of their purpose or the officer's own reason for travel, the officer genuinely pleased to help the two young Poles. His friendly demeanor carried a sense of their purpose and an understanding of their need to continue a quest. Bidding them farewell and safe travels, he watched the two depart to continue their journey. Ian and Artur headed in a southwest direction toward higher elevation that provided a spectacular view of the picturesque city below them. From there, they pointed south in the direction of Romania where the wanderlust of deep forest introduced their next chapter. Ian and Artur were closing in on their destination.

Historical Perspective

Unknown to Ian and Artur, yet another conflict was emerging between Hungary and Romania, two countries with a lengthy history of distrust and discord. When planning the route, they expected no extraordinary difficulty in travel between the countries. As far as they knew, leaders of both countries were aligned with Germany as part of the Axis, but neither was considered a hotbed of unrest or sympathy for the Axis among their civilians. However, the Romanian government was in the process of once again changing sides in the war.

Early in the war, a weakening of neutral Romania enabled a coup that brought the fascist Antonescu regime into power. Romania fell into the camp of the Axis, offering unequivocal support in the way of supplies and troops to the German Army as they mounted their blitzkrieg against Russia on the eastern front. However, by 1944 the prospects for victory clearly shifted toward the Allies, enabling another coup d'état to unfold. The exiled King Michael was the perfect choice, and Stalin propped him up to lead another coup that would side Romania with Russia for the remainder of the war.

By midafternoon, the two were well outside of Cluj and deep inside the heavily wooded countryside, believing to be in Romania. There was no sign of a village or people, simply an occasional shack peeking through lush trees in the thick forest. They came across an old shed which showed at least some sign of human activity. Outside the shed, a large pot hung on a crudely built wooden tripod, dangling over burnt-out embers. The shed had no windows or openings, but they were able to peek inside open slats dotting the ramshackle structure. Spotting no visible signs of food or supplies, they decided to move on.

They attempted to move in a southerly direction using shadows as a guide, but cloudy skies and uneven terrain mixed with thick forest made the task difficult without a compass. Eventually they spotted a clearing and some signs of civilization, distant farmhouses, grazing sheep, and lounging pigs chained to posts. The only other sign of civilization came from unusual-looking tire tracks, embedded intermittently along the countryside but not appearing in a continuous manner. After some study of the tracks, Ian bemused that the locals must be fashioning self-made sandals using worn tires for soles.

Daylight was waning. Closing in on a farmhouse hugging the edge of the clearing, they decided to approach with a request for food, perhaps gain some information on nearby villages, train travel, or anything to assist in their trek across Romania. The owner greeted them at the door and appeared to comprehend their request, motioning for them to wait out front while he went inside to prepare some food for the hungry travelers.

Ian and Artur sat on the ground outside the front door, eagerly waiting in anticipation for some food to energize them. After about five minutes, anticipation grew that their host might be preparing something special for them. But as the wait continued, doubt crept in. Just as they arose to check on their host or depart from the premise, two armed border guards appeared from around the back of the house. With rifles pointed at them, they understood the threats well enough to raise their hands high up in the air. Unbeknownst to them, they were suspected of being collaborators with Hungary, who was now considered an enemy of Romania.

CHAPTER 10

Escape From a POW Camp

Transylvania Region, Romania
September 1944

With hands clasped behind their heads, the two were marched at gunpoint to a military compound in the vicinity of their capture. About a dozen soldiers were housed in the building where the two were asked questions about their nationality and what they were doing in Romania. The interrogators appeared particularly distressed over the notepad, which was confiscated from Ian. Jabbing at the notepad held in front of them, the guards angrily shouted questions. Despite the language barrier, Ian and Artur tried to explain as best they could that they were simply civilians and not engaged in any conflict with Romania. The soldiers wrote down some notes before providing the two with a simple but much appreciated meal. Unable to effectively communicate further, they were told to stay quiet and wait for further instructions, under watch of an armed guard.

The next morning, a husky man who appeared to be a local villager was brought in to transport them further into Romania. Armed with a rifle and provided instructions from the soldiers, he motioned for Ian and Artur to get up, pointing them outside the building to commence their journey south. Ian observed the landscape slowly transform from valleys and rolling hills to higher foothills, with views of mountains appearing in the distance. Throughout the day, their guide tired from the combination of heat, elevation, and his heavy rifle. He continually found himself lagging behind his prisoners, suggesting they stop for water and rest. Each time, Ian and Artur offered to help the fatigued guide by carrying his bulky weapon. Every time, he good-naturedly refused their offer. By evening, they reached a small town near the base of the mountains, where Ian and Artur were asked yet more questions and held in a jail cell for the night.

On their third day in Romania, a younger and better-conditioned guide was assigned to transport them through the mountainous terrain. He appeared to be the same age or not much older than they were. Fortunately for Ian and Victor, they were accustomed to such difficult travel conditions. Unfortunately for the pair, their knowledge of the Transylvania region they now entered was based more upon folklore than actual awareness of their surroundings. They were entering into unfamiliar if not mystical territory.

Upon reaching a vista offering spectacular views before them, their guard stopped to take a break. As Ian and Artur sat down to drink water from the canteen, their guard casually walked over toward a precarious spot near the edge of a cliff, several strides from where they sat. Ian made eye contact with Artur as the two knowingly contemplated attacking and knocking him over the cliff. It was a daunting dilemma requiring a split-second decision. Although Ian had experienced death these past few years, he had never actually killed a man. Collectively, the pair managed to communicate and empathize that their guide was a young man much like themselves and only doing his job, that the plan could backfire and they could be shot, and even if they did manage to overpower him, their limited knowledge of the mountainous region could not guarantee survival. The pause enabled the guard to rejoin them without incident as the three concluded their reprieve before continuing the journey.

As the trek drove them deeper into the Transylvanian mountains, Ian spotted a remote castle. It appeared from out of nowhere, like a nightmare amidst the rising fog and jagged crags surrounding them. Looking over at Artur, he visibly shared his angst. The fortress grew more daunting with every step, sharpening into focus as a threatening symbol from a dark fairy tale, and Ian couldn't help but wonder if they were approaching the Castle of Count Dracula.

Dusk arrived by the time they walked through heavy doors that enclosed them inside the massive fortress. Before they were able to acclimate themselves to their surroundings, they were taken to a large empty room and interrogated, repeated questions echoing off the high ceiling. Again, there was anger raised from Ian's notepad, and again there was difficulty in answering due to their having little knowledge of the skirmish as well as the language barrier. Though they could not fully understand the questions, the country names of "Russia" and "Germany: were spat at them over and over. This certainly caused a dilemma in responding to the questions. First, Ian was unsure just who the interrogators were siding with. And second, from his own experience, he felt an intense disdain toward the leadership and principles of both countries. Both were aggressive in their pursuit to dominate Poland, and both were guilty of taking away his family's freedom and way of life.

Using sign language, common German phrases that the interrogators understood, or any means possible, they struggled to explain their situation in a way to avoid any form of condemnation. It did little good. Confusion reigned as aggressive threats continually hounded them. Confusion was soon replaced with doubt as they reluctantly signed official-looking documents that their questioners never stopped waving in front of them. Although the questioning and threats finally ceased, they had no knowledge or understanding of what they had just signed under threats and coercion.

Ian and Artur were led through a maze of hallways before entering yet another room in the castle where they joined a number of fellow prisoners, they being the only civilians among the uniformed Hungarian soldiers. Sleep did not come easy. Locked inside thick stonewalls immersed within the cavernous castle, they had little clue of the fate awaiting them.

Romanian soldiers were now assigned the task of transporting the larger number of prisoners held at the castle. Along the route, they picked up additional prisoners from various locations before finally arriving at a small town located along the lower elevation, a foothill of the mountainous region. There they were placed in a holding facility operated by the Romanian military. As part of the newest wave of arrivals, Ian and Artur were required to go through one final interrogation.

To their relief, one of their interrogators was a Romanian captain of Polish descent, enabling them to finally communicate and explain their situation. He arranged with the guards to take Ian and Artur to his home for the evening, providing a warm meal and sleep in a real bed for the first time since their departure from Poland. While this reprieve was welcome, it was also the first time they began to realize the seriousness of their predicament. During the evening, the captain informed them that the papers they signed were confessions to being spies for Hungary. Because of the signatures, he was powerless to do anything for the two outside of the hospitality he now offered. Ian and Artur realized for the first time that they were in serious trouble.

Early the next morning, all prisoners were collected and marched at gunpoint to the train station where they were squeezed into boxcars normally used to transport cattle. Just like the boxcars Ian observed holding those unfortunate families in Przemysl, there were no windows. A narrow slit along the top of each car provided the only opening, so it was virtually impossible to view the surroundings and see where they were going. Ian estimated the count of prisoners in their car to be fifty, so the three boxcars carried approximately 150 prisoners. Once again, Ian took note that he and Artur appeared to be the only Poles among the prisoners, and there were only a handful of fellow civilians. He also noted at least two uniformed Germans among the prisoners. The only other certainty they knew was that the train was transporting them all to a more permanent prison of war camp in the southern Romanian city of Pitesti.

Pitesti, Romania
Autumn 1944

Forced to stand for hours with no food or water and suffocating inside sweaty cattle cars, the prisoners spilled out when the train finally rolled to a stop in the industrial city of Pitesti. Upon departing the train station, the relieved prisoners were marched past the city center and through the town's streets. Sighting curious onlookers along the way, Ian and Artur purposely talked and sang to patriotic songs excessively loud in Polish, cryptically explaining their situation and quest, hoping to attract the attention of local Polish expatriates who might be able to assist them.

They continued the march until reaching a military compound just on the other end of town. The compound held a base for Romanian soldiers, and at one end of the compound sat three crudely made wooden barracks constructed to house the new arrivals. Three long, narrow rectangular barracks lined up in parallel, and a square-shaped guardhouse lay just outside their front entrances. A wooden fence roughly three meters high surrounded the entire compound, and a barbed wire fence about five meters beyond the wooden fence looked to stand about waist high.

After marching into the compound, the men were divided into groups and escorted into one of three prison barracks. Directed into the nearest barrack, a burly barracks guard, his round face contorted in a twisted smile, welcomed the new arrivals. He was housed in a small open space at the entrance, which contained a make-shift desk along one wall and a small cot along the opposite wall. Before allowing the men to pass, he conducted his own personal inspection and beamed with delight at the loot taken from his Polish prisoners. Gone were the watches and necklaces they'd been holding as potential contraband if confronted with an opportunistic encounter. The watches sure didn't help at the border, and the barracks guard clearly had no issues in confiscating their personal items for his own use. He grinned with an appreciative nod, as if the loot received was presented to him as a personal gift.

Suddenly devoid of all personal property, the pair warily entered spartan barracks lined with bunk beds on both sides. An open area offered free space with a crude table in the middle of the barracks where some men had already occupied the space to sit and play cards. They claimed a vacant bunk and assessed their situation.

Both men closely corroborated the landmarks and estimated distances outside the barracks. They noted that they were the only Poles among the Hungarian prisoners, but agreed to be careful and not assume that the guard or others don't understand what they're saying. They were initially not overly thrilled with being so close to the guard near the front entrance. However, upon further reflection, the two surmised that the arrangement might indeed prove beneficial. Satisfied with their initial assessment, the weary Poles lay down to rest from the exhausting day. Ian glanced around the barracks from the bottom bunk before closing his eyes. Clasping his hands behind his head, he reflected on their prospects for escape. "Say, Artur, do you suppose that anyone in town was able to hear or understand us?"

Several days later Ian and Artur were seated at the mess hall, dining on watery soup and bright yellow corn bread that tricked them with its appetizing appearance. The men were joined in lighthearted conversation with two Serbs whose company they had come to enjoy. Although the Serbs didn't speak Polish, their languages share a Slavic origin, and they were able to communicate quite well. The men were also united in shared ill-timed circumstances that brought them to the prison. The Serbs had gone to Hungary to attend university at a school just across from the Serbian border. Expecting to attend classes, they were instead drafted into the Hungarian Army and ultimately captured by the Romanians.

The four prisoners reflected on their unlikely circumstances and chuckled over the fact that Romanian soldiers on the opposite end of the hall didn't appear to be enjoying their meal. Although that did nothing to improve their own rations, they did take some solace in the fact that their captors were also suffering from similar dreadful offerings.

One of the Serbs suddenly stopped to alert them. "Quiet! Listen up…did you hear that?" Ian strained to listen through the noisy hall: "Polish prisoners! Searching Polish prisoners? Bajda, Wlosek!" They stood to grab the attention of the approaching guard, not sure what to expect, but felt relief upon viewing his reaction. The guard appeared bored and casually waved them over. He gestured outside, suggesting they had a visitor who was waiting in the yard to visit them.

Escorted out from the mess hall, they viewed a middle-age woman standing next to the guardhouse. She feigned a joyful welcome upon their approach, offering home-made cookies as the men joined in on her charade. Warm smiles and hearty greetings were exchanged as the guard wandered out of earshot. She maintained her cheery expression while informing them that she did in fact hear their plea for help as they marched through town. The men learned that she lived with her husband in a Polish community right in the center of town. Within the community was a social hall that housed a school and served as a place for residents to meet. The group even had their own doctor and nurse. The woman suggested that if they manage to escape the compound, they meet at a specific location where she would wait for them. She informed them she'd wait in that general location for about an hour past midnight over the following week. If the men managed to reach her, the Polish community would assist in their efforts to escape Romania and continue their quest.

When they got back to the barracks, they decided to waste no time, planning their escape for that evening. They had already put a good deal of thought into an escape, so now was just a matter of fine-tuning and executing. The close proximity of their bunk to the guard did indeed prove to be both beneficial and paramount to their plan.

During their first evening at the camp, Ian cautiously approached the guard in the middle of the night. Imitating loud snoring, he pointed to an empty cot next to the guardroom with a shrug and sleepy expression. Perhaps the friendly guard felt surprise or compassion, recognizing Ian as one of the Polish prisoners, but having a prisoner so close would probably mean one less prisoner to worry about on his nightly watch. So he did agree to the request, and Ian managed to combine some sleep with an observation of their guard's propensity to nod on and off into a deep sleep during the night.

Following that evening, Ian continued going right back to sleep on the cot next to the guardroom. And on this night, Artur lay on the bottom bunk, waiting for his cue. A few minutes after the guard nodded off, Ian eased out of the cot and peered out, motioning for Artur to enter. The men quietly slipped past the guard, cautiously opened the door, and managed to step out of the barracks undetected. It was a dark, moonless night.

Sensing nobody in or around the guardhouse, they crouched low and quickly moved toward the fence along the end of the yard. While working in sync to scale the wall, a light beam startled them, casting shadows along the wall. Now scrambling to clear the area, more lights directed toward them as they stumbled to reach the outer fence. Just as they reached the barbed wire, the entire area lit up and a crackle of gunfire sounded, its echo trailing above them. In his urgency to step over the barbed wire, Ian's pants got tangled, but he managed to free himself to a chorus of gunfire, ripping his pants before the lithe pair sprinted toward their designated meeting place.

Hearing the woman's shouts from behind a cover of heavy brush, they sped toward her. She stepped out to deftly guide them away as they easily distanced themselves from the approaching guards. She led them to her home where the exhilarated escapees were provided food and shelter. Her husband joined them at a table in the candlelit room and laid out the next steps. It was now approaching sunrise, but they still had time to be transported to the nearby hall under cover of darkness. There they were hidden in an underground storage area and told to sit tight while their Polish friends determined the next best course of action.

Over the following days, they learned that their Romanian guards suspected the local Polish community was hiding and aiding them. Their captors threatened the Polish community, warning them of severe repercussions if the prisoners were not returned. Ian and Artur contemplated their situation. They decided that, rather than bringing hardship to the community who aided them, they would turn themselves in. Early the next morning, they walked inside the compound gates, past the startled guards, and reentered the prison.

Remaining resolute in their desire to journey south and ultimately join Anders' Army, the men stayed on alert for another escape attempt. Each day began with the same routine. An early wakeup, standing at attention in the yard, stating their name and number to be counted, and marched to the mess hall for coffee and corn bread before handed assignments for a new work order. Some days they marched outside to conduct manual work in town; other days they were given tasks within the compound. Cleaning saddles in the barn, repairing a fence, clearing up the grounds. The work was long and hard, certainly not in line with required treatment of war prisoners as dictated by the Geneva Convention. Armed guards were always close by, but they remained on alert, keeping their eyes open and looking to seize an advantage when the opportunity arose.

Within weeks, that opportunity arrived. On a dark overcast night accompanied by the distant sound of rolling thunder, they managed to leave the barracks and prison yard without being seen or heard. Claps of thunder enabled moments of noisy movement while bolts of lightning provided intermittent light. With relative ease, they found themselves outside of town and in the countryside. Unfortunately, a heavy October downpour soon had them chilled and soaking wet. Rushing into a nearby cornfield, they covered themselves with stalks of corn in hopes of staying reasonably dry and warm. But it was no use; they were chilled to the bone for the remainder of the night.

Morning was met with continued drizzle. They resumed walking in the rain and mist, reaching a small town along the roadside. But almost immediately upon their entrance, a local policeman spotted them as if expecting their arrival. He intercepted them at gunpoint, pointing them inside to enter the police station. Entering the warmth of the station, the men actually felt relief. Before long, a truck from the prison arrived to escort the escapees back to Pitesti. Again, they felt a sense of relief on being back inside the dry barracks, but their barracks guard did not feel so fortunate.

The Romanian prison protocol seemed to have a peculiar twist. As with their first escape attempt, Ian and Artur were expecting some form of punishment after being caught. But instead, it was their barracks guard who was required to endure the punishment. He received multiple lashes and was then forced to stand for about an hour inside a small wooden crate, not even large enough for him to stand upright. After crouching in an awkward stoop for an entire hour, he stiffly entered the barracks where Ian and Artur sat braced for the worst. To their surprise, their good-natured guard simply sported a grin, as if to say, "You got me again." Ian wondered if he was actually enjoying the challenges posed by his Polish prisoners, who were the only ones attempting escape. Or maybe he felt the young Poles caught a tough break landing in a prison intended for Hungarian soldiers, or perhaps he felt that his punishment was somehow warranted for the spoils he took from the two.

Determined, the two kept their eyes open, but now well aware of the need to be better prepared. Sure enough, they received another visitor. This time from an elder charismatic gentleman who was a former captain in the Polish cavalry. The bearded captain had heard all about their prior attempts, and was both adamant and persistent in his ability to help them. He did not reside in the Polish community but in a remote area outside of town. He vehemently assured the men that if they could reach his house, their quest to join the army would prove successful. Smoothing his gray beard, he provided detailed directions and ensured them that he would remain awake every night in wait of their arrival. Ian and Artur enjoyed the visit but were not quite sure what to make of the colorful captain and his story.

Having seemingly remained in the good graces of the barracks guard, Ian resumed sleeping on the extra cot near the guardroom. With no better options, the men decided to take a chance with the cavalry captain. They kept their eyes open in search for the opportune time to make a break. One night their guard dozed off even deeper than normal and joined in on the chorus of snores heard throughout the barracks. Ian motioned to the alert Artur and the two quietly slipped out into the prison yard. Again, they scaled the wall, this time no spotlight or gunfire or rain. They managed to carefully clear the barbed wire, this time no tangle of pants to slow them. Having gained valuable knowledge of the local surroundings, they had little difficulty in following the memorized directions. Within an hour they reached the designated area outside of town. There they spotted an isolated cottage covered in foliage across from the identified landmark. Now it was up to the captain to prove that he truly was legitimate.

The captain proved to be more than legitimate. Almost before they could even make a sound he appeared out of nowhere at the front entrance as if one step ahead of them. Excitedly rushing his visitors inside, he guided them to an old wooden table and quickly arranged an assortment of dried meat, bread, fruit, and cheese. Ian suspected that his cupboards must have been left bare by evening's end. The three never slept or left the table as their host freely poured shots of vodka, discussing plans and reliving colorful stories of his escapades as a captain in the Polish cavalry.

Shortly after daybreak they were greeted to the booming entrance of a rickety old truck. The captain was expecting an old friend who had been patiently waiting to deliver a load of used goods to Bucharest. Their exuberant host directed the men to climb atop the overloaded truck, high enough to avoid being seen from other travelers. To further ensure their safety, he tossed up a folded canvas for good measure, and sent them off with a proper salute and farewell. The men returned the salute and slipped under the canvas, warmed by a series of the most unexpected friendships, but also hopeful that they'd seen the last of Pitesti.

Bucharest, Romania
Late Autumn 1944 – December 1944

The bumpy ride atop the old truck lasted through the morning, travelling 120 kilometers nonstop through small villages and country roads. Ian and Artur cautiously captured glimpses of Bucharest, the sprawling capital and largest city of Romania. Their destination was a neighborhood not too far from the main train station. Jumping down from the truck, they were offered water and light snacks from a friendly fellow Pole who was there to greet the driver. After some discussion, the two were discreetly escorted to a nearby corner building on a busy street, located at Six Strada Sevastopol. The building was run by a Polish underground organization and housed a number of men, providing food and shelter while arrangements were made for their release.

Ian and Artur learned there was no vacant space in an upstairs room, so they were led downstairs to an open cellar framed by thick brick arches. A handful of disheveled men sat around a makeshift wooden table in the middle of the dark cellar playing cards. Uneven stacks of coins, paper currency, and several old watches decorated the tottering table. Ian observed they didn't appear to be the friendliest bunch. None of the men even bothered to look up or acknowledge the younger arrivals upon their entrance. So the two settled on empty cots situated along the room's perimeter. Realizing they hadn't slept for days following their escape and ride from Pitesti, Ian lay down on a hard cot, but managed only sporadic sleep in the smoke-filled room. The players engaged in loud bravado under a dangling lightbulb all through the night. When Ian arose early in the morning, the scene before him had barely changed. The men vacated their same positions around the table. Only the stacks of money and jewelry had shifted.

Despite a lack of sleep, Ian felt a tinge of anticipation for an opportunity to depart the dark cellar and explore an enticing new city. Venturing out beyond their neighborhood, he was immediately drawn to expansive city parks that guided him to the city center. When he reached Victoria Street, he took in the array of shops, impressive government buildings, and a string of Orthodox churches lining both sides of an adjoining wide avenue. After some time wandering along the city streets, a revelation came upon him, one that he certainly should have observed much earlier. Although they did not appear in great abundance, civilians populated the city, few military personnel were visible, and few if any signs of war were evident. It was the first time since the beginning of the war (outside of Vienna with the security of signed papers) where walking along a city street seemed as normal and routine as walking through town as a schoolboy in Bochnia. Certainly much different from what they experienced in northern Romania where tensions were thick from the conflict with Hungary. Well aware that he and Artur had no legal papers and remained wanted escapees in a foreign country, he reminded himself to remain vigilant. But he also felt a sense of relief and normalcy in a city not occupied by foreign invaders.

Meeting up with Artur later that evening, he learned that his friend also made some interesting observations, along with fortuitous friendships that would soon prove most beneficial. In the same neighborhood was a much more luxuriously furnished building occupied by what appeared to be a Polish mafia organization. Unlike Ian, Artur's exploration that day was geared toward learning the neighborhood, where he ran across a group of these men at a nearby cafe. The group welcomed the outgoing young Pole into their circle, eager and interested in learning of his Romanian experience and escapades. They seemed to genuinely enjoy his company, sharing information about the neighborhood and some of the Polish men at Sevastopol. The group enjoyed the evening over fine wine and good food. Artur's new friends insisted on picking up the entire check by evening's end. It was quite late when Artur returned to the cellar. He and Ian shared their findings while the cardplayers resumed their all-night gambling.

Their handlers did not waste time. Early the next morning, plans were shared with Ian and Artur to receive papers that would enable legal status and safe passage inside Romania. They were provided instructions to visit the local police station, and told what to say and what *not* to say in order to receive the required documents while avoiding arrest. Not being fluent in the Romanian language and aware of the consequences if the papers were denied, Ian and Artur requested that their handlers speak on their behalf. However, when it was explained to them that their presence would only raise already heightened suspicion, Ian and Artur had no choice but to go alone. Before leaving, they were provided with further instructions and a valuable weapon to use in the event that they sensed imminent danger.

Approaching Bucharest's main police station, Ian's anxiety increased with the mere presence of the intimidating block-like structure. Walking up broad steps, past Romanian flags and through heavy doors, the two did their best to appear calm. It was little use. Ian sensed uneven glares from strict-looking officials and unfriendly police officers. They were taken to a cramped room off the main corridor and asked a variety of questions, answering as best they could, using the coaching they were provided. However, the questions become trickier, and the language barrier further complicated the interrogation. You can only feign confusion for so long, and just when it appeared that the police were losing patience, or that they may slip with a wrong answer, Ian and Artur decided it was time to unleash their secret weapon. Explaining their difficulty in answering the questions, they casually pulled out Romanian currency equivalent to about $50 apiece. Minutes later, Ian and Artur walked out of the police station breathing a huge sigh of relief with their registered documents securely in hand.

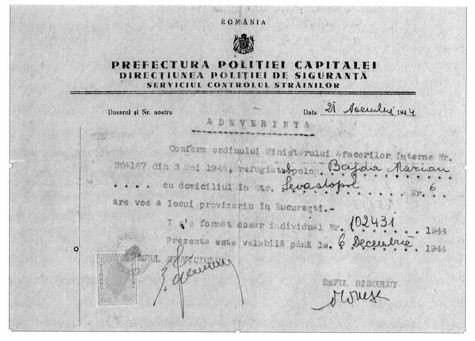

Ian's document enabling legal status in Romania. Ian and
Artur bribed the police to secure their documents.

That relief was short-lived. Later that afternoon after reentering the cellar at Sevastopol, they heard a commotion in the room above them. Aggressive shouts preceded angry footsteps that charged down the stairwell like rolling thunder. Ian wondered if the freedom they just bought was all for naught. A group of men burst into the darkened room, and they did not look happy. Nor did they appear to be the type of men you wanted to see angry. Ian smelled fear in the room. The cardplayers looked up for the first time, their faces dripping in terror. Artur, however, who stood right next to Ian, conveyed familiarity. One of the men acknowledged him with a handshake, and after careful inspection of the room, asked Ian and Artur to leave while they "take care of some business."

Asking no questions, the two rushed up the stairwell and quickly made their way outside where Artur identified the intruders as the group he met the prior evening, the Polish mafia organization who did business in the neighborhood. When they returned to the cellar later that evening, there was no card playing. The beaten men lay on their cots, no bravado exchanged but covered in blood and bruises. They had apparently done something to betray the trust of the mafia organization. Ian and Artur decided it was time to leave Sevastopol and Bucharest, and continue their quest.

After about a week in Bucharest, their generous handlers provided enough money for them to purchase train tickets to a nearby destination and still have some left over for other expenses. Feeling safe in their newfound ability to travel inside Romania, they selected the city of Craiova, located in the southwest corner of the country. From there, they would seek further assistance to safely cross borders to reach Palestine. They purchased train tickets in the early afternoon, but confusion and delays kept them waiting in the station throughout the day. It was not until late evening when their train arrived, and the two were met with a most unsettling scene. Their train was already overcrowded. Tired and angry waiting passengers rushed to squeeze inside the stuffy train. Ian and Artur had no choice but to join them.

Every coach car appeared overflowing with passengers. There was no room to sit. People and families sat atop one another in every available seat, bodies half out of open windows to maximize space and breathe in much-needed air. Ian and Artur did their best to fight past the standing crowd in hopes of finding relief in the next car. Their struggle to reach the exit door lasted well over an hour. They were not alone. Several others fought alongside them to reach the same exit. When they finally closed in, angry passengers tucked alongside the exit door were unwilling to make way for any passenger hoping to pass them; plus there was literally no place to go. Ian and Artur were determined. They climbed over swearing passengers, doing whatever it took to reach the door. They finally made it, but to little relief. The dangerous open connector between rail cars was also full, people hanging on to whatever they could so as not to fall off treacherous footing. Peering through an open door, entering the adjoining coach car was clearly not a viable option, the chaotic scene inside unchanged. The two gave one other a knowing glance. There remained only one option.

Searching for any hold he could find in the darkness of night, Ian scaled the rail car to reach the top, Artur right alongside him. The cold December air that welcomed them upon departing the overcrowded coach car now hindered their climb. Chilled fingers fought to retain their grip on makeshift steel handles. The two struggled to reach the top to great relief, but even that relief was once again tempered. They were not alone. The top of the rail car was overflowing with fatigued and tired passengers.

For three days, most of which was spent atop the overcrowded rail car, they struggled to stay warm and safe. The distance from Bucharest to Craiova is under 250 kilometers, a trip that should normally take well under six hours depending on the frequency of stops and weather conditions. Unfortunately, these and other factors were working against Ian, Artur, and their fellow passengers. The single line track required continual stops along the way, oncoming trains vying for the same set of tracks. Even when cleared for travel, their overcrowded train was all too often unable to make it up simple gradual hills that populate the southern Romanian landscape. Time and again, the train slowed to a halt before clearing a hill's summit. Passengers groaned at the overcrowded train's inability to make it to the top, surrendering to the need for retreat and another attempt. Sometimes they were able to make it on the second attempt, but more often it took three or four tries before the train barely made it, to the great relief of its fatigued passengers.

Ian and Artur struggled to find comfort atop the rail car. They had packed only enough food for one day of travel, so were forced to carefully ration what limited food they had. Travel at night was particularly treacherous. Passengers squeezed in search of an opening to lie down, and it was not uncommon for some to fall off during the night, given the combination of uneven tracks and frequent stops and starts. Every morning, passengers assessed the revised accommodations, more relieved than concerned over added space made available during the night. On their third day of travel, the two departed the train to overwhelming relief, hopeful that Craiova would be their gateway to Palestine, from where they would reach Italy to join Anders' Army.

CHAPTER 11

Receiving an Education

Craiova, Romania
December 1944 – August 1945

Three key events occurred while in Craiova: one having worldwide implications, one more personal in the young men's quest to join the Polish Army, and a third which simply became known among their tight circle of friends as "the knockout." It was not long before Ian and Artur made contact with fellow Poles in the city. They located an address provided to them while in Bucharest and entered a Polish community not so unlike the one they discovered in Pitesti following their first escape attempt. Lodging was simple enough. The two newcomers were invited to stay with four other young men, but viewed the accommodations as only temporary. They were eager to continue their quest, seeking any information they could to achieve their dream of joining Anders' Army.

Expecting help and information to aid their trek south, they were instead met with doubt and apprehension. Everyone they spoke to cast doubt upon their plans, tried to talk them out of their quest, suggesting they avoid danger and settle in Romania for the time being. "Stay here where you will be safe. Bide your time. There is only danger and conflict all around if you leave Romania."

They did have a point, but Ian and Artur viewed the local Polish community as much too conservative and narrow-minded for their liking.

On Christmas Day, they joined a lively gathering in the apartment of a young Pole whom they had befriended. They learned that his route to Romania was most interesting; unwillingly drafted into the German Navy from his home in western Poland, he managed to flee from his base along the Black Sea after the Russian military entered Romania. He introduced them to his roommate, a bright-eyed young

Romanian named Ionel. Also present were several others, including another Romanian whose father owned a wine shop in the community, an attractive Romanian woman named Oana, and several others who they recognized from the neighborhood. Ian enjoyed the outgoing group. It was good to be in the company of similar-minded young adults who were all at the crossroads of their lives during such turbulent times. Knowing of Ian and Artur's quest and unrest, the group focused on their options, but not without much banter and laughter.

Ionel in particular had much to share. Ian observed that he had an uncanny ability to attract attention from the entire room just before he spoke. As conversation turned to dealing with the sudden presence of Russians in Romania, Ionel spotted his opening. Taking a deep drag from an ever-present cigarette, his mischievous smile cued them all that he had something profound to share. "Let me tell you about dealing with the Russians. I went to their headquarters and asked to speak to someone in the main office. The person at the desk replied, 'Just one minute please.' So I waited and waited, still no assistance. I finally went up and asked the person at the desk if I can see the official now. The person was obviously bothered by my impatience, and replied, 'I said, just one minute please.' When I explained that I had already been waiting for over an hour, the desk person looked up and said to me, 'Young man, Romania is small country, one minute not so long. But Russia is big country, one minute last very long time.'"

With his arms spread wide in a comical gesture to exaggerate the Russian's explanation, Ionel had the festive room laughing even harder. Ian chuckled to himself, rather enjoying this young Romanian, whose ever-present humor was matched by both a passion for his homeland and strong views in what was happening in the world around them.

"Ionel, you don't have to tell me about problems in dealing with Russians. I'm more interested in how Artur and I can get out of Romania to join the Polish Army. Our plan was to go south through Turkey, but it seems that everyone we speak to is trying to talk us out of that. What do you know of the route directly west through Yugoslavia?"

"Oh, I would not recommend going through that territory. Tito is not only fighting the Germans but also his partisans face other enemies inside who are fighting his revolution. And if you've had problems with the Russians before, be advised that their Red Army is now also entering the fighting. Why not just stay in Romania?"

The prospects of staying put while Anders' Army was advancing north to liberate Italy before advancing to Poland did not sit well with Ian and Artur, and their host seemed to sense their unease. Pouring each of his guests with a fresh glass of wine from a newly opened bottle, he offered a temporary solution.

"I have a proposition for you. You can stay here for a few months with Ionel and me. With four of us we can further split the rent. And I've worked a deal with the high school for me and another Pole to take evening classes so we can earn diplomas. You can join us in taking classes, and with your degrees you'll have better options as well as buy some time to make your next moves before getting back on track to continue your quest.

"But we've missed several years of high school. How long will it take to attain the degree?"

"Not a problem. The professors have agreed to work with us on an individual basis. We will all take the final exams with other students during their normal schedule, and have our completed degrees within months."

The first thought that Ian registered was improved prospects for their aspirations; having a degree would speed promotion to officers in the Polish Army. Artur seemed to draw the same conclusion based upon his reaction. Almost in unison, the two agreed to the arrangement. They had each received an unexpected but most welcome Christmas gift.

Since they carried all their belonging with them, Ian and Artur simply stayed put and moved in that evening. Their new flat was located in an apartment building in the vicinity of the Polish community. Their flat, along with all others in the block C-shaped building, looked inward to an interior courtyard populated with a handful of barren trees, scant patches of grass on an uneven lawn, and a weathered bench. The three Poles and one Romanian did their best to rearrange the few furnishings, enabling sleeping arrangements in the tight quarters. While not the most opulent or spacious arrangement, it was certainly an improvement over drafty wooden barracks shared with scores of snoring prisoners. It also beat sleeping on hard hilly terrain, although Ian did miss sleeping under the stars.

As promised by their roommate, classes were arranged for them at a local high school that served Polish residents. The young men were invited to the school for lessons every evening from 4:00 p.m. to 8:00 p.m., following regular classes held for students during the day. A different professor came in every hour, each providing private lessons in math, history, languages, and Latin. Courses such as physical education and arts appreciation were skipped, the goal being to condense several years into months and have the evening students pass their exams in June. Such was the requirement for all students to earn their high school certificate.

The four eager students tackled their studies with vigor. They had already experienced so much in their lives and easily focused on attaining a diploma. For Ian and Artur, there was the additional impetus to pass the exams, knowing that the certificate would be required to eventually attend officer school in the Polish Army.

Ian enjoyed the school and particularly looked forward to the daily history lectures. Their wiry, energetic history teacher was Latvian, and he tailored the lessons to his students, explaining that no amount of lessons could ever replace the experience that the four had actually lived during those past five years. "You have all been living history!" Delivering lectures with an enthusiasm that had them all at the edge of their seats, he provided colorful and detailed descriptions of the people who had occupied the Polish lands throughout history. Including a Latvian tribe that actually became extinct around the twelfth or thirteenth century. With an energy and passion that could only be conveyed by a historian or academic, their teacher wondered aloud what might have happened to that lost tribe. He appeared quite adamant about one day finding an answer to that question.

Ian also enjoyed the math class, which came quite naturally to him. Their teacher often called on him to write calculus problems on the board and explain to his classmates the logic of how he came up with the calculated solutions.

With the arrival of spring, the young men often spent their evening hours in the courtyard where they were joined by a smattering of local teens and young adults from the community. Settling on a welcome patch of grass near the lone bench, music emanating from their friend's guitar, they attracted regular visitors from throughout the apartment complex and the neighborhood. Included among the regulars were the lovely Romanian woman Oana, a young German woman whose father taught German at the high school, and an attractive Polish woman whose family owned several buildings in the neighborhood. As an added attraction, the young Polish woman had a wonderful voice, and she enjoyed entertaining them all with familiar Polish songs.

Also included among the regulars was their Romanian friend whose father owned a local wine shop, and two guitar-playing Polish brothers whose family moved to Romania at the start of the war. Ian observed that the brothers and most Poles seemed to live quite well, their families receiving assistance from the Romanian government since the start of the war. The Polish government had arranged with Romania at the onset of war to store money from their treasury and provide assistance for Polish refugees. Ian couldn't help but wonder how his family's fate would have differed had they reached Romania rather than the border village of Podwoloczysko after escaping the Nazi blitzkrieg.

Not everyone in the neighborhood appreciated the camaraderie and gathering of friends introduced by the Polish visitors. One evening, shortly after 10:00 p.m., there was a frantic knock on their door. They scrambled out to see one of the Polish brothers in a panic and out of breath. Rushing him inside, their friend explained that he was attacked and chased by a gang of locals as he left for home following their evening gathering. Fearing that the gang was in the area awaiting his return, the four roommates agreed to escort their friend back to his home.

The four Poles and one Romanian kept their eyes open on the dimly lit street for any sign of danger, and almost immediately upon turning the corner from their apartment, they spotted trouble. Ian estimated at least six men grouped together in a cluster, more likely lingered beyond shadows cast by a dimly lit street lamp. They moved cautiously, determined not to be intimidated by the threat now staring at them. Ian felt a surge of confidence, knowing that with Artur by his side and everything they'd been through together, he could count on his friend to have his back and step up in any possible confrontation. It also didn't hurt that Ionel was quite adamant in voicing his displeasure over the treatment received by his Polish friend. "We need to teach these bastards a lesson!"

Approaching closer, one of the Romanians ran up and hurled a rock in their direction. Sidestepping the errant throw that just missed hitting them, Artur picked up the rock, visibly holding it in front of him. Ionel jabbed his lit cigarette in the air, releasing an angry tirade in Romanian spoken so rapid fire that Ian could barely make out a word he was saying. The group collected themselves and continued moving forward, Artur with the rock in hand.

The two groups moved slowly until separated by mere paces. Ian studied the outline of stony faces cast in darkness, and the rush inside him sparked like a fire lit in his belly.

A wave of emotions flooded his consciousness. Images of capture, a prisoner in a country that held allegiance to Russia, denied a quest to fight the same enemy as his captors, and now this gang blocking entrance to allow a fellow countryman access to his own home. Clenching his fists, adrenaline pumped through Ian's body as a surge of fury pounded throughout his entire being.

The largest of the Romanians, the one standing out in the middle of the tight cluster, never saw it coming. Ian's right fist unleashed an uppercut that caught the gang leader square under the chin, lifting his feet off the ground before sending him crashing. His entire body hit the ground with a thud like a giant oak slowly felled from its permanent roots. The rest of the gang appeared stunned. They said nothing, simply knelt beside their fallen comrade while Ian's party continued on their way.

When they returned after seeing their friend safely home, the area was cleared, nobody in sight. The following day they inquired about the well-being of the Romanian oak and learned from several youths in the neighborhood that he was okay. One of the boys gleefully added, with a degree of satisfaction, that the Romanian thug was sporting a left jaw swollen the size of a ripe grapefruit. The gang was never seen again, and their friends were never threatened again following the knockout.

Ian (back row left) and Artur (back row right) with three Polish friends in Craiova. Seated left is the brother of their friend who was attacked by the Romanian gang, and seated right is their roommate who was drafted into the German Army. Ian and Artur are wearing jackets provided to them by their handlers in Bucharest.

While the knockout brought about positive change for the neighborhood, a second event that occurred while in Craova brought out transformation of historic proportions on a world stage. By 8 May 1945, German troops surrendered all across Europe, effectively ending their occupation of Poland and across much of Europe. Images of relief and unbridled joy plastered daily newsstands, from pictures of victory in London to liberation in Paris. Although their neighborhood in Craiova did not experience such visible change, residents openly welcomed the news with renewed hope that a sense of normalcy and peace will be returned to their homeland. But for many, particularly from the perspective of Ian and Artur, the war was far from over. The Russians had already entered Romania and were poised to exert their influence here, over all of Poland, and across much of Eastern Europe.

The third event occurred in June. Following months of intense study and preparation, all four evening students passed their exams, receiving certificates that would enable them to continue studies in university or, more importantly to Ian at the time, attend officer school for the army.

There was a clear need to complete some unfinished business, but the four roommates were in a celebratory mood and planned an evening in honor of the recent positive events. Preparations were lining up nicely. Their friendly landlady, who also provided food for Ian's twenty-first birthday party, offered to prepare some tasty appetizers for the evening. Their Romanian friend, whose father owned the exclusive wine cellar in town, agreed to provide the spirits along with their cellar's finest wines. He was always happy to share his father's wine for gatherings at the apartment, but never at this level.

The combination of graduation and world-changing events mixed in with tasty food and fine wine made for lively discussion. Especially with a group of young people who, as their Latvian teacher so succinctly put it, had lived and were living history. Ian sat back to take in the scene; their Romanian friend circled the room, proudly pouring from a vintage of his father's finest wine, and Ian waited in amused anticipation as Ionel's gesture and a deep drag on his cigarette suggested that he had something to share.

"The French would like you to believe that they have the finest wine. But it's not true, Romanian wine is the best!"

The comment did not go unchallenged by doubting guests, particularly those of Polish descent. Undaunted, Ionel continued.

"The history of Romanian wine is well documented. Centuries ago, our king ordered to burn down vineyards because the wine was so tasty, peasants were getting drunk all day rather than toiling in the fields."

Much laughter followed, with suggestion that perhaps Romanian peasants were simply lazy and not such connoisseurs of fine wine. The lovely Oana, sporting a tasteful blue dress that still managed to draw everyone's attention as she swept into the room, held out an empty glass, teased the smiling Ionel with a soft-spoken comment voiced in her sweet melodic tone. "Now you wouldn't deprive this peasant girl from such delicious wine would you?"

For a brief moment Ionel's focus appeared to desert him, but recovered enough to fill her glass while continuing his argument.

"The French still view Romanian wine as inferior because a parasite invaded our vineyards in the 1800s. The vineyards had to be replaced, so the French looked down upon our grapes as 'not noble.' Yet the same thing happened in France in the 1700s. And who do you think came to their rescue? That's right, Romanian vines were brought in to help replenish their vineyards, enhancing their own wine. So how can they now view our wine as not noble? It's a double standard."

Energy filled the room with continued banter and laughter as the conversation moved to options for each of the guests upon the recent world events. Ian's senses were suddenly heightened by a change in the air, as if a door eased open to release a cool breath of mountain air. He looked up to see the elegant Oana walk toward him with a freshly opened bottle of wine. Moving with the grace of a sleek cat, Ian wondered if she was walking on air. Oana simply smiled and filled Ian's glass as he observed sparkling Latin eyes accenting soft feminine features, her look further enhanced with wavy hair loosely tied back in a delicate pink bow. He watched her fill empty glasses around the room before settling back next to Ionel, playfully ignoring the empty glass from his outstretched hand. "Too much wine will keep you from toiling in the fields."

Ian smiled, sensing that Ionel's future options appeared quite clear, and wondered if Ionel and Oana would one day marry. The room continued with talk of what would happen next on the world stage, where to go, how to get there. Everyone had a different viewpoint and opinion. Some wishing to go back to Poland but uncertain of what was awaiting them. Others suggesting a wait-and-see attitude, knowing that American troops and Allied victors were visible throughout Europe, shaking out a new world order.

A burst of smoke filled the air, alerting the crowded room that Ionel had something to share. The cigarette now rested by his side. He relayed a simple message. "Why don't you just remain here in Romania."

Artur was the first to respond. "Now don't get me wrong. Despite capture and being held prisoner in your country, I have learned to appreciate if not enjoy Romania. But you have complained about your country from day one, everything from continual changes in the government and corruption to its mismanagement of basic services. You laughed about our experience on the train, saying that is the Romanian way. And yet you now suggest that we stay in Romania?"

Ionel chuckled and nodded in agreement. "Well, it is true that we Romanians have grown to distrust both our government and outsiders, at least initially, but we have proven to be quite adaptable. Ours is a complex country full of contrasts. Carpe diem. Not only do we like to complain, we have also learned to accept and enjoy life. Take what you can now, enjoy life, and don't fret about the past or worry about the future, because as fucked up as it may be there is nothing that you can do about it, so enjoy the moment. And regardless of what happens, one thing we will always have is our pride and our independence."

What followed was a spirited debate between the rich histories and independence of both Poland and Romania. Artur, in particular, pointed to the fierce pride and rich independence of Poland's history. He relayed the story of Polish King

Jagiello's defeat of the Teutonic Knights in the battle of Grunwald in 1410, an epic battle that made Poland the major power across the entire European continent. Ian was equally versed in the history, having read the book *The Knights of the Cross* from his favorite author Henryk Sienkiewycz. He filled in details of how the Teutonic Knights, former Crusaders from Germanic lands with aspirations to conquer Poland under a false pretense of loyalty to a religious order, brought in knights from all across the European continent in an all-out effort to defeat Jagiello, who was aligned only with Lithuania. The room grew silent as he described the brave Polish knight Zbyszko, whose loyalty to the lovely Danusia was a symbolic backdrop in the tragic story of good vs. evil. Everyone in the room was quite impressed with the story, the women in particular moved by both Zbyszko's chivalry and Danusia's fate.

Not to be outdone, stories of Romanian heroism and history followed. Lighting another cigarette, Ionel proclaimed Romania as the one pure country on the continent, the only European country never conquered. "The Romans feared the Dacians. When Trajan brought in his legions here to defeat us, they were only able to take parts of our land. Dacia was split into territories, but never completely conquered and taken over by the Romans, otherwise we would be speaking their language today. The Dacian king was so proud that he commit suicide in defeat, so as not to be taken back to Rome as a captor."

Ian sat back to take in the conversation. He lifted his glass of wine, not sure why it was so much more expensive than what they normally sampled. His own experience with wine up until now was limited to what their friend typically provided and the homemade wine in Weikendorf. But upon savoring the taste, he gained a new appreciation for the vintage wine so enthusiastically brought over by their Romanian friend. Perhaps Ionel was right about the status of Romanian wines.

He allowed his thoughts to drift back home. He had witnessed first-hand the breakdown of basic freedoms and private enterprise under Russian rule. He recalled the attack at the home in Podwoloczysko, the bone-chilling image of Russian tanks rolling into Poland, the pending danger they faced in Tarnopol, the ghostly train in Przemysl holding families for transport to labor camps. He had seen families deprived of basic rights, either sent away or forced to live in overcrowded conditions while the Russian authorities took over private property.

An emerging picture burned even brighter, a vivid image of Bochnia. The Bochnia he knew as a boy. Alive and vibrant! He pictured his father walking home from the office happy to see his children. Smartly dressed in a tailored suit and carrying his briefcase, he would be warmly greeted by Mother. Jozefa would have a delicious meal prepared for the entire family. He pictured the fruit trees in full blossom.

He pictured Krystyna chasing after her brothers in the yard. And he recalled the joy and laughter of the entire family as they watched Stanislaw excitedly take his first wobbly steps in the flower garden on their front lawn.

Ian was more convinced than ever that Poland must not remain under Russian rule. Their country must be liberated and Poland's rich way of life restored. Just as Jagiello restored Polish independence from the Teutonic Knights, Poland's independence must be restored once again. Though their trek to Palestine was sidetracked, they had learned from recent radio reports that the Americans, under General George Patton, had liberated the western region of Czechoslovakia and were now stationed in larger cities around the region. Patton's heroism and bold desire to rid Europe of Soviet influence were well known. He was also well aware of General Anders' victorious campaign in Italy, and heard that he was now mobilizing forces in Italy to build an even stronger and more powerful Polish Army. Between the two, they would surely be the generals to lead Western Allied forces to a new world order.

Ian sensed all eyes upon him. "What about you, Ian, do you know what you will you do?"

Ian sat upright and answered in his typical unassuming manner, "Well, yes. I've always known what I will do," The room was silent. Artur, in particular, expressed a keen interest in hearing what he had to say. So Ian continued. He shared that he had unfinished business. That he left his home and family behind to join Anders' Army in Italy and liberate his homeland, to restore Poland to its once rich and happy way of life. After coming this far, he would not give up that quest. The next step was to join the Polish Army under the American occupation, making certain to avoid Allied zones occupied by the Soviets. From there he would make it to Italy and fight under the command of General Anders.

He glanced over at Artur, who now wore a broad smile, and held his glass high for a toast with his friend and fellow adventurer. "Na zdrowie."

All across Europe, soldiers, refugees, and families-in-hiding were on the move back to either their home or to a safe haven. Rail travel was free for passengers able to show proof of identity that they were returning to their homeland. Ian and Artur were committed to resume their quest but first had an important stop to make. One that carried an element of danger and risk, but one they both viewed as necessary.

First, they needed to take care of a few matters. Their legal papers only enabled passage within Romania, so they recognized the need for documents that would allow free passage to destinations outside of Romania. Because Polish government officials were still in exile, there was no Polish consulate available to process and prepare the required paperwork. Fortunately, the Swiss consulate was available to act on behalf of the Polish government and prepared the required documents for both Ian and Artur.

Further adding to their good fortune, the papers were prepared in French. Although this was not seen to be of any significance at the time, the distraction cast on a Polish document written in a foreign language would eventually prove quite helpful in their quest. For now, Ian and Artur bid their friends who remained in Romania farewell. They were back on track to join Anders' Army.

Ian's document prepared by the Swiss consulate.
This document is written in French

CHAPTER 12

Welcome to the Polish Army

Bochnia, Poland
August 1945

For the third time since fleeing Nazi invasion on the horse-drawn carriage, Ian returned home to the yellow stucco house. Rail travel was free, the papers allowing return to their homeland. The visit would be brief. They would slip in and out of Bochnia, remaining invisible to the Russian authorities. His purpose was to see the family, assure them of his well-being, and promise a speedy return as liberators of their homeland. He had no way of knowing it would be forty-nine years before he'd see Bochnia again, and that Poland would suffer from many trials before their liberation.

Poland was at least liberated from German occupation. Brittle signs of normalcy returned but were overshadowed by ominous warning signs. Bochnia was far from the city Ian knew as a child. He could feel it the moment he arrived. Visitors trickled into their home. Neighbors and relatives stopped to see Ian, and everyone speculated on the prospects for Bochnia and Poland. Their mood was not upbeat despite the newfound freedom to congregate. Most of the visitors exhibited a defeatist attitude. Only when they learned of Ian's quest to travel with Artur and join the Polish Army in American territory did their mood brighten. "May God bless and protect you, Marian. We will pray for your safe and joyous return."

Jozefa made certain to prepare a special dinner for the family that evening. Ian was leaving in the morning after just one night at home, yet as typical she made no fuss. Ian was well aware that despite hardships faced by the family, the table was filled more than normal. There was a good deal of news to learn and share.

His siblings eagerly provided updates. Zdislaw was signed up for school in the fall, Jerzy was excited to attend the high school which was once again open, and even Krystyna would be going back to school. Henryk was home from his work order for the Germans in Weikendorf, Austria, and also attending classes to receive a teaching certificate for math and science. Ian was happy for Henryk, but what his brother shared next not only caught him by surprise but also raised Ian's spirits with incomparable joy.

Henryk shared that Michal resurfaced in Weikendorf where they met one evening at the village tavern. Henryk learned all about their escape and return to Bochnia, and reported that Michal was accepted back into the community and doing just fine.

Ian's father Stefan also shared that because his job was not an elected position, he had his old job back at the county law department, although at a significantly reduced basis than that before the war.

"Father, that's promising news, perhaps things will settle down and get back to normal."

His father managed a tired smile. "Ian, you must continue your quest. Things will not be normal here unless there are drastic changes."

Stefan Sr. went on to share with Ian the list of names who were elected to temporary positions for every important post in town. Unfamiliar with the names, Ian asked his father to explain.

"First, every name that I've mentioned represents individuals who are inexperienced, most if not all are totally incompetent, and all will do whatever they are told to do by the Soviet authorities. Second, all these men are members of the Communist Party, and theirs were the only names listed on the ballot.

"Ian, this is only the beginning. If the Soviets continue to exert their influence and ideologies, we will be no better off than we've been since the start of the war."

Jozefa broke the silence that followed, scooping a second helping of vegetables with bits of sausage and dumplings onto Ian's plate. "Now is not the time to fret about the future. Eat up, son, you need to put some weight back on your frame if you're going to join Anders' Army."

Ian sat back, believing he should feel guilty for accepting a second helping despite his healthy appetite. "Mother, I have not tasted such a delicious meal in years."

Later that evening, Ian reflected that it was almost exactly one year ago when he snuck out of Bochnia with Artur to begin their quest. Much happened in that past year, but he was more determined than ever to continue the journey and complete what they set out to do.

The household grew silent and dark, a silhouette of his father conducting paperwork under a dim light the only sign of life in the twilight of a long day. Ian approached his father before retiring to his room in the attic. He had seen his father so many times in the same place, but this time his father appeared more lost in thought than engaged in his work. "Father, I promise I will continue my quest. I will also find Stefan, and when we return next time, it will be as liberators."

Stefan Sr. removed his glasses and looked up at his son, a tired faraway smile that soaked in memories of the past while also gleaning hope for their future. "I know you will, son. Your mother and I, we've always known."

Pilsen, Czechoslovakia
August 1945

Ian and Artur met up early the next morning and secured free train tickets to a destination in southwest Poland. From there, they purchased tickets to the last major city still inside the Russian zone, Prague. The westbound journey from Poland by rail revealed aftereffects of the war. Visible signs of bombing were evident as their train rolled into the Czech capital's train station. Purchasing tickets for their next leg on the journey was expected to be more difficult.

They approached the ticket counter with a request for free travel to reach their homeland, a destination inside the United States zone, Pilsen. An elder gentleman glanced up just enough to see their documents in hand before providing two tickets to Pilsen. Ian was not certain if the teller either didn't recognize the foreign-looking documents or was simply not overly concerned with the two young travelers. The two walked toward the platform, their confidence growing as they closed in on their destination.

Ian felt a surge of relief after boarding the train to continue travel west. Within several hours they should arrive in Pilsen. However, relief was replaced with concern as the train slowed down well before reaching their destination. The train rolled to a full stop on the Russian side of the US/Russian military zone. Russian soldiers approached the train, checking the papers of every passenger on board. A young soldier approached Ian and Artur and asked to see their papers. He looked to be about the same age as the two young travelers.

The two handed over their documents, and observed the Russian soldier take great interest in the appearance and language of the documents. He asked a few questions, which they were able to answer in Russian. He never asked their nationality, and they offered no additional information, simply answering his questions in a direct but casual manner. The Russian continued reading, almost in a show-off manner, as if he both understood and enjoyed reading French words on the strange foreign documents. Allowing sufficient time to show that he comprehended both documents in their entirety, he handed them back with a nod that could almost be described as friendly. "Okay, everything looks good."

It took well over an hour before the soldiers completed their inspection and the train continued on its way. Ian looked over at Artur, and the two exhaled into broad smiles when they realized that they were travelling safe inside the United States zone.

Pilsen showed signs of energy and rebirth, much different from what Ian experienced in Bochnia. People walked freely along city streets, stopping to shop or simply engaged in open conversation. Ian and Artur stopped to ask for directions, and it wasn't long before they come across a bustling military headquarters identifiable by the stars and stripes of a United States flag. The entire area was populated with American soldiers. A bustle of activity, jeeps carrying personnel, tents set up to house various areas of operation. Soldiers were visible everywhere in small groups, smoking cigarettes while casually joined in work and conversation throughout the area.

Artur stopped a friendly-looking soldier who strolled past them. Having some knowledge of the English language, he managed to inquire where they might find some information about joining the Polish Army. The soldier smiled broadly, obviously pleased with his ability to understand and able to help the foreign-speaking men. Speaking in his strange-sounding language, he gestured for them to follow with a broad wave of his arm. With long strides that almost required a jog to keep up, he led them to an area just outside of the expansive US base where they immediately recognized the familiar uniforms of Polish soldiers housed in a much more modest base of operations.

They approached several recruiters seated behind a table, and just like that, Ian and Artur each signed a document stating their intent to join the Polish Army. They were handed additional documents, more applications to be filled out. Upon completion of the forms, one of the recruiters took note of their completed education with an affirmative nod. He informed Ian that there was an opening in the artillery division, while Artur's background looked perfect for infantry. Gone was Artur's dream to serve in the Polish Air Force, but he readily agreed to the assignment. They were told to return in two days where an American army truck would send them with other recruits to a larger headquarter base in Munich. From there they would be provided with further orders and sent to Italy with other recruits to receive their training.

"Gentlemen, welcome to the Polish Army!" It took a moment for the words to sink in. Finally, they had done it. Ian and Artur were on the cusp of attaining their quest, and to become officially recognized soldiers of the Polish Army.

Munich, Germany
August 1945

Ian had viewed destruction in towns and cities throughout the war, but nothing prepared them for the scene that awaited them in Munich. Entire sections of the city were immersed in rubble. Their truck snaked through city streets that smelled of death and desolation. Yet other sections offered a renewed spirit, signs of life sprinkled around them. As in Pilsen, residents were visible walking along city streets, some stopping at makeshift shops to purchase goods. More common were ghostly figures, staring vacantly as if lost souls unaware of the life around them. Cleanup crews joined by American GIs could be seen clearing out and loading piles of rubble. The army truck came to a stop at the Polish Army base set up in the city, and the recruits filed out to receive their first order. After receiving a hot meal and listening to instructions, they were told the day is free. "But get a good night's sleep, we will be departing first thing in the morning for Italy."

Ian and Artur ventured out to explore Munich. Interspersed with entire blocks destroyed from Allied bombing arose sections of the city seemingly untouched. The men found a makeshift outdoor café where they could relax, reflecting on the journey that brought them to Munich, and wonder in what awaited them. Between the two, they were sure to play vital roles in liberating Poland as soldiers in the infantry and artillery. Emptying his stein with a long swig of the dark heavy beer, Artur announced that he was returning to the base to get some much-needed rest. Ian planned to venture and see a bit more of the intriguing city.

Ian grew lost in thought as he wandered the maze of streets. Visions appeared of the family leaving Bochnia by horse carriage to avoid German invasion. He thought of how they found themselves in hostile Russian occupation and, fearing for their safety, hoped of returning home. The yellow stucco home, a beacon of safety from the Nazi occupiers. Then forced to labor for the Germans, warm memories of the butcher's farm and Vienna, his friend Michal. Escape from the farm and into Slovakia.

He reflected on his good fortune in meeting up with Artur. He smiled thinking about the dizzying sequence of events that led them through the Carpathians and Transylvania, escape from Pitesti where they met unexpected friends. He was thankful for yet more good fortune, close friends, and an education received in Craiova.

He walked past a red brick factory that miraculously stood intact, untouched by mounds of fallen bricks that constructed a haunting landscape, and thoughts turned back to Bochnia. The scene brought back memory of the brickyard and flourmill in their neighborhood. He visualized Mulek running across the street to fetch him. Mulek, their factory home now empty. Did he and his family survive? Increased confirmation of the horrors in concentrations camps spread across Europe like a horrific nightmare; the infamous Dachau camp was not far away from where he now stood. Ian looked up to see the main Munich train station. Workers repairing sections of roof and train tracks damaged from bombs, a hub of activity seen in and around the station. He was drawn to the entrance as if pulled by a magnetic force.

Easing into the expansive station, Ian was surrounded by a whirlwind of travelers and activity. Standing on an upper level, he sensed a presence. It burned from below. Turning around, he glanced down to meet the gaze of a solitary figure standing on the lower platform. Despite the crowd and bustle of activity around him, the man mysteriously graced the platform as if alone on an island. At first glance, the emaciated figure below him appeared an elder gentleman, shabby clothes loosely covering his gaunt body. But there was a youthful spirit and unmistaken eyes. It was Mulek.

Ian rushed to the lower level to greet his friend, and the two embraced where Mulek stood, a tired suitcase held together by string his sole possession. There was no need to question his appearance as the horrors and conditions faced by Jews in German concentration camps had come to light. Mulek conveyed strength, informing Ian that his family was sent to Auschwitz. A faint smile in sharing that both his brother and sister also survived. His eyes turning distant, he acknowledged that they cannot account for the whereabouts of his parents. Ian likewise avoided going into great detail, simply sharing that he and Artur were headed to Italy where they would receive training as soldiers of the Polish Army. Mulek was also bound for Italy. He was waiting to board a train that would take him to a port city on the Mediterranean Sea. From there he would board a ship and begin a new life in Palestine. Promise of a Jewish state that offered hope and freedom, where he would be free from discrimination and persecution.

Ian took Mulek's skeletal but strong hand to wish him well. There was no need to say more, their eyes communicating familiarity and warmth, a joy and happiness in the brief encounter. A sense of finality as if somehow completing a necessary chapter in their respective lives. Offering their final goodbyes, Ian walked away knowing that he would never see Mulek again. Before departing the busy station, he turned to take one final look at his childhood friend. But there was no sign of Mulek along the crowded platform or anywhere in the busy station. Just as he mysteriously appeared out of nowhere from inside the crowded station, he now mysteriously vanished amidst the mass of travelers.

The Alps
August 1945

The city of Munich was still asleep when Ian and Artur climbed aboard from the back of an open-bed army truck in the crisp morning air. They were joined by a host of recruits who eagerly filled up the convoy of trucks, and the mood was light and jovial all around. With up to twenty men circled in the back of each truck, introductions and hearty greetings came easy, the men all sharing a common goal and destination.

For the next hour, Ian barely noticed the transforming landscape as the group joined in laughter and lighthearted conversation. Talk of their birthplace and journeys raised interest, and of course discussion of women and romantic encounters captured everyone's attention. Boasts of bravery and adventure were sprinkled in, some intended to attract attention or respect among their newfound peers. Not being one to boast or draw attention to himself, Ian sat back and allowed Artur to share their Romanian capture and escape, and even his abbreviated version captured unusually high levels of interest and curiosity. He felt no need to add detail or describe his own earlier escapades; identification of his hometown and having experienced both German and Russian occupation would suffice. Nobody mentioned hardship or tragedy. Now was not the time. It was a wonderful feeling to be out in the open air and joined by fellow (soon-to-be) soldiers of the Polish Army.

Eventually, the adrenaline subsided as several men nodded off and others sat back to take in the wonders that magically surrounded them. It happened as instantly as turning a page in a picture book. Ian was captivated by the surroundings. He had experienced the majestic beauty of the Carpathians, the mystique of Transylvania, and basked in the luscious mountain valleys of Slovakia. But nothing compared with the scenery that now unfolded right before his eyes. Every bend in the road captured a breathtaking view while revealing new wonders. Ian could not escape the heavenly splendor of the Alps; no planned holiday could possibly top the spectacle that rolled before him like a moving picture show.

As the convoy snaked along the scenic mountain range, the back of the truck turned serene. Nobody complained of the bumpy ride. Everyone seemed lost in thought. They travelled through the day with intermittent stops to stretch or eat a meal, but the Alps had a hypnotizing and calming effect on the troops. On the road, Ian observed subtle changes in the foliage, and when they entered Italy in the waning hours before nightfall, the transformation was even more obvious. The temperate climate from the Mediterranean transformed the look and feel of the Alps, but her beauty and grandeur was never compromised.

They spent the evening at a small northern Italy town before resuming the next morning to reach their destination in Ancona. By noon, the convoy pulled off the road at an army base, a chance for the men to enjoy a lunch and stretch their legs. Spotting a military cemetery on the premise, Ian hurried to eat his rations. He sensed a need to visit the cemetery before the convoy departed.

Rows of wooden crosses dotted the hillside, carrying the names of soldiers who died in battle. With grave sites grouped by nationality, Ian felt a sense of angst upon noticing the large number of Polish soldiers buried in the cemetery. His heart pounded as he approached the Polish section. Pausing to take a deep breath, he proceeded to walk down each row, carefully inspecting the name on every marker. His eyes moved to each cross with trepidation, followed by momentary relief when the name he was searching did not appear. Ian was not certain that Stefan was in Italy, but knowing his brother he had a strong belief that his presence was near. He sensed it, a heavy feeling that never left him, the dream a constant reminder. Although the visit failed to put closure on Stefan's whereabouts, he at least knew that his older brother did not die on this battlefield. Over the following months, Ian continued to visit military cemeteries throughout Italy. Every visit ended the same, a conflicting mix of instant relief bleeding into lingering uncertainty.

CHAPTER 13

Reunited

Marche Region, Italy
August 1945 – November 1945

After twelve months as travel companions, enduring peril and adventure across seven countries, encountering everything from an exotic Gypsy village and the Polish mafia to escape from a Romanian POW camp, Ian and Artur finally achieved their quest. But they would now be separated. They were assigned to separate units under the Polish Army's Second Corps. The two bid their farewell after departing the truck in the port city of Ancona. With a spectacular view of Ancona's shipyard and the Adriatic Sea sparkling below them, recruits were assigned to their respective bases spread across the entire Marche region. Both men went their separate ways eager to begin their next chapter. It was clear almost from the onset that something special was taking place. General Wladyslaw Anders had big plans for his army.

With a headquarters based in Ancona, Anders' Polish Second Corps had grown to about 110,000 soldiers, most of the units stationed in Marche. Ian was immediately drawn to the beauty of the entire region. Spectacular coastline spread north and south of Ancona, sandy beaches and sleepy fishing villages extending for what seemed the entire Adriatic coast. Not far south of Ancona, a steep mountain cut dramatically into the sea, where white pebbles replaced sand to form an absorbing vista visible from faraway distances. Driving away from the sea did nothing to reduce Marche's allure. Winding roads took them up and down rolling hills, where fertile land produced rows of vineyards that contrasted sharply with green foliage of all shapes and sizes. Frequent openings in foliage from higher elevations offered panoramic views of the Adriatic Sea. Sparkling blue waters appeared no more than a stone's throw away.

Sleepy villages spread out among the higher elevations decorated the region. Well-preserved remnants of medieval castles dominated their cityscape and typically served as the centerpiece of each town's winding roads. Again, the inviting allure of the sea's deep blue water sparkled below them. It was from this enticing setting that Ian and his fellow recruits were assigned to military bases spread across the Marche region.

Ian's group was dropped off in the coastal town of Porto San Apidro, where he was assigned to the Polish Army's ninth group of heavy artillery. He was in for a number of pleasant surprises. Polish soldiers were everywhere. They met up in cantinas, restaurants, and meeting places which were run by the Women's Auxiliary Corps. The Polish soldiers felt quite welcome in Italy, the presence of Italian comradery and friendly attractive women woven into the region's fabric. Ian eagerly participated in football matches, which were provided along with areas for training and other sports activities. There was even a theater group that performed comedies, dance shows, and concerts.

General Anders made sure that his men were well taken care of. His entire design for the Second Polish Corps culminated in the creation of a Little Poland in Italy. The corps printed gazettes, schoolbooks, periodicals, historical works, stories, and poetry collections for the soldiers. They even had their own radio station. Anders also took great measures to provide educational and job training opportunities for his men. Vocational schools were created, along with high schools, college preparatory classes, and technical schools.

Historical Perspective

General Anders' selection and the subsequent agreement to use the Marche region as the base of his Polish Corps operations was well founded. Following the liberation of Monte Cassino and Rome, liberating Ancona was a strategic move needed to achieve victory for the Italian campaign.

Following victory in Monte Cassino, supply depots in southern Italian ports, now controlled by the Allies, were too far away to properly supply Allied forces in their advance north. In June of 1944, the task of taking the Ancona port from the German Army was assigned to the Second Polish Corps. Acting as an independent unit of General Montgomery's Eighth Army, 43,000 Polish troops prepared for battle to liberate Ancona. Included under Anders's command was the Italian Liberation Corps, a 25,000-man strong force fighting for a free Italy, and a unit of Italian volunteers trained to fight along-side Anders' Carpathian regiment.

Facing heavy German resistance, Polish and Italian troops finally entered Ancona on 18 July 1944. Defeated German troops surrendered, and the citizens of Ancona flooded the streets to welcome their liberators. Within days, the port was fully functional and providing supplies for the entire Eighth Army, Ancona's docks able to accommodate both large cargo ships and oil tankers. General Anders' Second Corps took the port of Ancona almost completely on their own, alongside Italian troops who showed a willingness to fight for the freedom of their country. This created a special bond between the Poles and Italians that carried over well after the war.

In an emotional speech made by General Anders, he further cemented the unique Polish-Italian relationship with the following words:

"For your freedom and ours,
We the Polish soldiers have given
Our souls to God,
Our bodies to the soil of Italy,
And our hearts to Poland."

Ian wasted no time blending in to the welcome environment. Military vehicles operated by the Auxiliary Corps ran continually down the main roads, transporting Polish soldiers at no charge anywhere throughout the region. Most of the vehicles were driven by women in the corps, allowing for friendly conversation of their homeland, shared stories of their trek to Italy, and discussion of hope for their future. When not at his base for training, Ian explored the entire region, taking advantage of the many amenities made available to the Polish soldiers.

Within the first six weeks of his arrival, he successfully completed basic training with fellow recruits. Because of a completed high school education received in Craiova, he was selected to attend a noncommissioned officer training at a nearby base, just up the road atop a nearby hill. Approaching the base, Ian was greeted to the sight of a magnificent mansion that had been transformed into a training headquarters for the Polish Army. The elegant structure sat atop impeccably landscaped grounds with a view of the sea. Although the training program was scheduled for three months, one of the instructors quickly recognized Ian's potential, suggesting that he fill out an application for the fully commissioned officer school. The recommendation and timing would prove to be most profound. Ian was selected, and in November, booked his train ticket to attend officer school in the southern city of Matera.

At the Fermo train station, Ian dropped his bags on the platform in anticipation of a lengthy wait before boarding. He arrived early and checked his watch to observe that he had several hours before departure. Gazing around the platform, he heard laughter among a group of fellow Polish soldiers waiting to board the same train. Ian's senses converged in volcanic force when a distinct voice emerged as the focal point in the masculine exchange of military camaraderie. Recognizing the speaker, Ian's legs felt heavy as he approached the group; he could feel the beating of his heart.

The gregarious soldier initially viewed Ian with a certain level of indifference. But then a change came over him. His face froze and lost all color, as if he were viewing a ghost, the others around him not sure what was happening. The frozen soldier had been in Italy for over two years fighting to liberate the country, and before that had trained in Northern Africa for over a year following lengthy imprisonment in Siberia. He had no way of knowing what had become of his family. When he last saw them in Povwolcask following the nighttime attack at the house, his younger brother was just fifteen years old. A young man can grow up fast and physically change a great deal between the ages of fifteen and twenty-one, especially when confronted with the demands and hardships of war. Yet the soldier now standing before him not only carried a strong emotional bond to his past but also had grown virtually identical to him in appearance. It was almost as if he were looking at his own reflection in a mirror, fully aware that some unknown element was left unexplained.

Finally, it was Ian who broke the silence, and the words were simply "Hi, Stefan." Dumbfounded, Stefan suddenly grasped the reality of having his own brother, his own flesh and blood, standing directly in front of him. Having two hours available before boarding, he clutched his brother before leading him out of the station in search of the nearest café. There they purchased a bottle of wine and pieced together as best they could a puzzle whose intricacy was surpassed only by its improbable landing. Family, friends, death, survival—a world war viewed from a front-row seat across three different continents. Answers would evolve over time. What mattered in the cafe was that two brothers were alive and reunited. Before leaving for the station to board the train, they raised their glasses in toast to brotherhood and to their respective roles in the forthcoming liberation of Poland.

Matera and Rome, Italy
November 1945 – May 1946

Following six years of separation with both brothers confronting the unknown on a daily basis, Ian and Stefan were now united for six months of regimented training in an enticing setting. Despite the demands of officer school, the time spent together in Matera proved to be most memorable. When not in training, class, or on patrol duty, they managed to explore the captivating city and catch up on their respective experiences over the past six years.

Throughout Matera and the surrounding countryside, Ian was fascinated by the industrious Italians in what appeared the poorer southern part of Italy. Their resourcefulness was shown in a variety of ways. In the countryside, refurbished jeeps and military vehicles were visible everywhere, serving as farm equipment. Shells of German and Allied vehicles (the Italians showed no prejudice) appeared battered but still intact. All fitted with efficient Italian-made engines to power the vehicles for plowing and other functions on the farm.

In Matera, an ancient neighborhood known as the Sassi was built into the walls of canyons. Homes were designed so that only the front of each house was exposed, and terraced so that one could meander through the neighborhood up and down the canyon. A chimney was needed only for cooking, as the homes were naturally warm and dry in winter and cool in the summer. Entering one of the homes, Ian was fascinated by the coolness felt even on a warm and humid spring day.

During their free evenings, they visited local establishments and quickly settled on a favorite destination. As Ian and Stefan approached the lower base of the Sassi, they came upon a nondescript entrance that led to an underground bistro. Outside the entrance, several boys dressed in tattered clothing approached them, hoping to purchase cigarettes to sell for profit on the black market. The youth well aware that Polish soldiers received cigarettes weekly. Whiskey was also made available to the troops on a monthly basis. Stefan pulled out a handful of cigarettes and gave the boys his asking price. They deftly tugged paper currency from a tight roll, expecting the cigarettes in return. Speaking in fluid Italian, Stefan pulled the cigarettes away and admonished them in a language and tone that visibly startled the youngsters. Showing surprise in getting caught, the boys sheepishly handed over additional currency before running off to distance themselves from the observant Pole and in hope of finding less-suspecting buyers.

Entering the bistro, they viewed the interior of a vast cave sectioned off in various areas for dining and entertainment. An exotic setting with the perfect temperature year-round, cool in summer and comfortably dry during winter months. The establishment was clearly their favorite. The brothers sometimes joined by fellow officers in training, but more often a private getaway for relaxation while catching up on family and personal matters.

Conversation came easy over an assortment of local wine and pickled herring, and there was so much to share. When not reliving his journey from Russia and

Siberia to Italy, Stefan enthusiastically told Ian all about Sonia, a lovely and spirited Italian woman he met in Rome following the battle of Monte Cassino. She was still in Rome with her family but would join him at his base as soon as they completed officer training. Ian likewise shared details of his own journey through Austria, Slovakia, Hungary, and Romania. He also shared news and conditions of family in Bochnia, at least as best he could. The former Polish government was still in exile, Red Army troops and Russian officials having replaced surrendered German personnel across Poland and much of Eastern Europe. The brothers had refrained from sending letters to family in Bochnia, concerned for their safety. Any letter from family members, particularly from the Polish Army, would be looked upon with much suspicion. They were convinced that any correspondence would be intercepted, resulting in close watch at best, but more likely arrest of family members.

Ian and Stefan enjoyed the wine, cuisine, and atmosphere—so much to catch up on after years of separation. They also shared an eagerness to complete their training and begin the mission of regaining Poland's freedom and independence. The brothers recognized their good fortune in the turn of events that brought them together, and raised their glass to toast a future that would reunite them all. "Na zdrowie."

In officer school, both brothers continued to excel. In addition to the rigorous physical exercise, there were book studies and equally difficult exams in areas highly concentrated in math. Every morning began with a 5:00 a.m. wake-up call, followed by two hours of jogging and a variety of physical exercises. Breakfast was served at 8:00 a.m., much improved over those that Ian had grown accustomed to in Pitesti and on the road.

Ian particularly enjoyed the artillery exercises, a chance to apply physical training with math and engineering course work. Military trucks drove the troops to large open fields where teams practiced loading and firing artillery weapons. The region outside of Materea was the perfect setting for heavy artillery practice. Few towns or villages with stretches of open land over rolling hills, populated with date trees and clusters of rock formations. Ian took great pride in the accuracy of his heavy artillery team, loading and firing their forty-kilo rockets with precision and accuracy. Stefan was part of the lighter artillery team, whose ten-kilo rockets were designed to inflict more tactical and rapid fire.

Teams of four men rotated assignments to gain experience and practice in each area required. One soldier was designated leader for the entire operation, one loaded the weapon with the correct charge for the required distance, and two quickly loaded and reloaded the rockets. A spotter/observer would select a target, most often a formation of large rocks that lay approximately twenty kilometers from their location. The spotter then moved several kilometers away from the target to observe the operation. The team spent the next hour calculating exact distance using an intricate set of trigonometry calculations. A team member would walk to a spot from where they calculated distance to a distant landmark by applying a surveying instrument that measured angles. From there, the process repeated to another destination, the task more complex due to uneven topography over the rolling countryside, resulting in a series of different-sized right triangles overlapping on the paper grid. Once the calculation was finalized, the team efficiently positioned, loaded, and fired the gun within a matter of minutes. The designated team leader then observed through binoculars their accuracy, calculating the required adjustments, both in distance and direction. They proceeded to adjust the aim and trajectory of their heavy weapon, reload with the proper charge, and refire. Typically, the team scored a perfect bull's-eye by their third attempt. Ian was convinced that there was no better artillery team in the Polish Army.

Ian (second from left) and his artillery team pose
in front of their heavy artillery gun.

One morning, the convoy of trucks were separated on the drive to their shooting range. When Ian's truck arrived, the truck containing light artillery was nowhere to be seen. They waited about thirty minutes before their driver went back to check on the missing truck. Ian couldn't help but wonder if something had gone awry. If, after six years of separation from his brother, they would be separated once again due to a freak accident in postwar Italy. Ian went about his business as if everything was okay, but reflected on the bitter irony if something had gone wrong, fully aware of the dangers that Stefan had already survived over the past six years, not only across Russia and Siberia, but also across the Mediterranean and Italy. As a member of the Carpathian regiment in the Italian campaign, the Polish Army utilized Stefan's speed and agility to their advantage. He was assigned the task of stretching wire, often running deep into enemy lines to lay cable from a roller, allowing for radio communication between his unit and their commanders. It was a dangerous job, requiring speed and endurance, and if spotted, he was a visible and important target for enemy snipers. Fortunately, that irony did not occur. Ian breathed a sigh of relief as both trucks arrived following what seemed an endless wait. The lighter artillery truck had tipped over upon crossing a bridge, but both equipment and personnel sustained only minor damage.

The only other unexpected incident actually occurred in the classroom following an exam. Ian, Stefan, and a third student who was a good friend, all handed in their tests early, confident in their scores. Days later when receiving their results, all were surprised to learn that they were the only students to receive a perfect score, but each of their papers was marked with an F in bold red ink. Despite sitting apart from one another during the exam, they were accused of cheating, their instructor not believing that the two brothers and a friend could all legitimately receive a perfect score. Although falsely accused it was only a temporary setback. In May of 1946, the three men successfully completed their requirements and prepared for graduation. They were to become officers of the Polish Army.

On a sunny afternoon, with a view of the Matera castle perched high atop a hill in the distance, the men sat in folded chairs eager to receive their diploma and medallion. Among the speakers was General Anders, his presence was commanding. Wearing his trademark black beret, his trim physique cast a distinguished figure at the podium. He spoke in a relaxed manner that captured everyone's attention with powerful words that conveyed deep meaning. Without singling out his own son among the new officers, he spoke with a deep pride of the role that each of his new officers would serve in the Polish Army. The military band performed several battle hymns, concluding with "The Red Poppies on Monte Cassino," which was met with thunderous applause.

A joyous energy filled the air at the ceremony's closing. With the Polish Eagle medallion proudly pinned over his left breast pocket, Ian joined with friends to sign each other's programs, a souvenir so beautifully crafted by members of the press group. Biographies of the generals, names of the officers, pictures, stories and poems of battle filled the pages. Amidst handshakes, laughter, and autograph signing, nobody wished to leave the area.

Lieutenant Marian Franciszek Bajda

Ian sought out Stefan to get his autograph and to share with him an idea that had been percolating for some time. Each of the new officers was rewarded with a two-week pass before reporting for their first assignment. Lieutenant Marian Franciszek Bajda's first order was to travel back to Fermo where he would have the opportunity to meet with his men who were stationed in the nearby town of Porto San Giorgio. Stefan, meanwhile, was to join his men in the town of Ascoli Piceno, about fifty kilometers south of where Ian would be stationed. However, Ian was not ready to travel back to Marche just yet.

There was Stefan, as usual, surrounded by a large contingent of fellow officers. Upon spotting Ian, he left the group to approach his brother, beaming with pride. "We did it, Marian!"

"Yes, we did! Stefan, I have an idea. Do you remember the book I told you about, *Quo Vadis* by Henryk Sienkiewycz? That story inspired me to see Rome. Let's travel together to see Rome before reporting for our assignments."

Stefan smiled while putting a hand on his brother's shoulder. "I've seen Rome, little brother. And Sonia has already left there to join me near my base. I knew you would find your way to Rome. You will love it. And when you return to Marche, you'll meet Sonia and we will all be reunited."

Signing each other's programs, the brothers continued their celebration and planned their respective moves with heightened anticipation. Ian departed the following day, joined by several fellow officers on the train to Rome.

Ian's worst fears were quickly relinquished. Unlike the damage he viewed in Munich, Rome appeared exactly as he imagined it. Monte Cassino bore the brunt of destruction on the road to Rome. So much to the delight of Ian, the treasures that he had come to view remained intact, virtually unchanged since the beginning of modern civilization. It was as if he stepped right into the pages of Sienkiewycz's epic novel. He sensed the souls of St. Peter and the emperor Nero in the air around him.

Throughout the city, students could be seen with notepads, taking notes while observing the city's famous architecture. The new officers found lodging near the Farnese Square neighborhood and, to their great fortune, met up with a group of touring Polish high school students staying at a hotel in the same area. The group enthusiastically invited the Polish soldiers to join their daily excursions in the historical city, learning from tour guides the colorful stories and history associated with a variety of places of interest.

They viewed intricate viaducts over two thousand years old, built to transport water into Rome, the centerpiece of a ruling empire. They entered the enchanting Vatican City where an endless array of wonders awaited them. St. Peter's Basilica appeared majestically, the entire structure supported by impressive alabaster columns. Their guide lit a torch to display the opaqueness of the magical white rock, the students mesmerized while observing the flame visible from all around the column. Deep below in the basement, they observed an excavation taking place, the remains of St. Peter having recently been found, adding yet more intrigue to their visit. Above the basilica, they climbed a circular stairwell to enter an opening atop the dome, the highest point in the Vatican. Up to a dozen or so tourists could enter, where windows circled the structure to offer spectacular views across the entire city.

They visited the catacombs, intricate tunnels built under the city, a place where Christians met to practice their faith while avoiding persecution. Frescoes and Latin inscriptions remained visible on walls holding memories both painful and hopeful. Ian was well aware of the historic significance of the catacombs and the entire city, but now their stories came to life right before his eyes.

Following their daily excursions, Ian often went back to revisit the sites, taking in their history and grandeur. Of particular interest and intrigue was the Roman Coliseum. Seated alone in the imposing arena, Ian found himself in another world.

Twilight breathed warm as the sky transformed into a blaze of scarlet, streaking like fire beyond the western wall. "Panem et Circenses!" An echo from the emperor's chant arose in a whisper, rising above the winds of silence that swept below Ian's breath. The chant swallowed by a deafening roar from the hungry crowd. The emperor smiles knowingly, fully aware that his promise of bread and entertainment will keep the masses in line, providing intoxicating fuel for their bloodthirsty appetite. Below him along the Coliseum floor, vivid characters spring to life. Christians led out to be slaughtered by hungry lions. Gladiators in colorful garb and equipped with an assortment of weapons battle to the death. The display of blood mixed with the smell of fear and terror among both victims and combatants brings the crowd to a frenzy. High above in his place of honor, the emperor is overcome with the taste of bile. It has a bitter odor of vengeance. He hides behind a nervous smile.

The stillness surrounding Ian stirred once again, another voice captured in the wind. "Quo vadis Domine?" The bloody battle from below fades with the question, replaced by the distressed image of an isolated St. Peter somewhere outside of Rome. After fleeing Rome in fear, he has an encounter and asks, "Where are you going, Lord?" St. Peter, lost and confused, finds strength. Guided back to Rome, he finds the courage to resume his quest and minister in a city controlled by a powerful but vulnerable emperor, Nero, who is terrified of the humble servant.

Ian looked up, the vision vanished, the Coliseum now cloaked in darkness. Rising from weathered stone, he walked out of the ancient stadium in search of yet more wonders and answers to be discovered in the ancient city.

Marche Region, Italy
May 1946 – October 1946

Quo Vadis? Ian now felt even more certain of his destiny; he knew where he was going. He likened Stalin to Nero, tenuously ruling an empire in fear of people who held disdain for his ruthless hold of power. *Panem et Circenses* would not serve Stalin, the populace not interested in his hollow promises. However, Stalin did have one thing going for him. With great sacrifice from the Russian people and his Red Army, his support was instrumental to the Allied victory and he was pictured on the side of Allied victors. Stalin now stood with Churchill and Roosevelt as symbolic victors on the world stage. Surely the Western leaders would see through the Russian leader's bluster and ruse. They need look no farther than the fate of Poland and neighboring countries. Ian was biding his time while preparing for battle. His return to Poland was on hold, but Allied plans would materialize and become known in due time.

However, some doubt and trouble signs were surfacing. The presence and role of the Polish Army in Marche was slowly but steadily dissipating. The army was in the process of transferring troops out of Italy and stationing them all across England and Scotland, diminishing the role and base of operations in Italy. Shortly after Ian reported to his base in Porto San Giorgio, his troop count was shrinking and his duty gradually minimized to one simple operation. Once a week, he took a platoon of twelve soldiers to guard a motor pool containing military vehicles and equipment. Over twenty-four hours, teams rotated in two-hour shifts to keep watch over the vehicles and heavy artillery. Walking around the perimeter, Ian chose against disciplining the occasional soldier seen napping on the seat of a truck. He chose instead to enter the area in a noisy manner, alerting them to wake up and continue the watch. Outside of that weekly assignment, his time was virtually free, and taking advantage of free time, spent it in a most heartening and memorable manner.

The sun had yet to peek above the Adriatic Sea when Ian stepped out from his barracks and into the salt sea air, fishermen the only sign of life along the coastal waters. Within minutes, a military jeep stopped to pick up the Polish hitchhiker; uniformed military personnel never had to wait long for a ride near the base. Ian's first stop was to pick up Stefan at his base, fifty kilometers away in Ascoli Piceno.

From there, they hitched a ride to a neighborhood of spread-out homes on hilly terrain, all within a football pitch from the visible sea. They could already anticipate warmth emanating from inside the handsome rented house as they ambled down the street. Stepping inside, the home was alive with the scent of flavorful aromas mixed with lively music and colorful chatter. Sonia welcomed them with flair as her newlywed sister Bruna danced in the kitchen. Tony dutifully carried a basket, greeting his fellow Polish officers with a warm smile. A basket filled with fruits, fresh bread, an assortment of cheese, and wine was placed by the front door, prepared for a day at the beach. A chance to swim in the open sea, relax on the sandy beach, and share dreams filled with cheerful homes surrounded by family and friends.

The sun and salt water had an energizing effect that always left the group with a healthy appetite. Back at the house after a full day at the beach, flavorful sauces were prepared and mixed with rich pasta. A bowl of ripe fruit so polished they glistened. Wineglasses and dinner plates eternally filled, the group never left the spacious kitchen. Feeling his belly full and satisfied, Ian sat back to take in the lively scene. Stefan deftly twirled Sonia around the kitchen floor, moving with ease to the music. The two moved so graceful, choreographed in perfect harmony, their movements in perfect sync. Nearby, Bruna pulled Tony up from his chair and onto the makeshift dance floor. In contrast to Stefan, the tall and lumbering Tony lacked fluid movement, but more than made up for it with practiced steps and attention to his partner, pleasing the high-stepping Bruna who clapped in delight.

The music's dying tones did nothing to relinquish the room's kinetic energy; an animated conversation ensued between Stefan and Sonia. The language flew out of Sonia so fast that Ian was unable to make out a single word. Even though he'd now been in Italy for nearly a year and was quite adept at picking up new languages, Italian did not come so easy. Ian blamed it in part on learning Romanian. The languages were similar, and he used his knowledge of Romanian to translate common Italian words. Perhaps a larger factor was that understanding Italian was not necessary for survival. Not only was Ian a free man, but also Stefan and Tony were always nearby to translate for him. The group's conversations always moved back and forth between Italian and Polish, so Ian was easily able to communicate with the Italian sisters. Now he looked toward Stefan, waiting for the translation of Sonia's passionate oratory.

Stefan simply smiled. He lit a cigarette and allowed Sonia to begin anew, offering an occasional nod or word of agreement. When she finally allowed herself to breathe, they both looked directly at Ian, Sonia with hands clenched and a look of anticipation, Stefan maintaining his easy smile. "Sonia and I have an announcement to make. We've been waiting for the right moment to share this wonderful news. We're going to get married!" Bruna released a melody of colorful chatter, rushing up to embrace her sister. Sonia maintained her pose, still looking at Ian, her expression unchanged. Stefan continued. "And Ian, we would be honored to have you serve as my best man."

Ian could not conceal his emotions. Thoughts of Stefan's journey spun in his head. Captured by the Russians, Lubyanka Prison, Siberia, than amnestied to train or fight as a liberator across three continents. To have survived all those encounters and now make this happy announcement filled Ian with unbridled joy. He was also aware that they would soon be separated once again. A large number of Polish troops had already been transferred to Britain. Many of those troops took with them their newlywed Italian brides. Unfortunately, some of those women filed for divorce shortly after arriving in Britain. They had worked out a deal with their temporary husbands. It became apparent that some women viewed marriage as an opportunity to gain acceptance into England, which after the war held more promise for a young lady than their native Italy. British authorities were forced to modify their policy and no longer accepted Polish soldiers married to Italian women. Stefan and Sonia, as well as Tony and Bruna, would not join Ian and other Polish troops transferred to Britain.

Rising from his chair, Ian lifted his glass to toast the happy couple, "Congratulations to Sonia and to my dear brother, Stefan. Of course I am honored to serve as your best man! May God be with you!" Ian's toast was quickly followed by another as Stefan raised his glass to join the group in a tight circle. "To our best man, Ian! I could not be more blessed to have my brother join us on this special day!" The room was filled with dance and laughter. Other toasts rapidly followed. "To the liberation of Poland!" "Prosit!"

After the toasting wound down, Ian asked his brother, "Where will you live?" Stefan, still smiling, translated for Sonia. She twirled in a flair, her bright sundress rippling like ocean waves, and answered in song, "Hollywood, Ca-lee'-for'-nee-yaa!" The group laughed as Ian raised his glass to a final toast. "To Hollywood!"

As the blissful summer of 1946 folded into autumn, the last trickle of Polish troops transferred to Britain. Ian did everything he could to delay his transfer, but they ran out of time. In early October, one month after the last of his men transferred and within a fortnight before the wedding ceremony, he was required to leave Italy and report for duty in Scotland.

Although unable to attend the ceremony and be a part of their special day, Ian was later warmed and comforted upon receiving photos of the wedding. It was indeed a gala affair. A line of decorated jeeps could be seen driving to the church. Sonia's family members along with joyous friends were all smiles surrounding the happy couple. A beaming Sonia was beautiful and radiant, bedazzled in white on the sun-splashed day. Stefan struck a handsome pose in his Polish officer's uniform. He stood tall, as proud and as happy as Ian ever remembered seeing his older brother.

A wedding photo of Sonia and Stefan Bajda

CHAPTER 14

From the Mainland to the Island

Western Europe
October 1946

Ian boarded the impeccably furnished military train late in the evening; spacious boxcar quarters shared with three fellow officers offered quite contrasting accommodations to prior train travel experienced in Romania. Getting settled in preparation for several days of travel, Ian reflected on the cattle cars used to transport him and Artur to Pitesti, and the squeezed rooftop accommodations to reach Craiova. The military train traveled north along the Adriatic Sea before a sunrise greeted the men with breathtaking mountain views. Meandering through the Alps, the train moved steadily in a northwest direction. Travel through Austria brought vivid memories of the butcher's farm. The smile never left Ian's face as he viewed cattle grazing upon open fields along the Austrian hillsides. He imagined Henryk meeting up with Michal in Austria and openly wondered where Michal managed to surface following the German surrender. He felt quite certain that Michal was able to land on his feet somewhere with a promising outlook. He deserved that.

Cutting through southwest Germany, the train entered France where rolling hills and small villages populate the countryside. Signs of the war remained visible everywhere, particularly in the towns and villages. Paris remained intact, but others appeared as haunted ghost towns with lost, isolated souls barely visible amidst the smoke-filled rubble. Ian finally departed the train in the coastal town of Calais, where the choppy waters of the English Channel greeted him. The challenge of swimming the channel consumed his thoughts.

Boarding the ferryboat, he was pleased to get a seat toward the front and eagerly took in the brisk, invigorating sea breeze. As the ferryboat closed in on its destination, Ian continued visualizing the swim until a mystifying object appeared magically as if out of thin air. The lengthy object emerged from blurry to striking, the White Cliffs of Dover stood proud, an expansive chalky white fortress in stark contrast to the gray-blue sea and overcast sky.

From Dover, he boarded a passenger train to London. Viewing a shockingly damaged city as the train pulled into one of London's main stations, he was suddenly confronted with a buzz of anxious travelers. A maze of people enveloped the station, donning everything from business suits and decorated uniforms to tattered clothes—workers, families, soldiers, beggars, Military Police—all adding color to the chaotic scene.

After sorting through the crowds, he finally managed to purchase a ticket for Hawick, Scotland. From there, Ian recalled little of the trip. Thoughts and memories returned to his family in Bochnia. Reports inferred the situation was not much improved in Poland, where Stalin was continuing to exert his influence. He wondered how his family was managing. Krystyna would now be twenty, Jerzy and Zdislaw teens. Unable to send news, he knew that his parents must be concerned about their future and worried about his and Stefan's well-being. He prayed for their peace of mind, for them to have patience. To have faith that their sons would soon return home as heroes and their once happy life restored. The rhythmic sound of rail cars over uneven tracks was hypnotizing. With images of his triumphant return in the liberation of Poland, Ian drifted off into a deep and dreamless sleep.

Hawick, Scotland
October 1946 – Late 1946

Dreams of returning home were soon replaced by a nightmarish reality. Not long after arriving in Scotland, dreaded confirmation of an ongoing rumor was confirmed. Ian and other Polish soldiers felt a sense of betrayal and came to grips that there would be no liberation of Poland. As actions resulting from an earlier reached agreement from the Yalta Conference predictably played out, it was painfully recognized that the three primary Allied leaders had already determined the fate of their homeland. Poland, along with a divided (East) Germany, Hungary, Czechoslovakia, Romania, and Yugoslavia were all to be under the Soviet's control and influence.

Angry talk immediately circulated among Polish troops that Stalin must have gotten both Churchill and Roosevelt drunk on his finest vodka to have them sign such an agreement. The newspapers pointed out the foundation of the agreement, and intimated that timing of the conference was the reason why Stalin might not have needed the vodka. At the time of the conference in February of 1945, Red Army troops were less than one hundred kilometers from Berlin in their western advance. With the Allies so tantalizing close to victory, Stalin was smugly holding his trump card at the conference. As US delegation member and future secretary of state James F. Byrnes was quoted, "It was not a question of what we would let the Russians do, but what we could get the Russians to do."

Despite the temptation to author a quick and decisive end to a brutal world war, Ian was convinced that the eager western leaders were far too shortsighted and overly cautious in playing their own hand. This view was ultimately and predictably borne to light as the true Soviet intentions became known and Stalin's promise of free elections in Poland never materialized. Meanwhile, the Polish government-in-exile, the same men who risked everything to ensure that their country maintain sovereignty while playing an active and vital role to the Allied effort, became an afterthought. Unable to wield power or have any influence in the direction of their homeland, some returned only to be arrested as traitors and see Poland fall under a brutal Communist regime as the result of fraudulent elections.

As for General Anders, he would never step on Polish soil again. He was deprived of both Polish citizenship and his military rank following the Soviet-installed communist government of Poland. As much as he loved and fought for his country, General Anders chose to remain in Britain, almost certain that a return to Poland would result in imprisonment and likely execution.

Historical Perspective

Wladyslaw Anders lived the rest of his life in England, where he was a leader in the Polish community until his death in 1970. His body was laid to rest, in accordance with his wishes, amongst his fallen soldiers of the Second Polish Corps, at the Polish War Cemetery at Monte Cassino, Italy.

The collective mood of the troops drastically transformed, from energetic anticipation to somber disappointment. This was especially true for Ian. Ever since leaving Bochnia by horse carriage to flee the Nazi invasion, he had been on a personal quest to join the Polish Army, solely for the purpose of liberating his homeland. After leaving the house in the early morning with Artur over two years ago, he had only seen his family for one day. He promised his father that he would return with Stefan as victorious liberators, and he dreamed of that moment every day since. A dream of having the entire family reunited and enjoying their way of life as it was before the war.

With Soviet intentions following the Yalta Conference having come to light, the mission of the Polish Army drastically changed. Rather than focusing on military strategy and tactics, the need was to get the troops disassembled and acclimated back into civilian life. The Polish Army provided all troops with three options:

1. The army will pay for their return to Poland.
2. The army will pay for their education or support in finding a job in England.
3. The army will pay for travel to anywhere in the free world.

For most troops, the first option was not a viable one. With the grim prospects of living under a communist regime and under Soviet control, the only men who chose this were those who had wives and children back home. And even many of the married soldiers chose not to return, at least for the time being. The second option certainly had appeal, having already lived on British soil and viewing improved prospects for finding work in postwar England. This option further included an education offered by the army as an added benefit. The third option was also an intriguing one. There was a new world order and a sense of rebirth. Many countries were welcoming young men to be a part of their growth during a time of world peace and prosperity.

While Ian was expecting his time to be preparing troops for artillery combat in the liberation of Poland, he was instead required to counsel his troops and process paperwork to get the men acclimated back into civilian life. Many chose to attend school or find work in Britain. Some reluctantly went back to Poland, while others chose to immigrate to countries all around the world—the United States, Canada, South Africa, and South America being popular choices. Possessing an adventurous spirit, Ian was also intrigued by this option, and learned that Stefan and Sonia were contemplating immigration to Argentina.

Stefan had been doing research and learned that Peron was modernizing the country. Cheap loans were made available to start new businesses. Argentina also had the allure of an open country made up of broad plains reaching scenic mountains along the Chilean border, modernized cities with a unique culture combining both Latin and European influences. They wrote to Ian, informing him of their plans to settle in Buenos Aires, and asked him to consider joining them. It was an easy sell. Ian liked the idea but first needed to complete the commitment to his troops and continue his education to further increase his options.

Edinburgh, Scotland, and London
Late 1946 – Spring 1947

Toward the end of 1946, Ian applied for mechanical engineering school. Classes were held in multiple buildings on the grounds of a golf course, just east of the captivating city of Edinburgh, Scotland. Being quite industrious and embracing the opportunity to continue learning new things, Ian took the exam in hopes of acceptance to the school.

In addition to applying for the mechanical engineering school, Ian also applied for electrical engineering. Classes were held at an air force base in the city of Royston, Hertfordshire District, about eighty kilometers north of London. Ian took the train to Royston to take the exam.

Following a lengthy exam, Ian visited the NAFFI (Navy, Army, and Air Force Institutes) canteen for a chance to relax. NAFFI canteens were quite popular around British military bases. It was a place to relax, enjoy fellowship over drinks and a good meal at reasonable prices. There were also stores where you could purchase tax-free cigarettes, even toothpaste and basic supplies. Just one year earlier, Ian and Stefan visited a NAFFI resort in Bari to bring in the New Year of 1946.

Ian sat down at the canteen and immediately felt the glance of a fellow soldier. He turned to face a smiling Artur, and the two shared nods as if meeting up was an expected occurrence. The friends approached one another and broke into easy conversation, no different from what they did every day over an entire year on their quest. Ian learned that Artur finally achieved a part of his dream. He was now a member of the Polish Air Force. Unfortunately, Artur would never achieve his lifelong dream of piloting a fighter plane to liberate Poland. He, like others, was transitioning back into society.

Ian and Artur spent the rest of the day together. The two didn't reflect much on the journey that now brought them back together. Words were not necessary to cement a friendship forged from living a shared quest. A quest that drove them over mountains, enemy territory, capture, escape, an education, and preparation as liberators of their homeland. Things did not all go as planned. But they never lost sight of their vision and achieved their quest to join Anders' Army. Where it would now take them was unknown, but that didn't matter. The two shared an unspoken spirit of brotherhood, spending the day together in the same comradery which enabled them to survive danger on a daily basis across vast enemy territory.

Arriving back in Scotland, Ian learned that he passed both exams. He had his choice between attending either the electrical or mechanical engineering schools. After lengthy consideration, he chose the latter. He would remain in Scotland.

Ian (left) and a fellow Polish soldier enjoying the snow
at their base near Edinburgh, Scotland.

Ian in the workshop at a military base.

Before long, Ian came across another opportunity. When not in school, he spent time in the military office and noticed that many of the enlisted men were not taking advantage of their designated leaves, choosing instead to remain close to the base. This presented a wonderful opportunity for Ian. He arranged to use their unused passes, enabling trips across Scotland and England, sometimes taking along friends and often travelling solo. With the approach of a new year, Ian made plans to visit London. Throughout the war, beginning at the house in Podwoloczysko, Ian and his family would turn to Radio London for news on the warfront. As part of the programming, radio listeners were greeted at the top of every hour to the rich, comforting chimes from Big Ben, a resounding prospect for hope in a period of darkness. Now he would visit the iconic city and hear in person the most famous clock in the world, that familiar sound of hope in a period of renewed birth and possibilities.

Ian (at left) with a friend in London. Ian secured passes to make numerous visits to London and all around Britain during his stay in Hawick.

Because of the large crowds, Ian had to settle for a hotel room well outside the city center. He rode a bus into the bustling city and quickly melted into the crowd. New Year's Eve in London was indeed a festive atmosphere. Revelers and onlookers crowded the historic landmarks, people in a joyous state adding color to a rebuilding London. With so many places of interest, the options were endless, but the largest crowds were at Piccadilly Circus. People streamed out of bright red double-decker busses. Everyone in a celebratory mood, Ian took in the cornucopia of sights. With the midnight hour rapidly approaching, he received directions to the landmark that he had come to view. He would ring in the year of 1947 to the sounds of the clock that gave his family so much hope, Big Ben.

Crossing the bridge over the River Thames, Big Ben loomed into view high above the clock tower. With crowds not as boisterous or large, Ian enthusiastically joined the throng that had gathered. The countdown began, and the melodic tune from the Cambridge Chimes rang down from above, more popularly recognized as a phrase from Handel's *Messiah*. The melody captured memories of the war, streaming into Ian's consciousness. News of battles and developments after the Allies declared war on Germany were introduced with the familiar tune he now heard. As the full hour permutations from the clock's inner working continued, Ian recalled the long and helpless periods of dark, foreboding news. German Army advancements across Europe, sighting Russian tanks entering Poland, rumored atrocities in labor camps. The full hour chime now completed, the crowd grew louder and more electric in anticipation of the twelve bongs to follow.

Bong! Waves of events flew to the forefront with each pronounced bong from the clock. He recalled sitting inside the majestic St. Stevens Cathedral in Vienna. Bong! Escape from Austria with Michal, being swept downriver. Bong! Travel with Artur through the Carpathians, stumbling upon the Gypsy village in Hungary. Bong! Capture in the countryside, held captive in a Transylvanian castle, escape from the prison in Pitesti. Bong! Bong!

The crowd grew louder in anticipation. Young couples embraced, children perched on their father's shoulders, everyone glued to the clock that towered above. Bong! Ian's heart was racing. How wonderful to receive a completed education in Craiova. Bong! Joining the Polish Army in Pilsen and reuniting with Mulek in Munich. Bong! The Alps. Italy. Spending a joyous year with his brother, Stefan. Bong! His family back home in Poland, he had still not written to them for fear of their safety. But at least they were not under occupation during a time of war. Perhaps this New Year will bring hope.

Bong! Bong! There was momentary silence as the clock struck midnight. The year was 1947. The war was over and the possibilities endless. The crowd suddenly erupted, hats thrown in the air, men kissing young ladies, excitement all around him. Ian confidently walked back to the bus stop. He might as well have been walking on air. He felt a positive energy; anything seemed possible. Walking back to Piccadilly, he was surprised to see the crowds had virtually disappeared, the city quickly emptying. Reaching the bus stop, there was no activity. Every station cloaked in darkness.

Unaware that London busses stopped running at midnight, Ian was forced to make the long walk back to his hotel on the outskirts of the city.

* * *

As the Polish Army continued consolidation of their operations, soldiers attending school at Hawick were transferred to the village of Haverigg, England. In Haverigg, a former Canadian airfield was being converted to a barracks and campus, housing three schools to be run by the Polish Army. The entire complex sat right next to the sea. In addition to the engineering school, there would be an architectural school and another that covered general studies.

Before departing in the spring of 1947, Ian inspected a local map to get an idea of where his next assignment would take him. It took some time to spot Haverigg, which appeared a tiny village in northern England on the Irish Sea. Across the bay from Haverigg sat a larger town, Barrow-in-Furness. The map further indicated that all around the area were higher elevations surrounding a string of lakes, which prompts the area to be labeled "The Lake District." Not much more was around, but about two kilometers up the road from Haverigg he spotted the town of Millom. Believing in prayer and fate, Ian folded the map and wondered what might await him in the small coastal village.

CHAPTER 15

A Lasting Dance

Haverigg and Millom, England
Spring 1947

Iris and Pauline had been devising their plan for days. The converted airfield down the road now housing Polish soldiers was causing quite a commotion. Curious locals spotting uniformed Poles at the newly formed barracks were providing quite contrasting reports. The young men in town either downplayed or questioned their presence. "Who are those blokes? Why do they have to come here to get an education, are they that daft? Next they'll be taking up jobs and trying to steal our ladies." But the young ladies offered quite a different perspective. "Did you see the dashing Polish soldiers in their smart uniforms? I hear they're going to be hosting a dance every Friday evening. We just have to go!"

Iris and Pauline were now preparing for that very dance. However, it would not be easy. Uncle Will remained as cantankerous and as strict as ever. There's no way he would allow them to go. Why, he wouldn't even attend and give away his own daughter Ethel when he heard that she was marrying an Irish Catholic. Their Uncle Arthur had to give Ethel away at the wedding in place of Uncle Will. As was typical of Ethel, she refused to back down and proudly went ahead with her marriage to Steven Mulholland. So for Uncle Will to be that adamant against Ethel marrying an Irish Catholic, imagine how he'd react about them going to a dance with Polish soldiers, and Catholic Polish soldiers at that.

Although they were not quite as bold or witty as Ethel, they were nonetheless inspired by her actions and undeterred in their quest to attend the dance. They would simply have to go about it in a more subtle manner.

The night of the dance finally arrived. Iris and Pauline went about their business just as any ordinary day, containing excitement for the upcoming evening and doing everything in their power to deter Uncle Will from having a late night cup of tea. Uncle Will typically went to bed around nine every evening, allowing him to rise early in the morning. Just as planned, he trudged upstairs at his normal bedtime.

The young ladies immediately set their plan in operation. With outfits already picked out, they quickly dressed and made themselves up for the evening. Upon completing that task, they silently tiptoed upstairs to listen from outside his room. Sure enough they heard exactly what they were hoping for, Uncle Will's uneven snoring.

Freedom! Stepping outside into the balmy evening brought about a sense of relief and excitement. Adding an element of intrigue and anticipation was the unknown of meeting foreign soldiers, maybe even officers at an elaborate dance. The ladies hurried to the bus stop and practically jumped onto the bus, heading down the road to Haverigg.

As the bus rolled up to the sprawling complex and the ladies stepped out, live music from inside the dance hall could be heard. Entering the decorated hall, they were greeted to an elaborate and vibrant setting. Ladies dressed in colorful dresses complemented the smart khaki uniforms of Polish soldiers. A live band splendidly performed popular dance tunes inviting enthusiastic dancers to the floor. There was a constant hum in the room and electricity in the air.

Iris could see her friend Ida and rushed over to get the latest gossip and news of the dance. Sitting on folding chairs facing the dance floor, Ida excitedly shared events that had unfolded during the evening—pointing out whom she's danced with, what it was like dancing with a young soldier who barely spoke their language, who else was there, what they're wearing. Suddenly Ida stopped. Wide-eyed, she shouted, "Whoa!" Looking around, Iris viewed her cousin Pauline being whirled around on the dance floor by a tall, handsome Polish soldier. They appeared elegant and in perfect sync and seemed to be capturing the attention of everyone in attendance.

Iris stared at the dancers, could not believe that Pauline was the center of attention. When she finally turned back to Ida, her friend had another strange expression. This time Ida appeared to be trying to tell Iris something, but the words just wouldn't come out. Sensing a presence, Iris looked up to see a smart-looking Polish officer standing right in front of her, his hand extended as an apparent invite to the dance floor. Iris examined his face and observed handsome features with wavy brown hair combed back neatly and gentle blue eyes. He appeared a bit shy but well mannered, perhaps not sure how to properly ask a lady for a dance. Ida practically pushed her up off the chair, and Iris found herself on the dance floor within stepping distance of the whirling Pauline. While Pauline and her dance partner seemed to take up the entire floor, Iris and her partner found themselves in a bit more awkward state. He was quite a bit taller, and despite Iris being an accomplished dancer, the two were mostly out of step throughout the dance. It could have been uncomfortable, but every time she looked up, she was comforted by his warm smile and gentle manner. She made an attempt to engage in conversation.

"My name is Iris. Do you speak English?"

"My name Ian. English good no."

Finally, the dance ended, and Ian smiled a shy expression as he led her back to the chair before walking away. Slowly sitting down, Iris turned to her friend Ida with a wide smile. Before able to say a word, Ida was beaming again and replied, "It looks like he's coming back!"

Later in the evening, the two Polish soldiers escorted Iris and Pauline outside. The two couples were all smiles, having spent over an hour dancing and enjoying the evening. While Pauline and Ian's friend Edward went off to one side laughing and translating through pantomime, Ian took on a serious expression as the bus approached.

"Dance next week, you here be?"

Iris couldn't hide her smile. She nodded yes and grabbed Pauline to jump on the bus. The ladies took a front seat to open the window, blowing kisses and waving goodbye. As the bus rolled away, Edward could be seen slapping Ian on the back as the two close friends proudly walked back toward the dance hall. The ladies could not stop talking about their evening, not even concerned about Uncle Will. It was well past midnight, and he should be fast asleep when they get home. They would be fine just as long as they can keep the commotion down.

* * *

Several weeks had passed since the dance. As promised, Iris went back the following week at the dance hall. As expected, Ian was waiting to greet her.

Iris and Pauline now found themselves sitting atop their favorite spot on the bluffs overlooking the Irish Sea. Casually going about the business of setting up a picnic serving for four, their eyes searched out to the sea. Ian and Edward's heads could barely be seen, bobbing in and out of view from the undulating waves.

Pauline mused, "Have you ever seen anything like those two? Why I think they could swim to the Isle of Man." Iris agreed. "They're like two fish. I just hope we've brought enough food to satisfy their appetite." The two cousins had been on quite an emotional roll since the dance. Upon meeting their dates at the second dance, they seemed to pick right up where they left off, and it was as if they'd all known each other forever. Even the language barrier was not proving to be an issue. In fact, that barrier was creating situations both romantic and humorous.

Pauline gazed out to the sea with a dreamy expression. "Do you know what he did last night, Pet? We were in the taxi, and I couldn't for the life of me understand what he was trying to say. So he breathed heavily on the window and traced a heart shape. Then he wrote inside, 'I LOVE YOU.'" Pauline held her dreamy expression before snapping out of the reverie. "And your Ian! My, what a handsome gentleman he is! So polite and the way he looks after you…and how remarkable his English is getting."

Iris smiled in reply. "It truly is quite amazing how quickly he's learning the language. But I have to tell you, this really had me laughing. Last week he sent me a note that started with 'Expect letter you did not yet receive.' It was the most precious thing I've ever read."

The two merrily continued their conversation while finishing the setting. The picnic was now in place. An assortment of quarter-sliced sandwiches filled with everything from tomato and cheese to cucumber and onions, some mixed with a variety of meats. Crisps, cut-up fruit, and of course a thermos with ingredients and condiments for the perfect cup of tea. Satisfied with the setting, Iris returned her gaze out to the sea. The Isle of Man was not visible today, but there was also no threat of U-boats, and the Barrow shipyards were safe from bombs.

Closer to shore, the two men were finishing their swim. Iris's eyes settled on Ian. With smooth, powerful strokes cutting through the choppy waves, he quickly and easily glided closer to shore. She felt excitement in anticipation of his return, and a warm sense overcame her. For the first time in her life, Iris felt she had a purpose. She felt a sense of freedom, suddenly alive. She felt somehow liberated. The possibilities appeared as endless as the sea. Iris looked in wonderment beyond the horizon and for the first time in her life tried to imagine what lay beyond the expansive sea.

Pauline and Edward (left photo) and Iris and Ian (right photo). The two couple spent countless hours together, from the dance in spring of 1947 until Ian and Iris left for the United States in June of 1956.

Liverpool, England
June 1956

Brilliant shades of blue covered a canvas of sea and sky for as far as the eyes could see. Standing aft of the hulking *Brittanic*'s main deck, Iris shifted her view downward, only to be confronted by a wildly contrasting scene. A dizzying array of sound and activity swarmed the lower deck. Somewhere in that mass of humanity, Ian was hoping to learn more details of their lodgings. She was holding baby Celia in her arms. Two-year-old Andrew did not leave her side. Meanwhile, keeping five-year-old Julie in tow proved a more daunting task. Struggling to keep her children safe and at bay, she fought the tears, fought the urge to turn around and take one last look at the English landscape beyond the bustling docks.

Earlier in the day, Pauline and Edward sent them off from the bus station in Urmston, from where they caught the local bus to Manchester. The train ride from Manchester to Liverpool seemed surreal. Earlier in the week in Millom, the heartfelt farewells also felt surreal. At least there she had the comforting support of Ethel. "If it doesn't work out, she'll be right back," Ethel steadfastly informed the many family and friends who insisted on meeting one last time. But now it was real. They were actually aboard a ship that was bound for America.

CUNARD M.V. BRITANNIC   27.666 TONS.

The sound hit her like a jolt of electricity; her entire body shook. Unique and rich harmonics from bagpipers filled the air before fading into a constant hum, accompanying the words of a familiar and soothing song:

> *Speed, bonnie boat,*
> *Like a bird on the wing,*
> *Onward the sailors cry;*
> *Carry the lad that's born to be King*
> *Over the sea to Skye.*

Unable to resist the temptation, Iris slowly turned to face the English landscape one last time. She held her gaze, scanning the distant horizon. Panning left, somewhere along the same coastline lay Millom—images of Uncle Will and the one time bustling household, mischievous escapades with Pauline and Ethel, warm conversations with friends and townsfolk on her daily walks to the market. She was overcome with sadness and loss for never taking the time to personally thank Uncle Will for taking her into his home following the loss of her mother. Narrowing her focus to the foreground, she spotted a small band of musicians who were serenading travelers with their sweet, melodic sound in heavy Scottish accents.

> *Loud the winds howl,*
> *Loud the waves roar,*
> *Thunderclouds rend the air;*
> *Baffled, our foes stand by the shore*
> *Follow they will not dare.*

"Speed, Bonnie Boat," a beautiful, soothing Scottish folk song that Grandma would often sing. A sense of calmness infiltrated the sadness she was feeling. Speed, bonnie boat. Speed, *Brittanic*. They are sitting around a crackling fire in the cozy cottage. Wilf and Jean nearby. Iris sitting on Mum's lap. They ask Grandma to sing her favorite songs. "Speed, Bonnie Boat" with its haunting lyrics and soothing sound fills the room. The calm lingered. Pauline and Ethel would be sure to join them in America. She will write and tell them about the opportunities in America, and they will be sure to follow.

> *Though the waves leap,*
> *So soft shall ye sleep,*

Ocean's a royal bed.
Rocked in the deep,
Flora will keep watch by your weary head.

Ian would soon return from the deck below, and they'll be setting off on their voyage. What awaited them in crossing the broad and deep Atlantic Ocean over a near fortnight? How will they manage? They've been assured that the accommodations are wonderful, the food first-class: "Like a cruise ship, we have everything to make your voyage relaxing and comfortable."

Many's the lad fought on that great day,
Well the Claymore could wield,
When the night came,
Silently lay dead in Culloden's field.

The bitter taste of uncertainty lingered, but she would be strong. Her brother Wilf had left England to be with a German gal, and from his last letter sounded quite happy. Ian left his family behind. He had shown strength and conviction in the decision to come to America, and his belief and faith have had an effect. She looked at her children, the baby asleep in her arms, not a worry in the world. Andrew now relaxed by her side. Julie took in the activity and gleefully enjoyed the menagerie of sights and sounds. Her children gave her strength.

Burned are their homes,
Exile and death scatter the loyal men;
Yet ere the sword cool in the sheath
Charlie will come again

The decision was made. Although she did not want to leave her family behind, the vast horizon beckoned. As Ethel so adamantly assured, "If it doesn't work out, she'll be right back." Whatever happens, she always has her family and will always be welcome back into their homes. Her sister Jean was now married and living in Wales. Pauline, Ethel, they will always be there for her, just as they were when she moved into Uncle Will's home.

Speed, bonnie boat,
Like a bird on the wing,

Onward the sailors cry;
Carry the lad that's born to be King
Over the sea to Skye.

Somewhere above, Mum and Grandma were watching over them. She felt their presence. The calmness continued. Ian now approached from below, a smile on his tired face intended to reassure them. He handed over a pamphlet, information for the voyage. He then reached down and facing the open sea lifted Andrew high above him, their son's widening eyes expressing wonder and amazement for the first time at the spectacular scene. She had never before witnessed such a blissful and animated expression. It awakened her senses. Iris smiled, looked down at Celia before taking Julie's hand, and the five sought their lodgings on the ship that would take them to America.

Part 3

CHAPTER 16

America Fifty-Seven Years Later

Elyria Memorial Hospital
11 January 2014

The drive to the hospital from Cleveland's West Park had become more familiar over the past year, but no easier. My mother was now eighty-eight years old. A myriad of ailments including knee and hip replacements, shingles, and severe arthritis have taken a toll on her frail body. From Julie's earlier message, the doctors weren't sure what caused the latest mishap that brought her to the ICU, but they will take some tests to determine the cause. As I waited for the elevator doors to open just beyond the garage entrance, I was pleasantly surprised to see my father and Celia come to view with the slowly opening doors. Celia's beaming smile complemented an appreciative nod from my father. When we entered my mother's room, Julie already had a seat in the room as we all settled in. My mother appeared pleased to be with her family. I was instantly encouraged.

We spent the late morning in conversation before Julie departed to take care of things around her house. Celia left next, having been in the hospital with my father since early in the morning. I sat with my parents, careful not to ask the questions that I've been digging to understand regarding my father's escape from Pitesti. Although I did manage to learn some details when my mother was in dialogue with a helpful nurse.

The clock approached midafternoon, and I prepared to leave. It was a Saturday afternoon, a chance to take care of things around the house before going out for the evening. But I decided to stay longer when my father declared that he needed to leave and prepare dinner before five o'clock mass. He told my mother he'd be back around seven o'clock, leaned over to give her a kiss while making sure she had everything needed to be comfortable.

As he left the room, she turned to me with an expression as if to say, "Can you believe this?" She closed her eyes, somewhat frustrated and visibly tired. I thought she was asleep, until she quietly remarked with eyes closed, "I read the draft from your story. How did you know all those lyrics to 'Speed, Bonnie Boat'? I could only remember the first few refrains."

"The Internet! I've told you, you can find anything on the Internet."

I reached for my smartphone and did a Google search on the song. I read the lyrics aloud, and she smiled. She asked me to repeat the refrain about the ocean bed.

Though the waves leap,
So soft shall ye sleep,
Ocean's a royal bed.
Rocked in the deep,
Flora will keep watch by your weary head.

With eyes still closed, she appeared more at ease. I watched her for a few moments before getting an idea. I did another search, spotting a video by a group that sings the song, The Corries. I placed the phone on the bed close to her head and pressed the play arrow. Sitting back, I waited for the reaction.

Speed, bonnie boat,
Like a bird on the wing,
Onward the sailors cry;
Carry the lad that's born to be King
Over the sea to Skye.

She almost jumped out of the bed. A look of wonder and disbelief, as if a child receiving a totally unexpected gift that was wildly wished for on Christmas morning. "What the…what is that? Where is it coming from?" I quietly laughed, not wanting to interrupt the song. "It's the Internet, from my phone. Just relax and enjoy."

She slipped back and closed her eyes again, mouthing the words, occasionally shaking her head in disbelief. When the song ended, she looked at me with a look of unbridled joy and happiness that I had not seen for a long time. She simply expressed the phrase she would always use when caught off guard by a good surprise. "Uhsaaaaaaaay!"

Now wide awake, the thoughts and memories poured out. Stories that I had not heard for some time, but stories that I was well aware of, having heard most of them as a young boy. She reflected on the sadness from that song, leaving her family behind in England and wondering just what she was getting into as we boarded the *Brittanic*. She recalled viewing the Statue of Liberty as we reached the shores of America. Everyone rushing to take in the glorious symbol to a new country, but her thoughts more concerned on how she and Ian could possibly manage with three young children.

Although I knew what happened next, I egged her on, kept the conversation going. She shook her head, explaining the fall down the steep steps upon departing the ship. She was holding Celia but slipped and fell, her behind bouncing down the narrow steps as she desperately clutched her baby daughter. When she finally landed, people all around did nothing but make comments, outwardly worried about the baby. She wanted to cry, thinking, "Well, what about me?"

She recalled the overnight train trip from New York City to Columbus, Ohio. In need of boiling water to mix formula for the baby, she asked a porter for assistance. He seemed surprised at the request and simply filled the bottle with warm tap water. The next morning, my father was shocked to learn that his $200 in traveler's checks were stolen. They suspect they knew who stole the money but had no way of proving. We arrived in Columbus with virtually no money and only the clothes on our backs, along with whatever was stuffed in the suitcases.

My mother leaned toward me, more life in her eyes. Clearly feeling increased energy, she continued with little prompting. We stayed for two weeks in the house of an acquaintance, the only people we knew in the United States. Ian's former coworker from Manchester had immigrated to the States and was doing quite well, owning a nice home in Lexington, Ohio. He is an Englishman nicknamed Scotty, and they have a daughter who turns out was quite spoiled as a child. After observing the daughter's refusal to share toys with her children and feeling overly dependent on their hosts, Iris pleaded for Ian to find something. Anything! "And boy did he ever find something."

The white wood frame house in the small village of Johnstown looked decent enough from the outside, in fact had nice curb appeal with a generous porch accented by shady trees, but inside revealed a number of surprises. There was no toilet. An outhouse sat at the far end of a long backyard, as if standing proud for all to see. "I'll not be using that outhouse," Iris defiantly informed Ian. "Everyone on the street will know where I'm going!"

The staircase was so narrow that when they finally purchased a bedroom set, they were unable to move it up the stairs. The kitchen sink had no faucets but a pump that provided sulfuric-tasting well water. Even Iris's attempts to venture outside caused complications. As typical in England, she took her three children out for walks into the countryside but one day found herself isolated and in danger, cars whizzing all around her. She somehow managed to walk onto the medium strip of a busy expressway. The sight of a young mother stuck in a medium strip with two toddlers and a baby in the pram must have been quite a confusing sight to the auto-happy American drivers.

For a long time, my mom could not bring herself to bare this news with Pauline and Ethel. This was not what she was expecting, and would certainly come as a disappointment to the family members she desperately wished to join her in America. However, when she finally broke down and shared news of her mishaps and missteps, the cousins were beside themselves. Explaining in follow-up letters that they were indeed sorry to hear about the troubles that Iris had encountered, they shared that the letter also had them in hysterics. "Pet, we cannot stop reading and laughing from your latest letter. The image of you pumping well water and rushing to reach to an outhouse is absolutely killing us?'

We were interrupted. An orderly entered the room, explaining that he's to move my mother to another floor for tests. He was a pleasant-looking young man, appearing a bit shy, short and stocky in stature, and sporting a full black beard on his round face. He also came off a bit uncomfortable in helping my mother out of her bed and to the rollaway bed in the hallway. So I informed him that I'd help out and walk her out to the hallway. He appeared relieved. As we slowly made our way to the hall, my mother continued chatting, remaining in good spirits.

When we reached the hallway, we realized that the bed was too high for my mother to easily get into. The orderly walked around and contemplated that we'll need to come up with a way to get her up there as the bed cannot be lowered any further. I reflected that this shouldn't be too difficult. She is my mother, and I don't see why some potential hospital policy should apply to me. And besides that, my mother can't be much over one hundred pounds. So I reached down to lift her up in my arms, gently laying her on the bed. She let out a high pitch, an unexpected rise that may have felt somewhat liberating. "Weeee! That was fun!" The orderly walked around and appeared pleased. "Well, that problem is solved, but don't expect me to lift you when we get back."

I gave her a kiss on the forehead and walked toward the elevator, where I stopped to turn and look at my mother. She looked comfortable, a blanket now atop her and the content look remained.

"I can't get that song out of my mind."

"I know." She replied, "I keep hearing it too."

"You should hear the bagpipe version, it's really beautiful."

"I can only imagine. But I'd have to be in the mood for that. It would be quite sad."

The orderly lifted the brakes on the bed and was just about ready to wheel her out.

"They'll have you back here in an hour. And when you return, Dad will be in the room waiting for you." The peace remained on her face. She did not appear a patient about to be wheeled out for tests. "Yes, I know he will be. He always is! Love you, son!"

CHAPTER 17

An Eastbound Trek Begins

Turnpike and South Bend, Indiana
30 August 2014

"Hey, Andy, how would you like two tickets to the Notre Dame game this Saturday? Let me know soon because they're really good tickets, and we'd like to give them to someone we know will appreciate them."

With only a few days to make plans, it would have been easy to turn down the enticing offer from my friend and financial advisor Dan Bragg, but a vivid image burned bright in my mind. During the 2006 football season, I drove my father to South Bend to watch his favorite college football team, the Notre Dame Fighting Irish. We left Elyria early that day and arrived well before the expected noon kick-off, only to learn upon arrival that the start time had been moved to 3:30 pm. The following five hours (following a four-hour drive) can be best described as glorious, visiting and soaking in every ounce of the nostalgic campus culture. I chalked it off as a really cool bucket list item for my father, but why not do it again. I let Dan know I'd take the tickets. Little did I know the visit would sow the seeds for an even greater bucket list item, one that seemed almost surreal to even imagine.

My mother agreed it would be good for my father to get away for the day. Since her visit to the hospital in January, he had barely left her side, leaving only for daily one-hour visits to the college gym and stops to the store when not accompanying her to doctor's offices. Despite the required attention, the comeback that my mother made since her visit to the hospital was nothing short of miraculous. Shortly after her discharge from EMH, Celia arranged with both Julie and I to make a concerted effort to help out my father in caring for Mom. Sometimes a brief visit to simply say hello and enjoy a cup of tea. Other times helping with chores around the house, picking up a lunch, or making dinner together. With each visit, her strength and outlook grew. Even though the doctors had diagnosed many of her ailments as debilitating with no hope of improvement and in obvious pain, there was a renewed spirit, improved memory, and spunk that we'd not seen for some time. Every visit ending in enlightened conversation, new stories and memories from the past coupled with observations of the present.

When I arrived early that Saturday to pick up my father, he was already by the door, all packed and ready to go. Celia was in the kitchen with my mother. They also appeared to be looking forward to their own day together. They made sure we had everything for the trip, from packed lunches to rain gear given the potential of inclement weather.

Blue skies and puffy clouds accompanied the drive along the turnpike to South Bend, shadowing easy conversation that flowed continuously. I shared the story of Louis Zamperini from a book that I had just completed, *The Unbroken*. My father listened with fascination, offering his own thoughts of what enabled Louis to survive, and smiled when I offered that he and Louis would have made quite a team if paired up during the war. He shared further memories of his own family and the war, and before we knew it, signs with driving distances to South Bend informed us that we were nearing our destination.

The magic of Notre Dame's campus picked right up where it left us in 2006. We sat on grass in the expansive mall enjoying a steak sandwich, soaking in the color surrounding us. The sound of beating drums and trumpeting brass provided a magnetic pull, guiding us to the chapel that was a must-see on my father's list of places to visit. Walking inside thick oak doors, noise and brightness were replaced by coolness, serenity, and a golden symbol providing a beacon of light toward the altar. Filtering sunlight from stained glass windows created a path as we walked toward the altar before my father sat down at a pew. I took a few photos and noticed the peaceful expression on his face, wondering what he was thinking.

Walking outside the chapel, we met up with the tail end of the band and joined in the procession. The band guided us to the stadium, crowds of onlookers and late-arriving fans opening a path as drum rolls accompanied by brass sounds induced great delight to everyone in sight. We followed the music directly to the stadium where we were among the last spectators to enter, finding our seats just moments before the singing of the national anthem.

The game itself was a blowout. Notre Dame scored early and often against Rice University, providing their fans with many reasons to cheer. Even the downpour brought more excitement than agitation. During halftime, dark clouds appeared from the southwest, inviting a welcome breeze and cool shade from the scorching sun. By the time the rains came, Notre Dame's offense was on the field and moving to score. Heavy raindrops showered confetti with the resulting touchdown and were blown away almost as quickly as they arrived.

We left at the start of the fourth quarter, making the thirty-minute walk back to the car to avoid heavy traffic. Back on the road, conversation flowed easily, moving between Notre Dame's prospects for a national championship and questions about my family in Poland. The question seemed innocuous when I asked it.

"If you could go back and visit just a few places you were during the war, where would you want to go?"

He gave his thoughtful expression, but the moment of reflection was so brief I was convinced it was a question he'd already pondered. "Well, you know I'd really like to go back to Austria. I've been wondering if that butcher's shop is still there. Possibly still run by the same family. And I'm certain I could find that spot where we swam across the river into Slovakia. I never told you, but that mound along the river was similar to the mound along the creek behind your house on Schwartz… that river valley in Slovakia was spectacular…I would have to go to Romania. It would be really interesting to find that castle in Transylvania…oh, you should see the Alps! There is no place more beautiful…it would be interesting to see the village Podwoloczysko…Rome is really something…"

I interrupted him to throw out an idea that was percolating. "Well, you know, I can request a sabbatical from the college for a full semester. Perhaps you can join me for a few weeks."

The turnpike drive from Indiana to Ohio is flat and straight with little variation from open fields and isolated homes. But for the following three hours, it was filled with a medley of images across the European landscape. Everything from the carriage ride across Eastern Poland to mountain views along the Adriatic Sea sprang to life. I could sense the contained excitement in my father's voice, but I fully understood his seriousness when he outlined the one obstacle that we'd need to overcome.

"Your mom really needs me right now. She's at the point where I need to be with her all the time. Even during the night, I get up with her when she goes to the bathroom to make sure that she's not going to fall."

"Well, I know for a fact that Marissa would make herself available to stay with Mom. Lauren would also be available to help out, and of course Julie and Celia. And I'm sure that Brittany and Kelly would help out any way they can."

A look of relief instantly crossed my father's face, as if the one hidden solution magically appeared. Of my four daughters, Marissa was the one who gave me the most cause for concern through her teen years. The runt of the litter, she was quite small and appeared almost scrawny as a toddler. She had a knack for not listening but managed to talk her way out of the constant trouble she was getting into. I knew she had a special skill as early as two years old, one that both humored and concerned me at the same time. With my young daughters all running around the house well past their bedtime, I brought to their attention in no uncertain terms that they had best be in their beds before I got to their rooms. Feeling confident that the scrambling noise would result in an empty hallway, I approached to see my nemesis stare me down from across the darkened hall. The tiny figure stood unafraid if not defiant, a sight to see in her oversized nightgown and a stuffed Barney dangling by her side. Before I could utter a word she beat me to the punch, and the words were "Get your butt over here!"

Finally! The opportune time to discipline her had arrived. Her posture and face shifted as my look of surprise turned to anger, her mind obviously clicking, but there was no way that a two-year-old can talk her way out of this one. I steadily approached and asked her to repeat, "What did you say?"

Her defiant face transformed into the sweetest thing that a father could imagine. She dropped her Barney and held her arms out to be picked up, stating in a whimsical expression as if to suggest, "Why would you question me?" "I said...hey buddy, come over here."

I never was fully able to get Marissa to listen or hear me out. Growing up, she never paid much heed to my continual requests and demands: "do your homework, quit straightening your lovely wavy hair, enough of the makeup, why have us pay all that money when your grades aren't so good and you can go to community college?" She predictably dropped out of college sometime during the second year, but then a miraculous change took place. She found herself.

Gone was the hardened image, replaced with a sweet personality that matched her petite glamorous looks. She could suddenly care less what others thought of her love for Disney characters and the TV show "Full House." Since she loved being around children, she looked up babysitting jobs on the Internet, and it wasn't long before she found her niche. Families quickly realized that their children were happy and well behaved when she was around and their houses spotless. Marissa's mild compulsive behavior to have everything clean and put in its place was perfect for the job. Her services were in demand, and the title of babysitter eventually replaced by the title of nanny.

With circumstances taking her to Virginia, Marissa was now a nanny for a wealthy young family who owned a house along the ocean in Hampton, Virginia.

The job included generous lodging and vacation time. When I approached her one day about possibly looking after her grandma for a short period, she instantly lit up. "Yes, of course! I'd love to look after and be with Grandma!" Marissa and my mother share a unique bond, my father mentioning on more than one occasion that the two are a lot alike in many ways.

My father would certainly not agree to have just anyone watch my mom, and there's no way my mother would be okay with my father leaving her for any length of time. However, the one person that could make this all work for everyone concerned was Marissa.

Darkness arrived when we pulled over into the Ohio rest stop just east of Toledo. I didn't really need the Starbucks coffee to keep me alert on the road and could see that my father was also wide awake. We picked up a few snacks at the gift shop, loaded up on gasoline, and the conversation immediately picked back up when we reentered the turnpike. The road signs indicated names of local towns and driving distances to eastbound destinations. There was no sign for this destination, but we might as well have been en route to Podwoloczysko in the Ukraine, a Polish border town close to the Russian border before World War II.

CHAPTER 18

Liberated

Sandy Ridge, North Ridgeville, Ohio
8 November 2015

Unseasonal November sunshine sparkled off the Sandy Ridge wetlands as my father and I hiked around the park's perimeter. Things over the past year did not go the way I envisioned since our drive back from South Bend.

I was denied the 2015 fall semester sabbatical that I applied for. The formal letter I received in March of 2015 stated,

The plan of retracting your father's steps during World War II is certainly very interesting and would be quite educational for you. However, the resulting book would not contribute to your particular academic discipline, and would not further the academic mission of the College.

Fortunately, I received an informal heads-up from the campus president prior to that letter, which provided valuable time to conduct some last-minute changes. My associate dean, Dr. Pam Ellison, scrambled to revamp the summer schedule of business courses. She secured agreements that enabled me to teach two online classes, freeing up time to both instruct and take my much-anticipated trip to Europe. The reduced stay would not allow time to write or travel to Britain and Germany, but I had time to research and visit key areas of interest. I immediately booked a round-trip flight to Cracow, Poland, allowing for six weeks of travel within eastern and southern Europe. I also authored a letter to the college provost, respectfully acknowledging their decision but seriously questioning the committee's rationale for denying my detailed proposal, one of only two requests not approved. My disappointment from the denial was short-lived. I was already making plans for Europe.

Unfortunately, my father did not join me. We continued discussing plans, but my mother's health was not improving. Her dependence on my father was growing, and when we finally brought up the idea of him joining me for two weeks, her reaction was expected. In his quiet way, he confided when the two of us were alone that he would not accompany me on the trip. "Your mother needs me to be here with her. It would not be fair to her or others to leave her. You go ahead. We'll be just fine."

The six weeks spent in Europe was nothing short of life changing. I spent the first few days with my second cousin Michal, Henryk's grandson. He drove me to Premyzl. We hiked mountains in Slovakia, enjoyed local craft beer, spent one evening in Kosice, and awoke at 4:00 a.m. to drive into Miskolc, Hungary. We entered a desolate train station where we said our goodbyes as he directed me to the platform for the train to Cluj. There would be many more train stations leading along a trail of learning and unexpected adventure. Cluj, Bucharest, Budapest, Vienna, Weikendorf, Venice, Ancona, Matera, Rome, the Alps, Linz, and back to Poland. My trip ended, joined by my daughter's Brittany and Lauren and my sister Julie, with four glorious days spent with family members in Bochnia.

There we stayed at the home of my cousin Marian (my Uncle Zdislaw named his four sons in reverse order of his siblings: Stanislaw, Zdislaw, Jerzy, and Marian). A home built on the same property where my father grew up. The yellow stucco house was replaced by a modern two-story structure. Every evening was spent with my cousins and extended family on the overflowing back deck, where music accompanied dancing, dining, laughter, and easy conversation. It was all surreal, the entire sequence of events, people, and places feeling more like a dream.

Midnight struck when I arrived back at my house in Cleveland following a day of airports and international flights, but I was unable to sleep. All I could think about was the excitement of driving early in the morning to see my parents in Elyria. To let my concerned mother know that I was okay and to share everything that I learned and experienced with my father. I knew that they were just as eager to see me, for their own separate reasons, as I was to see them.

Three months later, the discussion points were not exhausted between my father and me; they were exponentially expanding. The thought was not lost on me during one of the few quiet interludes on our walk. It struck me that only a few years ago, our conversation typically bordered between forced dialogue and awkward silence. Now I looked over at him and could see his mind racing. I slowed the pace as he showed just a hint of unsteadiness from the brisk walk.

"How are you doing with Mom? That's a lot of work for you, and as we've told you, there are agencies who can help out when we can't. They'll bring someone over to look after her to help you out. You also need to take time out and do things for yourself."

"Oh no, I'm just fine. It's my job now, and what else would I do?" After a brief pause, he continued. "The only difficulty is to see her frustration. She wants to keep doing the things she always has, but it's difficult for her."

A flock of geese flew overhead, and we stopped to observe them land in the open water. My father smiled as he told me about the pigeon business that his brother's Henryk and Stefan operated before the war. They created an opening from the attic to the rooftop and built a home for the pigeons. On market days in Bochnia, they sold their prized pigeons on the square, enabling the purchase of goods for themselves and the family. My father beamed with pride and fondness. "That Stefan, he could sell anything." He then shared how Henryk would develop photos using glass. He created a dark room in the home and used glass and various other methods to create different effects from his photos. I mentioned how much I'd love to use a photo taken by Henryk for the cover of my book. Just several days earlier, I spoke to Michal on Skype, and we discussed the idea. If Michal was unable to find a suitable photo taken by his grandfather, he promised that he'd try to create one for me that met my definition of a new word for him, "wanderlust."

Leaving the wetlands area, we walked along a path through a wooded area to reach the parking lot. Barren trees increased visibility, so we stopped to observe a deer and her two young fawns. We stayed there for an extended time, simply taking in the peaceful feeling of the forest and in no rush to drive home.

It was there that for perhaps the first time in my lifetime I heard my father voice a confession, or at least as close to a regret as anything I've ever heard from him. "You know, the one thing that I really miss is spending more time outdoors, in the forest. I always felt a sense of peace and safety in the forest."

Images flashed into my mind. My father and his Ukrainian friend Michal finding safety in the forest after crossing the treacherous river into Slovakia. My father and Artur seeking refuge in the forest trekking across Poland, Slovakia, Hungary, and Romania.

I asked him, "When you look back at everything you experienced during the war, is there anything that wished you did different? Anything that you regret or would change."

Following his trademark thoughtful pause, he answered with conviction and clarity, "No. Everything happens for a reason. Things were supposed to happen the way they did. Who knows what would have happened had Artur and I not been captured. We may have ended up in much more danger. We would not have met the people that we were destined to meet."

I let the thought sink in. It brought to mind the conversation we had when I shared with him my disappointment in not receiving the requested sabbatical. He explained that there was a reason for the denial. That destiny will lead me to new and different discoveries, people, and events that are supposed to happen. Those words proved to be most profound and true.

I saw that he was deep in thought, enjoying the serenity of the forest.

"If you could go back to Poland, is there anything you'd like to see again or experience?"

There was no thoughtful repose. He answered with the enthusiasm of an adventurous teen, "Do you know, I'm reading a book, *Bochnia, City Tour Guide*. This author, he makes you feel like you're right there, describing the people who lived there, the architecture of the buildings, everything. Do you remember my high school teacher Jan Kot I told you about who swam in the '36 Olympics, the one who trained by swimming upstream for hours in the Raba River? I just learned that he was a member of the Underground during the war. He was really something. I tried to swim upstream like he did but just couldn't do it. He swam like that for hours. The book is written in a way that takes you down each street, describing the notable people and buildings. You feel like you're right there. Reading this book, I'd like to go back and see these places."

Looking at him, I viewed a fifteen-year-old teen who viewed escape from the Nazi blitzkrieg on a crowded horse-drawn carriage as an adventure. I saw a man who never sat still, risking danger to escape occupation or prison so that he could follow his dream and help to liberate Poland, a man who defied all odds to survive danger and join Anders' Army. I saw a man who was inspired by the works of his favorite author as a boy, Henryk Sienkiewycz. The fire and spark have not left him. Nor has the desire to adventure and learn. I also saw a man whose dedication to his wife and family have proven to be the most important things in life while on this earth.

That dedication between husband and wife remain as strong as ever. Following dinner, my mother encouraged us to take the walk as my daughter Lauren stayed home with her. I pictured an image shared by my second cousin Marc when I visited him in Austria this past summer. He fondly recalled as a little boy in Wales hearing so many stories of Auntie Iris from his Grandma Jean. In one, little Iris would chase after Jean and Wilf, wanting so desperately to join her older siblings. Her little legs just couldn't keep up. They moved so fast that her knickers would fall down as she fought to continue. I'm not sure if she did reach her older brother and sister who must have been beside themselves in laughter, but she kept on fighting. Guided by Grandma, she met up with a Polish soldier, and together they forged a life in a new country, providing their children with immeasurable love and wisdom.

My thoughts were interrupted by a steady breeze that released a lingering scent of fresh pine, as if transcended from a heavenly breath. My father remained in thoughtful repose, and I couldn't help but go back to his words—destiny leads us to new and different discoveries, people, and events that are supposed to happen. I saw a man who was both at peace and alive.

"Perhaps you will go back to Bochnia. To see these places again. The yellow stucco house may be gone, but family and memories are still alive from our past, and I believe may be guiding us today."

We started walking once again through the forest path, and for the second time on our walk, there was a quiet interlude. Words were not needed. I knew what he was thinking, and I believe we both took solace in the knowledge that a father's dreams and thoughts were both understood and shared with his son.

Epilogue

Stifling heat arrived far too early that July morning in the summer of 2015 when I came upon the road sign for Weikendorf. My plan was to locate the butcher shop where my father worked for the Germans from late 1942 to August 1944. From there, the estimated ten-kilometer walk across open fields to the Morava River seemed within easy reach. Observing little promise of shade along the narrow road, I wished I had come better prepared, perhaps rented a car. I reminded myself that Dad had no such luxury to reach the Slovakian border, nor would I.

A distant yellow church spire surfaced beyond checkered fields of proud sunflowers. There stood my destination inside Weikendorf, a church facing Marktstrabe Street. My father and I spent considerable time viewing the church and what he thought might be the butcher shop on Google Map's street view, but there was no familiarity as I approached the landmark, only guarded anticipation. Could someone from my father's past still live in that house?

An elderly groundskeeper was the only person on the church grounds. He spoke no English but seemed to convey familiarity with the surname Schuster. Following a brief tour of the grounds, he counted fingers and a thumb to indicate the fifth address down the quiet street of row houses. When I knocked on the door, doubt grew in my mind; this is either the wrong house or nobody lives here. Just when it appeared that nobody would answer, a middle-aged woman opened the door, a look between nervous and surprise that someone would come knocking on the door. Trying to convey friendly intentions, I introduced myself as a visitor from America conducting research for a book. It was only when I referred to the name Schuster that she reacted, motioning for me to wait as she closed the door and went back inside.

Her nervous expression did not wane when she returned, but she gestured for me to enter. She led me past the foyer and into a large outdated kitchen, pointing to a door on the opposite end. Inside the room, a bedridden woman looked up as if I were an alien. She was seated with a tray in front of her, working on a crossword puzzle while watching TV. I realized that I was intruding on her normal routine, so tried my best to reassure her with an explanation for my visit. I threw out basic words that did nothing to change her puzzled expression. Finally, I connected the words *Marian* and *Poland*. That did it. Her expression changed. She straightened up and grew animated, excitedly repeating the name Marian over and over.

For the next hour she spoke nonstop. Unfortunately, I comprehended very little from her rapid-fire German, but there were breakthroughs. She asked her caretaker to bring in a box of old photos, which opened yet more doors. When I pantomimed that my father and Michal swam to safety after escaping the farm, she smiled broadly. And when I shared photos of my father with his granddaughters, her eyes visibly teared. I stayed for about an hour, eager to make the walk to the river and not wishing to disturb her day any further. I asked if I could take her photo, but she insisted that I instead take a snapshot of her wedding photo to share with my father. Walking out the front door, I heard her continually talking to the caretaker, repeating the name Marian over and over.

That memorable day in Weikendorf, Austria, was just one of many that brought me closer to my father as I retraced his journey all across Europe, capturing the entire trip in my travel blog abajda.com. What made it even more meaningful was to actually meet someone from his past. Searches for Mulek and Artur have thus far yielded no positive results.

As for family members, others have gone on to join Minnie in heaven. In fact, it strikes me that the only person outside of my parents and Anna still known to be alive from their story is Ida, my mother's friend who sat with her at the dance where she met my father. No other siblings or cousins immigrated to the United States, and only one from their past is known to be alive. Irena, the older sister of the two cousins who escaped with Ian's family on the horse-drawn carriage, Alexandria and Zofia, now lives in a nursing home.

Fortunately, I did have the opportunity to meet many of my family members before they passed, on two trips to England and one to Poland. So I am able to provide a glimpse into their lives after my parents immigrated to the United States. I also experienced a most revealing encounter with the only grandparent who was still alive after I was born.

My British Family

My first trip back to England was in my early twenties. I still remember nervous anticipation as the plane began its descent like it was yesterday. The view from my window seat revealed distinctive foreign farmland growing closer, irregular-shaped lots populated with grazing sheep, bordered by neat stone fences on hilly terrain. Somehow, I felt I was returning home. I took the train from London to Cardiff, Wales. My cousin Phillip met me, and I tried to contain my excitement that he was the first cousin I ever recall seeing. We drove through winding narrow streets to a bowling green in the village of Mountain Ash, where his father Rhys Jones was competing in a friendly match with his mates. Phillip asked me, which of those gentlemen do you suppose is your uncle? I picked him out right away. We walked to the cozy house up the hill, which literally felt like climbing steep stairs. And when I saw my *Aunt Jean* for the first time, I had to do a double take. Although not identical in appearance, it was like looking into the eyes and soul of my mother.

Mountain Ash and Wales left wonderful memories. Long hikes across the valleys and countryside, sharing a room with my second cousin Marc, stopping for refreshing pints in centuries-old pubs, wild horses roaming freely, the goodbyes heartfelt and sincere. But the anticipation of my next stop was growing. I boarded the northbound train in Cardiff, destined for Millom.

Once the train reached my birthplace of Manchester and a number of passengers departed, I made sure to grab a window seat facing west. I wanted to take in every possible view of the sea and surrounding landscape for the remainder of the trip. Lush green meadows contrast with jagged rocks, together dominating the uneven coastline as we approached Millom. An overcast mist hung in the air. Again, my heart was racing as the train gradually slowed to a stop, repeated signs hanging below the platform roof announcing the town of Millom.

Departing the train, I intently studied every face inside the station. Could this by my *Aunt Pauline*? When it became apparent that nobody was there to greet me, I ventured out of the station to gather my bearings. Millom is a small town. Someone will direct me to the house. I collected my luggage and walked toward an arching stone bridge that crossed the tracks and led to the town square, where I made out a lanky figure atop the bridge running toward me. She was wearing a long raincoat, a closed umbrella in one hand while waving her free hand in a frenzied manner. Finally I make out the voice and heard a thick northern English accent. "Andrew! Andrew!" She finally reached me, clearly out of breath, and threw her arms around me, a smile so warm I immediately knew it was Auntie Pauline. "Why, you're the spitting image of your Uncle Wilf, the way he'd stroll out from that train station when he'd come home on leave."

Unfortunately, I never did meet my *Uncle Wilf*. His whereabouts remain a mystery, nobody having heard from him for decades. The last my mother heard was a letter received from him just before leaving for America. He was living in Germany with a woman he met after the war. To this day, I lament the loss of the sole possession she had from him that she entrusted with me. Five well-used wooden dice used for gambling, packaged in a narrow blue box. Each of the dice's six sides containing the numbers 9 or 10, or the face figure from a card deck: king, queen, joker, and ace. I spent many evenings rolling and studying those dice, imagining the stories that must have accompanied the many games played during the war. Being such a symbolic item from an uncle that I feel a natural connection with, I pray that they will one day magically appear. Perhaps hidden in an old box containing long-forgotten memorabilia.

I also missed the opportunity to meet Pauline's husband, my *Uncle Edward*. My parents often speak very fondly of him and still hold his memory dearly. Not only was he a skilled dancer, as evident at the dance where my mom and Pauline met their future husbands, but also he was quite charismatic and skilled in a variety of areas. Edward was to be my father's best man, but apparently wasn't feeling so well that morning, Ian and his mates having gone out the night before the wedding. Edward was both athletic and artistic. My father was still amazed at how he would carve the most intricate animal figures from a simple block of wood within a matter of minutes. His artistic talents did pass down to his children—Danusia, Janek, Mirek, and Anna—who all inherited some of his artistic skills. Edward passed away shortly after the birth of Anna.

Aunt Pauline's house became my home base as I met family and ventured into other parts of Britain. While in Millom, Aunt Ethel came over to visit often. Sometimes we'd all walk to the bluffs overlooking the Irish Sea. It never was clear enough to view the Isle of Man, but the Barrow shipyards loomed prominent just across the bay. Aunt Pauline enjoyed telling stories of my mother as a girl, articulated in a wide-eyed manner that had me chuckling right at the onset. At times she laughed so loud telling a story that I could barely make out what she was saying. It was quite apparent that she, Ethel, and my mother participated in many escapades in the years leading up to and after the war. She also dreamily told the story of how Uncle Edward wrote "I Love You" on the window inside the taxicab.

My *Uncle Frank*, who promised my mom that he and his wife would adopt her after he married, never did marry. He did however maintain his giving spirit. He presented me with a brown sweater, lined with orange and white around the collar. I thanked him and shared that it was the exact colors of our home football team, and that I'd proudly wear it on game days. He seemed quite pleased in hearing that. Years later, I finally decided to give it to charity, offering it with a bag of clothes to be donated, the sweater still in its plastic wrapping. Although I never wore the sweater, I like to think that it became a favorite article of clothing for an appreciative young man. Maybe even worn during Cleveland Browns football games. I do believe that Frank's giving spirit was appreciated and passed on. Conversely, the wool sweater that Pauline knit for me became an instant favorite. I literally wore it out, having to finally scrap it after years of wear and tear.

I didn't see too much of my *Aunt Mary* while in Millom, although she made a point to stop by and visit me at Pauline's. As shared by my mother after moving with family in Millom, Mary appeared more reserved and matronly in appearance from her sisters, didn't say much, and typically stayed close to her home taking care of the house.

* * *

My mother only made it back to England twice. On her fist visit, Pauline and Ethel waited outside the gate and immediately recognized the legs of my mother as she departed the plane, her upper half obscured by mobile equipment handling baggage on the tarmac. Unable to conceal her excitement, Ethel rushed past the barricades to greet her cousin. With long pent-up emotions after years of separation, she couldn't wait any longer. The trip proved to be a most memorable reunion.

My second trip to England about eight years after my initial visit could never match that emotion, but was equally memorable. Although not aware at the time, it was a final opportunity to say my goodbyes to the aunts and uncles who still survived: Pauline (who was in poor health) and Ethel. I also could not have known that it would be a final farewell to my cousin Janek.

As Pauline in my first visit, Ethel was a most gracious host. "Just make yourselves comfortable, let me know what you need washed, and feel free to come and go." Years later I thought about her and decided to write a letter, sharing warm memories of Millom and my mother's happiness in the special bond with my daughters. Her son Stephen wrote to my mother about a month later, explaining that she died peacefully. He also pointed out that my letter has remained proudly positioned on the mantel since the day it arrived.

After the passing of Pauline, Ethel, and her sister Jean, my mother never did go back to England, I believe wanting to remember Millom the way it was growing up as a girl.

My Polish Family

With tight visa restrictions between the United States and countries under Soviet control during the Cold War, it was many years before my father returned to Poland. When he did return, both his parents were gone, and only two brothers were still alive. He did run across Victor one day in front of the yellow stucco house. Victor was taking a walk, and the two ran into one another, just as they did many times prior to the war.

Unlike the familiarity I felt with England and my family there, I knew relatively little of my Polish family at that time. I do recall viewing a picture of my Uncle Stefan in his army uniform as a young boy, and was struck at the striking resemblance between him and my father. As planned, Stefan and my Aunt Sonia did immigrate to Argentina where he started a business in Beunos Aires. As fate would have it, Stefan and Sonia were unable to have children, so they wrote to my parents in England with what had to be a most personal and difficult request. Right before my younger sister Celia was born, they wrote to ask if my parents would consider giving their expected child up for adoption. The request was of course denied, though I do tease my mother that she probably replied with "Well, we are open to discussion about the boy."

I used to wonder what it would have been like if my sister was in fact adopted and we were to meet at a later time. Unfortunately, that meeting would likely not have included Uncle Stefan. I realize now how much I would have loved to meet my Uncle Stefan and how emotional that would have been for my father. The two never reunited after parting in Italy. Stefan passed away in his thirties, the time spent in Russian prisons and a Siberia labor camp having taken a toll on his health. Had my sister been adopted, meeting her might have taken place in Utica, New York, when I was in my late twenties. Aunt Sonia came to America for the first time to visit her sister Bruna, who also married a Polish soldier (Tony) and had immigrated to the United States. Following a seven-hour drive, their entire family rushed onto the front porch as we pulled up the driveway. When my father stepped out of the car, my Aunt Sonia fainted, falling into the arms of Tony. The resemblance of my father to Stefan so striking that she momentarily believed she was viewing the ghost of her husband.

Outside of reviving Aunt Sonia, my recollections of that weekend centered around a large kitchen in the two-story wood frame house. We spent virtually the entire weekend in that kitchen, which was constantly filled with the most delicious-tasting food I believe I have ever dined on. Rich pastas mixed with savory sauces, polished fruit, fresh pastries, all accompanied with an assortment of juice and wines. Colorful stories of Italy during and after the war came to life around the large wooden table, spoken in English, Polish, and Italian; it was difficult to keep up. I vividly recall the barrage of wet kisses from those Italian sisters, along with a free flow of laughter and tears. It was also obvious that my Aunt Sonia felt a connection, if not a strong bond, with my outgoing sister Celia. Perhaps she looked at her as the daughter she never had.

* * *

The other memorable visit before travelling to Poland was from my *Aunt Krystyna*. I recall feeling a bit uncomfortable to have a nun stay with us for several weeks, living at home from college for the summer. But any unease was quickly removed the instant she appeared from the Jetway. She was covered in a bright blue habit, standing tall and regal, and appeared to glide rather than walk. The radiant smile on her attractive face was contagious; even the people around her seemed buoyed. She was unlike any nun that I ever recalled from twelve years attending Catholic schools.

Working outdoors during the day and embracing summer activities, I did not see a whole lot of my Aunt Krystyna during her stay, but I thoroughly enjoyed the time spent with her. The days I did come home, children from the neighborhood appeared to pop out of the woodwork in hopes of seeing her. She'd greet me with a warm smile and ask questions in Polish, playfully laughing at my inability to answer. One day I came home and she was the only one there, so I sat with her in the family room to spend some time together. As we attempted to make conversation, she said, "Mowia Andrzej," which sounded to me like "Move Andrew." So I moved to the other end of the room. She grew more animated. "Mowia Andrzej!" I thought maybe I smelled offensive from being sweaty and working outside all day, so I left to take a shower downstairs and freshen up. Later my father asked why I didn't speak to my aunt upon coming home from work. After explaining that I thought she was asking me to move, I learned that the word for "speak" in Polish is "mowia."

During her visit I learned more of my grandmother *Jozefa* and came to recognize the impact she made on others throughout her life. Among the items that Aunt Krystyan brought with her were large black-and-white glossy photographs accompanying an audiotape of my grandmother's funeral. St. Michal Basilica was packed with lines of people, ordinary folk mixed with dignitaries dressed in everything from business suits to elaborate robes. Clear audio captured the moment; emotional oratory echoed in the cavernous church; brief moments of sobs or polite laughter interspersed with silence from the attentive congregation. I didn't understand the words, buy my father and Krystyna sat silent and intent throughout the lengthy eulogy, occasionally providing translation for the more memorable comments. More black-and-white photos captured a long procession to the cemetery, Jozefa's casket transported by horse-drawn carriage. It seemed the whole town was there. When asked what was the gist of the eulogy, my father simply explained that she was recognized as a great woman who touched the lives of so many people. I went to bed that night with a whole new sense of wonder and appreciation for my grandmother. Little could I imagine that I would one day have my grandmother reach out to me in the same cemetery where photos showed her body being laid to rest.

* * *

The idea struck me in an instant. I was in my mid-forties when I suggested to my father, "Let's take a trip to Poland." By this time, he had been back twice, both times with my mother and once including my two sisters. This could be a unique father-son memory, and I could meet family members while learning of my heritage. He gave me an inquisitive look before we heard my mother state, "You should both go." Just like that, the decision was made.

I really didn't know what to expect, leaving all the planning to my father who quickly made arrangements with his two surviving brothers, my Aunt Krystyna having by this time passed away. As we hopscotched across Europe with a number of layovers before arriving in Poland, I was immediately struck by the change in my father. I saw him as I'd never seen him before. My father was alive with the wonderment of a child. Not a thing was missed, his excitement visibly grew, and I suddenly felt like the responsible adult needing to keep an eye on his travel companion. Quite a departure from a normally contemplative father and his more spontaneous son.

My *Uncle Jerzy* (George) met us at the Warsaw airport and would be our guide for much of the trip. I had met my Uncle George on two earlier trips to the States. A soft-spoken and humble man, he was clearly a well-respected priest, a theology professor and author of countless books, having delivered lectures throughout the world. As we would learn, he was recognized throughout Poland and able to gain access to a wide array of places of interest. He was also a man used to having things done his way, and that was not without its challenges for my more free-spirited style. But that was of minor concern; this trip was about my father and my family.

With his vast contacts, Uncle George arranged for us to have a vehicle, and I was the designated driver for the next few weeks. After several days in Warsaw, our next stop was Bochnia.

The drive from Warsaw to Bochnia was eye-opening. Nothing escaped my attention on the scenic roadway, passing small towns and villages, distant castles, antiquated farm equipment, and hourglass-shaped stacks of wheat dotting open fields. We pulled over to a rest stop where the setting again reminded me that we were far from America. The rest area was an opening cut into thick forest, vehicles parked in front of a colorful structure that appeared to be an elaborate gypsy wagon. Smoke wafted from a well-used outdoor grille used to smoke thick links of sausage. The smell was enticing. We stepped inside to order a light lunch. White lace curtains contrasted bright red decor, framing tall pine trees visible through open windows. Observing no bathroom inside, I ventured out in search of the restrooms. However, all I could see was a well-worn path leading into the forest. There was a temptation to continue walking, a wanderlust inviting new wonders at every corner, exotic foliage mixed with an assortment of the most ripe and delicious-tasting berries. I assessed that I'd best do my business and head back before getting lost in the forest. Poland was beginning to capture my soul.

The landscape slowly transformed into rolling hills as we spotted the first signs indicating driving distances to Bochnia. It was beginning to feel surreal to me, so I could not imagine what my father was thinking. Every time I viewed him in the rearview mirror he was intently peering at the surroundings, seeming transfixed in thought. When we finally arrived at the hostel on the outer edge of town, it was past dusk and growing dark. I clearly sensed that my father shared my energy and excitement of arriving in Bochnia.

We arose early to attend Mass at a church close to the house where my father grew up on the opposite end of town. The church was overflowing, and I was conscious that family members were spread out among the congregation. As soon as Mass ended, we were surrounded by relatives of all ages along the sun-splashed entrance. We spent the rest of that day in the house where my father grew up, the yellow stucco faded and the flower garden in need of tending, but once again a vibrant, happy home.

The following days were a whirlwind of visits. Always a table filled with an assortment of meats, ripe tomato slices dipped in vinegar and dill, crackers, tea, and juices. And always my father was the center of attention. I viewed him in an entirely new light. Although I didn't understand the language, he spoke freely in a fluid manner, holding everyone's attention. There were many questions followed by yet more intense listening. Many of his comments were met with *ooh*s and *ah*s or heartfelt laughter. Sometimes I recognized my name (Andrzej, sounds like Ahn-Jay, but somehow the natives manage to pronounce it by sounding out every letter), and everyone's attention would shift toward me. I simply smiled, having no idea why I was suddenly the focal point of their interest or laughter. I had not the slightest inclination at that time the blessing I have today, that I would be back and grow so close to those same cousins and family members.

My father was clearly in his element. One day he took me to his high school, pointing out class photos framed in the hallways. Although not familiar with his story at the time, *Mulek* was singled out as his neighbor and best friend. When we entered a classroom, he beamed in delight, sitting in the "exact same desk" where he sat as a student. The smile never left my father's face as he remained in that seat for a lengthy period of time, visibly reminiscing in the moment.

Another day we took the train to nearby Crakow, the cultural capital of Poland. As we approached a tourist area near a castle in the central part of the city, we stopped to view a lively band. My father excitedly explained their folk music and costume as typical of the Polish Highlanders who populate an area we would soon visit in the Carpathian Mountains. I paused to shoot some photos while taking in the music and sound. When I turned back, my father was nowhere to be found. Aware of the vast crowds and realizing how easy it would be to get separated in an era before cell phones, I yelled out his name in an attempt to locate him. Seconds later, I heard a distant voice coming from the band. "Andrew! Over here!" There stood my father, surrounded by band members, decked out in a colorful vest and a feathered Highlander hat, grinning from ear to ear and acting like a member of the band.

"Dad, you've got to let me know when you're going to do something crazy like that."

He couldn't stop grinning. "Hey, how about that. They let me be a part of their band! Can you believe it? I always enjoyed their music and lifestyle. I always had an appreciation for the Highlanders."

Back in Bochnia, we spent one day hiking the grounds of my father's boyhood house, the yellow stucco home, walking past the factory and into the forest where my dad and Mulek spent so much of their childhood before the war. We viewed the peaceful chapel in the birch forest and walked the path to view the twin ponds visible below the valley. Outside the house, my father pointed toward the direction that he and a friend (I did not know of Artur at the time) left Bochnia in the early morning hour. I could almost feel the emotion that they must have experienced.

Down the road, we explored the town, touring the historic salt mine with its intricate carved rooms. I visited small shops and watched people in the square, trying to imagine what it was like for the locals forced to view four young men hanging from lampposts at Christmastime during the Nazi occupation (at the time, that was all I knew of life in Bochnia under German occupation). We walked inside the police station where I learned Henryk was held after turning himself in to the authorities. I felt the magic entering St. Michal's church. Bochnia felt like home.

Outside of Uncle George, my father's only other living sibling at that time was *Uncle Henryk*. We only saw him one time, visiting his cramped home just a few blocks from St. Michal Church. He and his wife struck me as an unassuming couple, but the warmth he exhibited upon reuniting with my father was crystal clear. Uncle Henryk was a tall man with rugged features and a genuine smile that made you like him instantly. His wife didn't say much, fashioning long dark gray hair and all dressed in black. She quietly went out of her way to make sure that we were all comfortable with a full cup of tea and food on our plates. When Uncle George stood up to proclaim that it was time to leave and they walked us to the front door, I couldn't help but think that this may be the last time my father would see his oldest brother. Watching them embrace with a final goodbye outside the front door, that thought would prove to be prophetic.

That first trip to Poland allowed me to view the country through the eyes of my father. We visited ancient castles, toured Warsaw, and spent days in and around Zakopane to view majestic mountains. We rode a trolley to a peak high atop the Tatra Mountains. Walking along the rocky summit well above the tree line, my father and I stumbled on a stone border marker that divides Poland from Slovakia. As I shielded from the brisk conditions, my father pointed to a border guard barely visible through the thick fog. He appeared almost ghost like, stooped with a flowing cape protecting him from the wind. I asked in amazement how my father so easily spotted the guard. I would have never noticed him and even then could barely make him out. My father simply shrugged, noting that he became quite adept at spotting border guards during the war, reminiscing that he and a friend crossed the border not too far beyond the mountain range where we stood. I was not aware at the time exactly how that crossing fell into the sequence of events that both preceded and followed. But it is a memory now etched in my mind of what my father experienced in his quest to join the Polish Army.

Before leaving Bochnia, we visited the hilly cemetery to search for gravestones of family members. We were alone that overcast morning, enveloped in a misty haze. As my father and Uncle George searched one section of the densely lined cemetery, I wandered around, taking in the serene beauty under protection of centuries-old oak trees. Approaching a summit that offered a lingering vista of the surrounding countryside, I sensed an excitement coming from my father and uncle. They located their mother's marker. I heard my father's voice calling for me.

Casually walking toward them, I viewed the pair standing in front of a prominent headstone, now engaged in quiet conversation. I don't recall much of any thoughts going through my mind as I approached, simply wanting to pay my respects out of respect for my father. When I reached the rich-looking headstone, I soaked in the words before me:

Jozefa Bajda
UR. 26.VIII.1892 ZM. 8.III.1969

Suddenly it hit me. This is my grandmother. At the time I knew very little of her. I recall the Western Union Telegram informing us of her death and the photos that Aunt Krystyna brought over on her visit, but little else. There are no memories, as I never knew her, despite the fact that she was the only grandparent still alive after I was born. But right then, something came over me, waves of emotions. My lips quivered in a manner that I couldn't stop. Tears flowed freely, and my entire body shook uncontrollably. I tried to control myself, not wanting my father and uncle to see me in such a state as they were standing behind me. A part of me wanted to reach out and touch the headstone. It was as if my grandmother was reaching out to me, pouring out her love to me. I fought to contain myself as much as possible before turning away to drift into the background, careful to avoid eye contact with my father and uncle.

I ventured far enough away, allowing myself to regain composure before the three of us joined up to leave the cemetery. For years, I never said anything to my father about that encounter, but I viewed my grandmother much differently when he finally provided details of his story during these past few years. Every time he mentions her name, the admiration, love, and respect he feels for his mother is clear. Somehow, I better understood the emotions he experienced.

During these past few years, I learned that my father kept in constant contact with his mother right up until her death. Their frequent letters shared continual details of life's happenings on both sides of the Atlantic, even if some cryptic writing was always required to throw off the intervention of prying Party eyes. There was certainly a great deal of news that must have been difficult to share. Henryk was forced to sell off large portions of family property to the government so that he could find the means to pay exorbitant taxes, enabling Jozefa to stay in her home, the yellow stucco house. Zdislaw seemed to be losing hope for a promising future despite a supportive wife and four young sons. His failing health was not helped by increased consumption of the one commodity which was readily in supply in Soviet-controlled Poland, alcohol. Krystyna's health and spirits were also not so good. She was forced to give up her beloved teaching job for the children she so loved. Party authorities designated her for work assignment to a factory up north, where the manual work, dreary conditions, and damp climate were not in agreement with her debilitating medical conditions.

However, there was also news shared in those letters that exhibited fierce pride and spirited joy. When Henryk was approached by Communist Party members to accept a significant (and finally well-paid) teaching position that required him to conform to Soviet standards, he responded to the alarmed officials with a simple direct answer, "You can go to hell!"

Jerzy was certainly a source of pride. As the photo sent to us with his close friend Karol Jozef Wojtyla (Pope John Paul II) hinted, his connections and contributions to the Catholic church were significant. He quickly became a respected activist wielding wide influence in the one area of Polish society the Soviets found difficulty in breaking, the Catholic church. Even Krystyna was eventually the beneficiary of improved news, although it would come after the death of Jozefa and after the fall of the Iron Curtain. She would leave her factory job and go on to start her own school in Cracow, preparing young children for their first Holy Communion.

I also have to believe that my grandmother Jozefa was most warmed and comforted by news across the Atlantic from her son Marian. She often shared with my father how much she longed to see and hug her grandchildren in America, reflecting on the crowded and noisy conditions with four highly spirited grandsons living in the house. My father recently shared with me that as bad as things appeared following the Nazi invasion, his mother never complained or worried, always looking out for her family and searching for means to survive. Now it's quite clear to me that my father both learned and inherited much from his mother. Although I knew little of my grandmother up until recently, I now realize that we were all in her continual thoughts and prayers. That she was somehow watching over us and providing guidance with a strong and loving hand. On the day when I finally visited her gravesite, the pent-up emotions after years of separation were released and brought to the forefront.

I recently mentioned to my father, "I don't know if you were aware, but something came over me that day at the cemetery when we visited your mother's grave."

"I know," he said calmly. "She was reaching out to you, to her grandson."

Nothing else was said. We left it at that. For me, it is comforting to know that my grandmother was finally able to reach out and touch the grandson that she never got to hold and hug.

A Proper Farewell

St. Michael church sits along a narrow winding road just past the village of Burgh by Sands. Centuries-old drystone walls line both sides of the road. On one side, the old stone church stands smartly behind neat rows of weathered gravestones. Across the street, yet more gravestones are visible beyond wildflowers and overgrown shrubbery. Somewhere in that cemetery lies the gravestone of my grandmother, Minnie. A visit to that lonely cemetery is long overdue.

My mother never visited the gravesite. When I asked about it, she teared up, still finding it difficult to explain the days following her mother's death. She struggled dealing with the loss of her mother. Nobody could talk to her. As the family prepared to make the trip to Burgh, Grandma made a decision. She quietly told my mother that she didn't have to go, that she'd stay back in Millom with her. The two didn't speak much while the rest of the family attended the funeral. At one point, Grandma called her over to sit on her lap. The two simply sat together for a long time, lost in their collective thoughts and memories.

I now know that I have to visit the cemetery at St. Michael's church and find the gravestone of Mary (Minnie) Graham. I'll take with me a poem that my mother wrote and leave it as a reminder from my mother, a loving daughter who never let go of her mother and Grandma.

Acknowledgements

I am forever blessed and grateful not only for the love and wisdom that my parents have bestowed upon me, but for their health and longevity, which has proven to be a special blessing in so many ways. As I continue to learn even more of my family's past with every visit, I also grow closer to them in ways I could never have imagined.

Just recently, my father told the story of how he and two others in Weikendorf secretly constructed a homemade distillery to produce moonshine whiskey behind the butcher's stables. He went into great detail explaining the operation, and even recalled the names of his two Polish accomplices, Edmund and Jozef. When I commented how that would have been interesting to include in the book, he simply shrugged it off, commenting that lots of people made moonshine whiskey. He followed with his modest smile, rating the whiskey as quite strong but not so tasty.

All of which leads me to the realization that I will never fully understand the true depth of what my parents experienced during this tumultuous period of world history. I also feel compelled to state that the story I have written is true, and all the people and characters are real, with an exception that I will soon explain. As a writer, I took very few liberties, and those were made only in an attempt to explain the full range of emotions and feelings they were living. Notably, Ian's dream the morning they were waiting to escape across the Morava River, and the re-creation of quotes to fill in detail of their story.

While reliving their past over the last few years was not always so easy for my mother, she still spent countless hours answering my questions while reliving heartfelt memories. As for my father, he dove into this project head-on. He was forever patient, always taking the time to talk and answer questions during my regular visits. His memory and recollection of his brother Stefan's journey during the war was another unexpected treasure. It would have been fascinating to learn of my Uncle Stefan's story firsthand, but I am so grateful that my father retained so much information and was able to so vividly retell his brother's experience during the war.

There were summer evenings where my father and I talked long into the night, and he'd always walk me to the door on my way out. I'd drive away in the early morning hour, my father standing outside to wave goodbye. It was clear that he relished these times together to relive his past. The more we talked, the more doors opened and the more their memories awakened. I recall the surprise when my mother recited the poem that she wrote at her mother's bedside as if it was written yesterday. Up to that time, she seemed to be experiencing some slight memory loss. Now, several years later, her mind and memory are as sharp as they've been for a long time. As for my father, his memory remains as sharp as ever. Dates, addresses, names, all readily available. As we all continue talking, the more they both recall people and events they had probably not thought about for decades.

While my parents Ian and Iris made this book possible, I would be remiss if I did not mention several people whose contributions made a profound impact on the book's final outcome. During the summer of 2015, I spent six weeks travelling across Europe to conduct research for my writing. Travelling outside of Poland, I booked eight stays using Airbnb. Every single host was extremely accommodating, but two stood out, not only for their generosity and friendship, but also for the information and insight they provided. Had I not met these wonderful hosts, my story would have lacked key components that proved invaluable in tying together the pieces needed to weave a cohesive theme for my writing.

The first person I'd like to recognize is my friend from Bucharest, Ionel Tanase. Almost from the moment I booked the room in Bucharest after viewing the neighborhood and reading his wife Oana's profile, Ionel took an interest in my project. After reading a brief description of my reason for travel, he called me before I even left the States. He was there to greet me when my train pulled into Bucharest, and we spent that hot summer evening dining and walking to the many places of interest in the Old Town neighborhood. Several days later, he drove me to a high-end restaurant that now occupies the building at 6 Strada Sevastopol. The owner of Restaurant Mignon was expecting us, and served an expensive bottle of Romanian wine in the same cellar where my father and Artur stayed following their escape from Pitesti. The setting now much different than what my father experienced, but the thick brick arches still prominent and immediately recognized by my father when I shared the photos with him.

I thoroughly enjoyed the time spent with Ionel. I found his colorful personality and stories not only entertaining, but learned so much of the rich Romanian history and the psyche of her people. His friendship and support were so inspiring that I decided to include him as a character in my book. My father did in fact have a Romanian roommate in Craiova who did in fact try to talk them into staying in Romania, but my father could not recall his name. So I used Ionel's name and character as that person, and included his stories to help explain the likely mindset of a young Romanian man during World War II.

On the morning that I left Bucharest, Ionel and Oana picked me up at four in the morning to drive me to the train station. Entering the station, we found ourselves in quite an emotional state as I boarded the westbound train for Budapest. Waving goodbye as the train slowly pulled out of the station, I decided right there that I would also include Oana as a character in the book. Ironically, Oana grew up in the city of Craiova, which is the same location where they are both featured in the book.

The other person I'd like to recognize is a spirited lady from Ancona, Angela (Angie) Mariani. Like Ionel, Angie expressed immediate interest in my reason for travel. Before I even arrived in Ancona, Angie was hard at work, searching for Polish survivors from Anders' Army who may still be living in the Marche region.

Angie also possessed a fun outgoing personality, and she drove me to various places of interest throughout Ancona and the Marche region. We visited a military cemetery, toured a museum that housed photos and memorabilia highlighting the contributions of Anders' Army in the liberation of Ancona, and dined in outdoor restaurants offering scenic views along the Adriatic coastline. Although I had heard my father mention General Anders, it was only through Angie's efforts that I came to fully understand and appreciate the actual significance of General Anders in the Allied war effort.

While I explored the area around Ancona during the day, Angie was busy doing research. She located and contacted active survivors from Anders' Army in both Rome and London, working to arrange for my future meetings with them. Then she surprisingly came upon a gem. Living in a village not too far from Ancona was a married couple who had co-authored two books that commemorate the accomplishments of the 2nd Polish Corps in Italy.

She arranged for a visit, and we drove to a scenic village to meet with the authors Beata Jackiewicz and Raimondo Orsetti. Seated in an outdoor garden, they shared with us two beautifully crafted hardback books filled with interesting facts and fascinating photographs. IL II Corpo D'Armata Pollacco Nelle Marche 1944/1946 Fotografie, and Loreto: IL Cimitero Militare Polacco.

They described hosting famous Polish dignitaries and the widow of General Anders in the same garden following publication of their books. Just as we rose to leave, they presented me with the two books, which I recognized to be in limited print, as gifts for my father. They also presented me with several smaller books, one of which was written in English and I used to gather information about the Italian Campaign for my own writing; General Wladyslaw Anders and the 2nd Polish Corps in the Marche Region, Italy, 1944 – 1946.

My time spent in Ancona made a great impression on me concerning the significance and contribution of General Anders during the Italian Campaign. From that foundation, I sought more knowledge and also learned of his role in forming the 2nd Corps as a Polish Army on Soviet soil. Had it not been for the diligence and interest that Angie took upon herself to conduct research for my book, the entire role of Anders' Army may have been little more than an afterthought in my writing. Because of her, the historical perspective of the 2nd Corps became a key component to my story, and helped to explain the significance that my Uncle Stefan made to the Allied war effort. For these reasons, I am eternally grateful to my good friend, Angie Mariani.

At various points throughout the book, I provided an historical perspective to help explain the background behind events taking place. Virtually all of this information was provided by my father. However, to validate his accounts, I purchased two books that I used to provide further detail and corroborate facts and figures. The books that I used were *The Eagle Unbowed* by Halik Kochanski, and *No Greater Ally* by Kenneth K. Koskodan.

I had much consternation over my desire to include lyrics from the song, *The Red Poppies on Monte Cassino*. The music for this Polish battle hymn was written by Alfred Schutz, and the lyrics by Feliks Konarski. My hope was to include the song's lyrics to honor the brave soldiers of the Polish 2nd Corps who fought and died for their country's honor and freedom. Unfortunately, following numerous attempts, I've been unable to locate the owner to request permission, so have chosen not to use the lyrics. If anyone has knowledge of the rightful owner, please contact my publisher so that I can request permission for use in a revised edition.

I would also like to thank and recognize my family in Poland, who made my visit to Poland in the summer of 2015 so memorable. I would love to recognize everyone whose company I so thoroughly enjoyed, but at the risk of leaving anyone out I will simply acknowledge my cousins whose families made my stay so special; Marian, Jerzy, and Ryszard Bajda. And of course, I must recognize and thank Michal Bajda, whose company, guidance, and friendship were so vital and so much appreciated in my trek through Poland, Slovakia, and Hungary.

There are two fellow professors at Cuyahoga Community College who I also owe so much for their friendship and contributions. Before leaving on my trip to Europe, I encountered extreme difficulty in arranging for travel from Slovakia to

Cluj, Romania. Air travel was not feasible, auto rental not available, and local travel agents or websites of Euro Rail Services were little help for this leg of the journey, so I was getting desperate in my search for any possible travel accommodation. Fortunately, Dr. Geza Varhegyi came to my aid. With the help of a cousin in Hungary, he provided me with a detailed schedule for the Hungarian Rail System, including times with specific instructions for where and when to change trains. He also convinced me to visit Budapest, providing maps and pamphlets for this fascinating city. Not only did this information prove invaluable in enabling travel through Hungary, but the decision to visit Budapest was one for which I am forever grateful for my own personal reasons. After meeting with Geza, travel plans were finalized and the stress level significantly reduced for my much anticipated trip to Europe.

The other person is English Professor Sara Clark. Sara reviewed an early draft of what I thought was near completion, and provided detailed feedback along with much-needed encouragement to take my writing to another level. I've kept that document (including her comments) as both a painful reminder of just how much work was needed at that time, and a thankful reminder of my overwhelming thanks to Sara Clark for her genuine friendship and true professionalism.

I would also like to recognize and thank a former Cuyahoga Community College student. Scully's support and enthusiasm for my project was truly inspiring, and her absorbing questions so invaluable. Because of her deep understanding of my work and story, Scully also came up with a title which I chose to use for the book, Captured in Liberation.

Finally, this entire work may not have been possible if not for my daughter, Lauren Bajda. Lauren continues to visit her grandparents on a weekly basis, stopping to visit them every Sunday, just as she did when she first returned from Alaska. Had Lauren not asked my mother if she was ever accused of being a spy, who knows if my father would have opened up when he did. Because of Lauren, the power of family is further validated and her grandparent's legacy will be passed down for generations to follow.

About the Author

Captured in Liberation is Andrew Bajda's first book. Bajda is an assistant professor at Cuyahoga Community College in Cleveland, Ohio, where he is lead faculty member for the Small Business (Entrepreneurial) Program. Andrew has developed numerous workshops and programs designed to promote social entrepreneurship while also encouraging personal growth and development. In 2013, he was nominated as teacher of the year for the Ohio Association of Two-Year Colleges. Earlier, Bajda won the Bessie Award for teaching excellence in 2009. This award is presented annually to a faculty member in recognition of exceptional professional competence, reflecting the esteem of colleagues and students for teaching that helps people succeed.

Outside the classroom, Bajda is an avid world traveler also who enjoys spending time with his family, including daughters Brittany, Lauren, Marissa, and Kelly. He is currently formulating an outline for his second book, a fiction that will focus on the power of diversity.